PRAISE FOR
The Battle of Mogadishu

"Descriptions of battle scenes are vivid. In some cases, personal emotions come to the fore that make the stories ring true."
—*Aviation Week & Space Technology*

"[*The Battle of Mogadishu*] provides enthralling reading."
—*Richmond Times-Dispatch*

"Straight from the warhorse's mouth. This isn't a Hollywood film. This is life and death."   —*Omaha World Herald*

THE BATTLE OF
MOGADISHU

THE BATTLE OF MOGADISHU

Firsthand Accounts
from the Men of Task Force Ranger

Edited by Matt Eversmann and *Dan Schilling*

PRESIDIO
PRESS

BALLANTINE BOOKS • NEW YORK

2005 Presidio Press Trade Paperback Edition

Published in the United States by Presidio Press, an imprint of The Random
House Publishing Group, a division of Random House, Inc., New York.

Presidio Press and colophon are trademarks of Random House, Inc.

Originally published in hardcover in the United States by Presidio Press,
an imprint of The Random House Publishing Group,
a division of Random House, Inc., in 2004.

Library of Congress Cataloging-in-Publication Data
The battle of Mogadishu : first-hand accounts from the men of Task Force Ranger /
[compiled by] Matt Eversmann and Dan Schilling.
p.   cm.
Includes index.
ISBN 0-345-45966-0
1. Operation Restore Hope, 1992-1993—Personal narratives.
2. United States. Army. Task Force Ranger—History.
I. Eversmann, Matt.   II. Schilling, Dan.
DT407.42.B37 2004
967.7305'3—dc22   2004048417

Printed in the United States of America

www.presidiopress.com

2 4 6 8 9 7 5 3

Map design: Mark South

Book design by Joseph Rutt

This book is dedicated to the nineteen American soldiers killed in Mogadishu, Somalia, on October 3–6, 1993.

CW3 Donovan Briley
SSG Daniel Busch
CPL James Cavacco
SSG William Cleveland
SSG Thomas Field
SFC Earl Fillmore
CW4 Raymond Frank
MSG Gary Gordon
SGT Cornell Houston
SGT James Joyce
SPC Richard Kowalewski
PFC James Martin
MSG Timothy Martin
SGT Dominick Pilla
SFC Matthew Rierson
SGT Lorenzo Ruiz
SFC Randy Shughart
CPL James Smith
CW4 Clifton Wolcott

FOREWORD

Matt Eversmann was the first serious interview I had for my book *Black Hawk Down*.

In August 1996 I flew to Columbus, Georgia, not knowing what to expect. The Army had agreed to let me interview a dozen Rangers at nearby Fort Benning. In all my years as a newspaper reporter, I had never written about the military. I had never served in the military. The truth is, the only people I knew who had gone into the military were knuckleheads from high school who hadn't gotten into college. They tended to be roughneck ne'er-do-wells. I remember thinking on the plane ride down how hard it was going to be to elicit the kind of information I wanted. I needed detailed accounts of what had happened to each soldier during the battle, and beyond that I wanted to know how they felt about it—now and, more important, at the time. The kind of people I knew who had become soldiers would have been too impatient to reflect like that. The battle had happened three years earlier. For what I wanted, I would have to really push them, guide them through the whole process.

I checked into the Red Roof Inn in Columbus and showed up for my first interview at Fort Benning Monday morning at 8 a.m., ready to go to work. In walked Matt. He was tall, rangy, with thinning hair and kind eyes. He sat across from me, and after a minimal introduction he started telling me his story. I haven't listened to the tape in years, but I know I asked very few questions. Matt's story just unfolded, with a richness of detail and reflection beyond my wildest expectations. My tape recorder was running, and I took notes, struggling to keep up. When I asked

questions it was because Matt said something I didn't fully understand—it was my first exposure to military jargon.

And in those first two hours, my opinion of soldiers did an about-
face. Here was an extraordinarily articulate, reflective young man. His
story raised the fine hairs on the back of my neck. When Matt left, another came in, and then another. That interview began a process that
lasted several years, as I collected story after story, among them those
of Mike Kurth, Dan Schilling, Raleigh Cash, John Belman, and Tim
Wilkinson, and began to assemble the story of their battle. One after the
other, they dazzled me with their passion, intellect, recall, and experience. I admired these men. I was not envious of their experience—I
have no deep-seated longing to be shot at. But I admired their courage,
their commitment to our country and to one another. I admired the pu-
rity of their motives and the strength of their convictions. Each story
was extraordinary. I felt privileged to listen. I came to feel, as I have
written elsewhere, that far from my prying this story out of them, these
young men were entrusting me with something precious and important. My job would be to blend them all together into a coherent whole,
picking the parts I needed to tell the broader story that became *Black
Hawk Down*.

In most cases, the portions of the stories I used were just a small fraction of each soldier's or airman's compelling personal tale. In all, just a
small fraction of the experiences of Eversmann, Kurth, Schilling, Cash,
Belman, Wilkinson, and all the others made it into my book. In the
years since, when I have met with readers, they are surprised by my
ability to recall each and every character in the book. What they don't
realize is they had been given only a fleeting glimpse of all these men,
while I had the pleasure and advantage of speaking with each of them
at great length.

This book allows readers to share in that experience. Anyone fasci-
nated by the battle fought in Mogadishu on October 3, 1993, will welcome this opportunity to delve deeper into the lives and experiences of
these six men.

It is also a very fortunate choice of stories, because each of the voices
in this collection is strong and unique: Matt Eversmann, one of the
older, more mature Rangers, wrestling with the burden of command;

Raleigh Cash, who, left out of the assault, led a convoy out into the raging battle; Mike Kurth, one of only two African American Rangers to take part in the battle; John Belman, who was roped into the biggest firefight of the battle after the first Black Hawk went down; Tim Wilkinson, the Air Force pararescueman whose extraordinary courage (and unfailing sense of humor) was such an inspiration to the men who served with him; and Dan Schilling, a well-educated, articulate Air Force combat controller whose near-total recall of the event was invaluable to my understanding of the battle.

The experience of the battle was different for each man, and only by immersing yourself in their accounts can you begin to understand the full complexity and power of the event, one that ended many lives and irrevocably altered the course of so many others. For fans of the book and movie *Black Hawk Down* it is a chance to examine the raw material of those works.

The remarkable success and resonance of this story are owed primarily to these men, to their deeds, their memories, their experience. No matter how skilled the writer of nonfiction, you are always getting the story secondhand. Here's a chance to go right to the source.

This is the real deal. These men were there.

—Mark Bowden

ACKNOWLEDGMENTS

I cannot speak with any authority on the book-writing process so I have no idea if this went well or rather poorly. I can say that this book followed a most circuitous path from conception through fruition. As this book goes to print we are now with our third literary agent as well as our third editor. I must first offer thanks to Chris Evans, as this project was initially his idea. Both Chris and Faye Bender of Anderson Grinberg patiently walked me through the process and helped get the project off the ground and rolling. During this operation several inexplicable personal events almost crippled the project until Sylvia Peck at Doris Michaels Agency took interest in resurrecting the manuscript from certain failure and whipped it back into shape. Sylvia attacked this project with the same dedication and resolve of any soldier I know. Without Sylvia's enthusiasm, attention to detail, and tireless service, we would have failed. Sylvia is now at the helm of the DaVinci Literary Agency. She is her own boss and we wish her the best. I know that she will be a success. Mark Bowden deserves special credit and thanks, as he alone braved unfamiliar territory to write *Black Hawk Down*. Mark has kindly helped us with this book from start to finish. He has answered rookie questions and made us feel like peers. He is a class act and living the American dream. Ron Doering at Presidio Press might be the most patient man in the history of editing. He kindly explained the publication process to me and has spoon-fed us professional guidance throughout the operation. Joining the project as the third editor, Ron inherited a difficult task. He was enthusiastic and was determined to make this book a success. He, like Mark, took us at face value and never made us feel like anything less than authors. I hope that the end result of his labor is worth it. I have to thank my colleagues—Dan, Tim, Mike, John, and Miles—for taking the time from their daily schedules to write or tell their stories. Dan has been a trusted agent and coeditor who contributed far more time and effort than any of us. Balancing a successful business and writing a book was a seemingly simple task for Dan; without him, this would have been a much more painful experience. Overseeing all of this was Doris Michaels, the president of the Doris S. Michaels Agency. Doris took a chance and let us write our story. My wonderful wife, Tori, stood behind the scenes and pushed me through this odyssey from the very beginning. She was the one who encouraged me to step out of my comfort zone and write this piece. During this project, my first daughter was born. Because of all of these wonderful people I have mentioned, Mary Van Arden Eversmann, along with all of her friends to be, will read and learn about the brave men who committed themselves to victory on Sunday, October 3, 1993. Most important, I say thank you to all the men of Task Force Ranger who answered the nation's call. Each of them is a hero. They are the best that America has to offer and I am a better man to have worked with them. May God bless you and your families, always.

—Matt Eversmann

This small collection of stories, while typical of our Task Force in many respects, is but a snapshot of a larger group. In reality there are at least four hundred accounts of bravery and dedication authored by the men of Task Force Ranger. In time, I hope that all these stories will be publicized. For those that won't, may they be passed on to family, so those who matter most might know what extraordinary people their loved ones are who have committed themselves to defending this country.

My deepest appreciation goes to Matt for including me in the project. It started with you and you embody the best traits of professional soldiers: integrity and dedication. Your soldiers are lucky to have you. There are three professionals who require recognition. Sylvia Peck is single-handedly responsible for resurrecting our book from oblivion and contributing countless hours to its improvement. You convinced me it was worthwhile to put our stories to paper when I felt strongly otherwise and that there was value in our words. Thanks, Syl, you are the ultimate in an agent and friend, energetic (an understatement) and funny. Ron Doering and his staff at Presidio committed to us and turned our mass of words and photos into a first-class work. Third, but by no means last, I'd like to thank Mark Bowden. Mark wrote the definitive account of our operation in Somalia and agreed to introduce our book. You've become a friend and adviser.

John Belman, Raleigh Cash, Mike Kurth, and Tim Wilkinson deserve credit for having courage enough to expose their stories, and all the good and bad that goes along with revelation, to public scrutiny. Thanks for coming on board with us, guys; I hope it's worth it. To Pat Rogers, who's no longer with us, and Tim I'd like to add my personal thanks for years of friendship and the great and not so great times we shared in special ops. To the men of Air Force Combat Control, you make everything happen in the often disjointed world of joint special operations, but receive no recognition. You deserve better.

My deepest affection goes to the following: my parents, Will and Ruth, whose fifty-four years of marriage taught me what commitment is, and who exposed me as a child to the open spaces of the West that I now value so much; my son, John, who is a great globetrotting companion and a world-class man in his own right; finally, and most importantly, Elizabeth Maria, who understands much, travels far, and tolerates my seven-day workweek and unconventional recreation habits. I would not be where and who I am today without you.

—Dan Schilling

CONTENTS

INTRODUCTION

If one were to look at any given day in Somalia's recent history, one would likely find famine, drought, brutal dictators, warring clans, and chaos. It is a country where fighting is a way of life, whether over boundaries like the Ogaden desert near Ethiopia or simply getting enough food to survive. In the late 1980s a severe drought crippled Somalia. The fundamental infrastructure disintegrated. The world was bombarded nightly with news of mass starvation and death on the Horn of Africa. In 1992, the 1st Marine Division, along with a small number of Special Forces and Combat Controllers, arrived on the shores to provide relief. The operation was a success. With the worst drought in Africa's history finally over, Somalia was presented with the opportunity to attain some semblance of normalcy.

Unfortunately for Somalia there was no "normal," not by Western standards. There was also no functioning government. By late 1992 there were two warlords vying for power in Mogadishu's political vacuum. On June 5, 1993, during a routine inspection of weapons storage facilities, twenty-four Pakistani peacekeepers were ambushed and killed by militia loyal to a warlord named Mohammad Farrah Aidid. In response, a resolution was passed by the United Nations Security Council to apprehend those responsible for the atrocity, including Aidid and his Somali National Alliance. At the direction of the Joint Chiefs of Staff, the United States Special Operations Command formed a task force with one purpose: to capture Aidid. On August 26, 1993, Task Force Ranger, composed of Army, Navy, and Air Force special operations personnel, moved into the main hangar at the Mogadishu airport. Five weeks later, on a Sunday afternoon, the task force launched Operation Gothic Serpent, its seventh and final mission.

The Somalis have a distinguished history of fighting. At the time of Task Force Ranger's arrival, the average Somali militiaman had ten years' combat experience. More directly of concern to us was that Mogadishu was a city of over a million people, many if not most heavily armed. Many of us knew going in that this warrior tradition, combined with a lack of hope for stability or improvement to welfare, and fanned by international neglect, would create a formidable foe. The Somalis were not fighters prone to easy capitulation.

We were to assault a building with an address in downtown Mogadishu. At 3:32 p.m. our helicopters lifted off from the safety of the airfield for the three-minute flight to the target. The quarry of the day were several of Aidid's lieutenants, who were meeting in a neighborhood known as the Black Sea. It was densely populated with Aidid loyalists. We planned on finishing the entire mission in a half hour or so. As most people familiar with our story know, the operation changed from an assault to a desperate rescue operation after one of our helicopters was shot down.

This book is an anthology of firsthand accounts from six men who saw combat on October 3 from six very different vantage points. But while each chapter represents the individual's perspective only, each and every man acted for his buddy, his team, and the task force. The Special Operations community, regardless of service branch, job title, or skill set, is without exception about teamwork. It is the manner in which we accomplish everything. The pages that follow allow us to tell the stories of brave men who might not have been mentioned in other works. These are men with names like Lamb and Watson, Telscher and Joyce, Fales and Rogers, Weaver and Carlson. The list is four hundred long. Unfortunately, this book still cannot tell of them all. Those not identified remain heroes who answered the call of the nation.

In Shakespeare's *Henry V*, the king's rousing Saint Crispin's Day speech steels his troops for the impending battle. Those moving words tell of dedication, courage, and selfless service. For the families and friends of the members of Task Force Ranger, we hope that this anthology conveys those same values. It is also our hope that the stories contained herein will prove useful to future soldiers by way of lessons learned the hard way. And in the end, despite the bad luck and misfortune that come with combat, these stories tell of what America's soldiers accomplished in the face of the most dire circumstances. To the larger civilian population of this country, we hope you may take heart that people like these do exist, are human beings, not numbers, and will not rest at night until you do.

MOGADISHU

Pakistani Stadium

Hawlwadig Road

21 October Road

Armed Forces Road

Cliff Wolcott's Crash Site

Target Building

Bakara Market

Olympic Hotel

National Street

Mike Durant's Crash Site

Maxuud Harbi

Via Lenin

K4 Circle

Mogadishu Airport

Task Force Ranger Base

INDIAN OCEAN

N

1 kilometer

PLANNED ASSAULT
VEHICLE ROUTE

INITIAL RESCUE
ATTEMPT ROUTES

RESCUE CONVOY ROUTES

THE BATTLE OF
MOGADISHU

OPERATION GOTHIC SERPENT

Matt Eversmann

There were four blocking positions used by Task Force Ranger to surround the target building. Matt Eversmann was in charge of one of them, Blocking Position 4. The twenty-six-year-old staff sergeant had twelve Rangers assigned to his squad that day. There were several three-story buildings around the target, and Eversmann and his men would have to insert by fast rope. They were charged with setting the blocking position on the northwest corner of the target. Their job was very straightforward: isolate the target building so that no enemy could get in or out.

Most of all I remember the smell, that godawful, nasty smell. As soon as the ramp of the plane cracked open, that sick smell swept through the entire aircraft. It was disgusting—kind of like sulfur and something pretty rotten mixed on top. The smell, that lingering scent of burning garbage and who knows what, combined with the African heat was my welcome to Mogadishu, Somalia.

On August 26, 1993, I arrived at a small airfield on the Horn of Africa as part of a task force of soldiers who were given the mission to capture a local Somali warlord named Mohammad Farrah Aidid. At the time I was a young staff sergeant with about five years' worth of experience in the Army. My first four years of service were spent in Watertown, New York, with the 10th Mountain Division, and I had been with the Ranger Regiment only since March 1992. In my seventeen months of training with the regiment, I had deployed all over the world. We trained with the British Parachute Regiment in the United Kingdom. We traveled to South Korea to experience the harsh Korean winters and mountainous terrain. We even trained with the Thai Rangers in Lop Buri, Thailand. We traveled all over the globe to develop our combat skills. Now, after five years of good, hard training, I was on my way to battle.

Between August and October 2, 1993, Task Force Ranger conducted six combat missions. On our thirty-eighth day in country, we conducted our seventh and what would be our final mission. We launched a raid from our base at the Mogadishu airfield on Sunday, October 3, at around 1530 hours. That mission would go down in history as the fiercest ground combat seen by American forces since the Tet offensive in 1968. During what would become known to the men there as the Battle of the Black Sea, eighteen soldiers made the ultimate sacrifice, and some seventy others were wounded in action, many seriously. The fighting continued when one member of Task Force Ranger died during a mortar attack a few days later, on October 6. Much has been written and plenty said about that mission. I have read and heard about as much as I can about it and am convinced about one thing and only one thing: that mission—that horrifying event, that brutal experience, that episode of complete savagery—will be, without exception, one of the finest examples of American tenacity, selfless service, courage, and commitment ever witnessed in modern times.

Most soldiers, and infantrymen in particular, live with one question all the days that they wear a uniform. It doesn't matter if they are newly commissioned second lieutenants from the school on the banks of the Hudson or eighteen-year-old high school graduates right out of basic training. Somewhere deep inside their psyche, every single man who joins the infantry wants to know how he will react when the bullets start flying. When you get right down to it, I do not think I have ever met a man who didn't want to go to war in some way, shape, or form. Many wax philosophical about the thought of combat and all that it entails, but I've never met a guy who, deep down, didn't want to go for the test. Why else would men subject themselves to the endless hours of training? Why would they put up with the long periods of separation from loved ones? Why would they suffer for the low pay and the stress? Why would they push themselves to the extreme day after day? I can think of only one reason: to go to war, to get a shot at the title, to pass the final exam—whatever cliché one uses to describe battle. That's what soldiers do, I thought; that's why we exist, to go to war and win. At least, that is how I looked at it in 1993.

In December 1989 I was waking up at Fort Benning, Georgia, two-thirds of the way through Ranger School. My class had come back to Benning from the swamps of Florida to begin our two-week exodus for the Christmas holiday. Bright and early on the morning of December 21, 1989, the commander of the Ranger Training Brigade held a formation. With no introduction he said, "Last night we invaded Panama. The regiment jumped in to seize an airfield. Several casualties were reported." I was in shock. At that time, so early in my career, I didn't know too much about the 75th Ranger Regiment. I knew enough to know that if there was a fight anywhere in the world, the Rangers would be the first ones to go.

I fully expected that my unit, the 10th Mountain Division based at Fort Drum, had already been called to action, and I was upset that I was not with them. But I soon found out that all my mates were still in Watertown, away from the fight. We would have to wait for the next one. Interestingly enough, a couple of my Ranger buddies actually signed out of the Ranger Training Brigade for leave and wound up deploying to Panama for some follow-on operations with the regiment, resuming the last phase of Ranger School later on. I was amazed at their mettle: go off to war, do the mission, and then return to school. The word *impressive* hardly does justice to them.

When the Gulf War started, I was still at Fort Drum. I remember scheming with my roommate, Mike Evans, to get assigned to a unit that would surely get called to the fight. We desperately wanted to go to war, and felt stifled in the light infantry. I say this not as an indictment against the 10th Mountain Division. Not by a long shot. They were a very good unit. They just weren't suited for the mechanized, desert battle that we expected would take place an ocean away. Even though our forces would go on to decimate Saddam Hussein's Republican Guard, I was still zero for two.

In November 1991 I took the plunge and reenlisted for an assignment with the Ranger regiment. I flew to Fort Benning, successfully passed the assessment course, and was assigned to the Third Battalion. There are three battalions that make up the 75th Ranger Regiment. The First Battalion (1/75) is in Savannah, Georgia, at Hunter Army Airfield, the Second Ranger Battalion (2/75) is near Seattle at Fort Lewis, and the Third (3/75), stationed at Fort Benning, Georgia, would be my new home.

I remember arriving at 3/75 as a brand-new staff sergeant with absolutely no special operations experience whatsoever. Though I had been to several good Army schools—sniper, airborne, Ranger, and SERE (survival, evasion, resistance, and escape)—I felt that I was still way behind the curve compared to my peers. It was pretty intimidating to assume a leadership position only to find that many of the subordinates were combat veterans of Panama. They proudly wore their combat infantryman's badge over the left breast pocket of their uniforms, and I heard the stories of the Rio Hato and Torrijos Tocumen airfield assaults that the men had been part of. Every day I would see the tiny gold stars centered on the suspension lines of their airborne wings. The "mustard stain," as we call it, signals a combat jump. They had been to the show. These men were larger than life, and I did not want to make any JV mistakes in front of them.

The best course of action for me, it seemed, was to listen and learn everything I could from these men. As I got to know the men of 3/75, I realized that they were certainly a different breed of men, a different caliber of soldier. Not necessarily better, just different. It was impressive to see young privates and specialists performing tasks that I previously would never have seen executed by anyone below the rank of sergeant first class. They were *expected* to perform difficult and dangerous things because that is what they would have to do in combat. Everything we did in that unit was focused on our combat mission. Young men were given a lot of responsibility and taught to be problem solvers. I heard the regimental commander, Colonel David Grange, say, "We teach these men how to think, not what to think." It was all starting to make sense.

More than anything, I was fortunate to fall ass backward into the arms of some very talented young men who took the time to help me learn the skills necessary to survive the rigors of life in the regiment. For that, I am eternally grateful.

I learned how to parachute out of airplanes in pitch darkness. We took marksmanship to a new level, and for the first time I started to really learn how to shoot my M-16. I learned how to use explosives, though I am definitely not the guy you want making the charge to blow the doors. I learned how to fast-rope out of helicopters in order to fight in an area otherwise unreachable by air. I learned how to navigate with a compass and by using the terrain. Most of all I simply . . . *learned*. Everything was new and everything was exciting, and I felt like sooner or later the chance would come to see if I could answer that eternal question.

Mathematically, I figured that since the First and Second Ranger Battalions had jumped into Grenada in 1983, in Panama in 1989, and in Iraq in 1991, the longest I would have to wait would be five or six years. When describing the necessity of repetitive training, the command was fond of saying, "It is not a question of if we go to war, it's a question of when." Prophetic.

In August 1993, after a hellacious tour of the world, we landed in El Paso, Texas, for another training mission. On the night of a particular airborne mission, I remember that the battalion commander was not present for the parachute issue. As we rigged and began the jumpmaster inspection, someone said he'd overheard that there was a real-world mission going down and the battalion commander, Lieutenant Colonel Danny McKnight, was receiving the warning order. I thought that was all bullshit—just wishful thinking. A little while later, as we stood around the aircraft, the night's mission was canceled and everyone was sent back to their tents.

Sometime that evening the platoon leader, First Lieutenant Tom Di-Tomasso, and the platoon sergeant, Sergeant First Class Chris Hardy, told us to pack our bags because Bravo Company was deploying to Fort Bragg, North Carolina. That was it. No information—just pack our gear and be ready to load the aircraft when they call. It was hard to tell what was going on. It could be just an exercise from our higher command to pick a company at random and test their skills. I did not recall anything particularly disturbing in the news—at least nothing out of the daily CNN newscasts. I could not think of anything, at least nothing from the nonstop news spectrum, that might have "real-world" stamped on it.

The more we thought about it, the more we thought it was probably just an exercise.

Later we loaded into a C-5 Galaxy and flew to North Carolina. In the dark of the night we arrived at an isolated site out in the middle of nowhere. It was still hard to decipher what was next for us. I figured that there was a fifty-fifty chance of a real-world deployment. After getting ourselves sorted and our gear checked, we were given the training plan. We would be doing some fast-roping from MH-60 Black Hawk helicopters and quite a bit of shooting at the range. It was awesome: fly, rope, and shoot, day and night. A couple of days into the training, I was finishing up at the range with a few other Rangers when I heard a collective roar from the tents where we lived. When we arrived at the tent, Lieutenant DiTomasso told us that we were going to Somalia to catch Aidid. *Here we go boys—this is it.* I felt fear, excitement, disbelief, and probably every other emotion wrapped up in one as we began to plan to take our turn in history.

Before we left the safety and comfort of America, I remember seeing a verse of scripture chiseled into a memorial wall. It was from the book of Isaiah, chapter 6, verse 8: "And then I heard the voice of the Lord saying 'Whom shall I send and who will go for us?' And I said 'Here am I, Lord, send me.'" What could possibly be more meaningful to a young soldier in preparation for a real-world mission? Selfless service, a calling to a cause greater than oneself. It was inspiring to think about joining the noble ranks of the warriors that had made the journey before me. Though I obviously had no idea what would lie ahead, that verse set the tone for me and, I believe, the entire task force. *Send me, send us, we are here.*

There were two plans of attack to catch Aidid. The first was to capture him while he was traveling in his convoy of cars. The second was to catch him when he was inside a building. That was it, either A or B. It made good sense to me and seemed like a very simple plan: the man would be either inside or outside. We would take him out whenever and wherever he showed himself.

The task force was broken down into three separate groups: the assault force, the blocking force, and the ground convoy. We would have an assault force of Special Forces soldiers to do the work inside the target building. Almost simultaneously the Rangers in the blocking force would set up a perimeter around the target. Finally, the Rangers in Humvees and five-ton trucks would drive through the city and link up for extraction once we had Aidid in our hands. The assault force and the blocking force would fly to the target site in MH-60 Black Hawk helicopters and MH-6 Little Birds. Once at the objective we would either land or—if no landing zone was available—slide down thick nylon ropes to the street and assume our battle posture accordingly. It was pretty simple at my level, though I know that this choreography took quite some planning for the pilots, crew chiefs, and command.

Once we were on the ground, the blocking positions would seal the objective and the leader at each position would be able to monitor the ground action on an FM radio.

Each blocking position consisted of twelve to fifteen Rangers that, as a "chalk," flew each mission with the same pilots and crew. I was assigned to BP4 (Blocking Position 4), which was transported in an MH-60 Black Hawk helicopter nicknamed, much to the delight of Plano, Texas's own Sergeant Casey Joyce, the *Texas Express*—its call sign was Super 67. The crew was the best in the world and proved it every single time the rotors turned. When they flew, they flew with a purpose that screamed to the entire world their motto: "Night stalkers don't quit."

Whichever course of action we executed, our battle position would be the same. Half the Rangers would exit the bird on the port side, and the other half would simultaneously rope from the starboard side. Once the last Ranger landed on the ground, the crew chiefs would release the ropes, and off they would fly to provide overhead cover for us. It was comforting to know that these Black Hawks were armed with 7.62 mm miniguns that could fire at a rate of four thousand rounds per minute, more than ten rounds a second per barrel. There is no joy for those on the receiving end of a burst from those guns.

Once we were all on the ground, we would fall into a loose L-shaped perimeter, wrapping ourselves around a corner of a building or block. That way, the ends of the "L" could make a visual recognition with the two other blocking positions, thus completing the square around the target. Sometimes we were relatively close to the other two BPs, and other times we might be spread out almost a block away. Still, the key was the visual link-up. Once we were in position, we would scan our sectors searching for the enemy. The urban battlefield is three-dimensional (that is, it contains multistory buildings), so each of us had to scan up and down as well as left and right. Each side of the L had at least one automatic weapon and at least one grenade launcher. The rest of the Rangers carried M-16s or CAR-15s. But our most casualty-producing weapon was the M-60 machine gun. Like the miniguns, this was a 7.62 mm belt-fed machine gun and could easily lay waste to the enemy when engaged. Until October 3, it had been untested in BP4. Our machine gunner had not fired his gun in anger because we had yet to make significant contact.

Each blocking position was assigned either a medic or a Ranger who had been through the emergency medical technicians course, as was the case with BP4. We also had a trained forward observer whose job was to coordinate the air cover for our blocking position. If we were to come into heavy contact, the FO would relay our situation directly to the Black Hawks and call in a rain of fire on the enemies.

On Sunday, October 3, 1993, there were thirteen of us on board Super 67 in Chalk Four as we set out on our mission. The only thing unusual as we began was that I was in charge of the blocking position this time.

We call it the "fallout one" drill. It is a simple exercise that we practiced over and over where the leader takes a backseat and allows the second in command to take charge. We accepted the fact that leaders could be killed just as easily as any other soldier so every Ranger had to be able to make decisions on the battlefield regardless of his rank and position. For me, this was put into practice when my chalk leader was called back to the States for a family emergency and I was the next in line. It was almost that simple. There was certainly added stress for me, being put in charge, but the men were superb and I felt very confident that they would perform no matter what happened.

Sometime that Sunday morning all the leaders of the task force were summoned to the operations center for a briefing. The intelligence was not confirmed, but all fingers pointed to a possible meeting between some of Aidid's top lieutenants. This would be a good grab if we could get them. Though we had been unsuccessful at catching Aidid, we had been successful at dismantling his infrastructure. We had grabbed his money man a week or so before. We captured some of his other staff officers and were tightening the noose around his neck. When the opportunity for more captures presented itself, we were ready to go. Day or night, it made no difference. To me, it seemed obvious: get them on the run, keep them moving and off balance, wait for the inevitable mistake, and then catch them whenever they showed themselves. I didn't have the slightest reservation about going into the city during the day. The threat was always very real, and the possibility of getting into the mix was a reasonable bet every time we launched a mission. But I felt that we had the advantage of being the best-trained soldiers in the world. We had the best aircraft and the best pilots and crew, bar none. Speed, surprise, and violence of action would be our calling cards and would help cancel the numeric advantage that Aidid had over us. Yes, I definitely felt very good about this operation.

Sergeant Jim Telscher and Sergeant Casey Joyce were my right-hand men. The sergeants were my two team leaders. Jim had worked for me for almost a year, and Casey had been with me for a couple of months. They were capable young men whom I admired and trusted wholeheartedly. Sergeant Telscher was also our demolitions guy. He had a knack for knowing everything there was to know about using C4. Casey was "Mr. Dependable"—always there to lend a hand, always calm and collected, and always there to listen and offer opinions at the right time. Having two stand-up men like these made my job very easy. They would make their men do the right thing. They enforced the standards with a calm and thoughtful demeanor and kept me from making bonehead mistakes. Any fears that I had were calmed by the fact that I had the very best team leaders that the Regiment had to offer.

Rounding out my chalk were Specialist Kevin Snodgrass, machine gunner; his ammo bearer, Private First Class Todd Blackburn; and First Sergeant Glenn Harris, who lent his expertise as a rifleman, as did Sergeant Scott Galentine. Specialists Dave Diemer and Adalberto Rodriguez were my squad automatic weapon (SAW) gunners, and Privates First Class Anton Berendsen and Marc Good were my 40 mm grenadiers.

Staff Sergeant Jeff McLaughlin was my FO, and Specialist Jason Moore was my radio telephone operator, or RTO. Together we had done missions before and were ready; there was no doubt in my mind that we would be able to handle whatever came down the pike.

By the time I left the operations center with the mission diagram in hand, the words "get it on" were echoing throughout the hangar. As I walked to get the rest of my kit, the hangar was a buzz of excitement. Last-minute precombat checks were being completed. Men checked their buddies as they adjusted the Velcro straps on their body armor to get it good and tight. Weapons were slung and double-checked. Finally, we made sure that our American flags were carefully attached to our uniforms. These flags had Velcro backing and could be worn on the sleeve of the uniform, but I always wore mine just above my heart on my left shoulder strap.

I told Jim and Casey it was going to be a long rope—not particularly good news, as fast-roping from great heights, cool as it looks, usually is not much fun. There were two- and three-story buildings on either side of our insertion point. The ropes might be every bit of seventy feet. There was always a certain amount of bragging about who roped higher, a kind of badge of honor to say that yours was higher and obviously much more difficult than the other guy's. The reality, though, is that it basically sucks no matter how high or how low you are. It is like jumping from a plane: you just have to grit your teeth and do it, and it only hurts for a second.

With nothing more than a passing comment about how it sucked, we left the wire, locked and loaded a magazine into our weapons, and headed toward the helicopters. We knew that once we lifted off, we had to be ready to engage the enemy, even while flying. Super 67's blades were already spinning by the time we arrived. Our crew chief confirmed the dreaded seventy-footer with a smile and bade us enter his domain. His last instruction to me as chalk leader was not to forget to take off my headphones. I thought this was an odd bit of advice before a mission.

It was a tight fit on the aircraft, but not too uncomfortable. We were by now veterans of a hundred flights or more, which included six real-world missions prior to that day. I took the seat in the middle of the helicopter between the two crew chiefs, put on the headset, and adjusted it as I watched the men filter into their respective positions. Both doors were open, the ropes already rigged and attached to the bar, and the men were ready. Across the helo common radio channel the code word to begin the mission was echoed. *Irene.*

It was a beautiful, sunny day, as I remember. The flight was only going to be about three or four minutes. We would take a long flight around the city and make our approach from the north. As soon as we lifted off, the pilots said that the Somalis were burning tires in the streets. Some people thought that the tire burning was an elaborate communications system used by the Somali bandits to signal the thug militia. Others suspected that the burning tires and garbage were nothing more than obstacles to hinder an imminent attack by the Americans. Whatever the reason, it made no difference to me. We were there to do a job, and this was just another problem to solve.

"One minute" came across the headset. The safety straps keeping us in the helicopter were unhooked, and each team prepared for the signal to toss the ropes. As we made our approach to the target, the Black Hawks and Little Birds broke from formation and headed toward each desired insertion point. Super 67 was the last Ranger aircraft to move to position, the piece of the puzzle that would seal the objective. Seventeen different aircraft were dancing over the city below, ready to rain fire on the enemy at the first sign of trouble. I still had my headset on, waiting on any last-minute guidance from the pilot. It was that last second when you realize the fear has left you and your mind is focused on the very next sequence of motor skills that will allow you to make your body move to accomplish whatever task it needs to do—in this case, the automatic action of removing the headset, donning my goggles, slipping into my Kevlar helmet, moving to the side of the helicopter floor, grabbing the rope with both hands, and pushing off the deck to slide to the objective.

I watched each of the men gaze toward the crew chief on their respective doors. All eyes eagerly awaited the visual signal to throw the ropes and begin the drill. I noticed an unusual amount of brownout on both sides of the aircraft—the helo's rotor wash raised a huge amount of dust from the dirt roads. We were flying in at an altitude of sixty-five or seventy feet when all of a sudden we came to a halt. We were stopped at a hover in a cloud of dust when I heard the pilot say, "I can't see shit."

I remember listening to the pilots talking over the helo common frequency during the flight. I was just making sense of his last words to me when I realized that we had come to a stop. I don't remember anyone shooting at us then, but sitting in a stationary helicopter at seventy feet above the ground wasn't the best place to be. We couldn't have given the Somalis a better target. Time just stopped. The Rangers in charge of throwing the ropes had their eyes glued on the crew chiefs, waiting for their signal to toss the ropes. The rest of the men were scanning the ground looking for armed Somalis, as were the crew chiefs.

The crew chiefs were also charged with security for the aircraft. During the flight, and certainly on approach to the target, the crew juggled about twenty tasks at once. As door gunners they had to watch for the insertion point, watch for the enemy, keep track of us, and all the while let the pilots know what was going on around the aircraft. If my job was difficult at this point in time, these guys' problems were magnified by a factor of about ten.

We continued to hover for what seemed like ten minutes. In reality it was probably more like thirty seconds. I heard the pilot who was flying say again, "I can't see shit." There must have been some discussion between the pilots and the crew because after a short pause the command to throw ropes was given. We were on our way to battle. The last thing the pilot told me was that we were short of our desired insertion point. He told me to look up at the nose of the aircraft and follow that direction about two or three blocks and we would be in the right place. That was fine with me. The ground was safety. Once on the ground we would make sure we were all accounted for, set a quick security perimeter, and then move to the objective. At least now we were moving. We would have momentum. The sooner we started the mission the sooner we would finish and head back to the airfield.

As chalk leader I would be the last man out of the helicopter. I remembered what the crew chief had said to us at the airfield, so as the men of Chalk Four started their descent I carefully took my headphones off and placed them on the seat behind me. As I started to adjust my goggles, the elastic strap that holds them securely against my head broke. This would be just one of many attempts by that bastard Murphy to take this mission south. I tossed the goggles aside and put on my Kevlar helmet. I was securing the chin strap when the helicopter suddenly keeled over a few degrees. Kneeling on the floor of the bird, I felt enough of a jerk for me to almost lose my balance. I slipped on my heavy leather gloves and waddled to the door of the aircraft.

The fast ropes are secured to the helicopter by a big clevis pin attached to a retractable metal pipe that runs across the ceiling and out the doors of the helo. There is a space between the body of the aircraft and the hanging rope of about two feet. It's just far enough away that a Ranger has to reach a little farther than comfortable outside the door to grab it. Once the rope is securely in his hands, the Ranger will swing his body out and around so that he is facing the aircraft as he begins to slide down toward the ground. All the while, he is feeling for the rope with his feet. Unlike on a firemen's pole, the only parts of the body that touch the fast rope are the hands and the feet.

As I started my descent I was looking up toward the belly of the helicopter. I wanted to make sure I knew the direction of flight and therefore the target. I remember the air was so cloudy and thick with dust, and without the benefit of eye protection it was hard for me to see. The seventeen other aircraft also stirred up debris, so it was no wonder we couldn't see anything. Bless those pilots for holding our Black Hawk steady while we were on the way down. Despite my leather gloves, the nylon of the rope made my hands burn, so I looked down to see how much farther it was to the ground. It seemed like I was on the rope forever.

When I saw the ground, my heart sank. At the bottom of the rope was a crumpled tan-clad body. *My God, someone's been shot. Who is it? And is he dead?* were the first thoughts through my head. That was my first real feeling of fear, a feeling of helplessness, as if I couldn't defend myself. I had always thought that making a combat parachute jump must be scary as hell since you are floating down into harm's way, watching a firefight in a hot drop zone all the while. This was as close as I got to what that situation must feel like, except I couldn't see or hear any shots. Thank the Lord, I finally got my feet on the ground, literally straddling the body. The medics were already working on him. It was

Todd Blackburn. As I made a quick check for the rest of the men it dawned on me that we were under fire.

We were in the middle of a four-way intersection and were taking fire from the north, the east, and the west. The fire wasn't that accurate at first, but unlike during previous missions, the Somalis were not just spraying their weapons at us with reckless abandon; this time they were aiming. The objective was only a few blocks to our south, but Murphy was with us again; we wouldn't be making the movement to the objective as quickly as we had planned.

Private Good was busy giving first aid to Blackburn. I couldn't believe that Blackburn was even close to being alive. He was bleeding out of his mouth, nose, and ears, and his body was horribly contorted. It was one of those surreal moments—there would be many more that day—and one that never in my wildest imagination would I have thought I would witness. Good and another medic had opened Blackburn's airway and were stabilizing his neck when the fire started to get heavier. As I checked the intersection to see where the men were, I realized that we had definitely landed right in the middle of the worst part of town, and the Somalis seemed none too pleased with our intrusion. As I checked the men I asked my RTO to call the commander, Captain Steele, to give him a sit rep and request an immediate extraction. All Specialist Moore got was nothing—no response, no acknowledgment. We had no communications with headquarters.

My first thirty seconds as the leader of Chalk Four sucked, plain and simple. We were in the wrong spot, had no commo, had an urgent casualty, and were being shot at from three directions. Things were going south in a hurry. The good news was that the Rangers from Chalk Four were performing phenomenally. I had no combat experience other than the previous missions, but watching them fight was a thing of beauty. They hit the ground running and were doing their job. We were dealt a bad hand of cards, but what really amazed me was just how fast the Somalis started to fight. It seemed that we were on the ground for a few seconds and then *bam*—the heavens opened up with small-arms fire. It really was like the movies, with the dust kicking up in the road as a hail of bullets ripped open the dirt. It was actually kind of wild to watch.

We moved Blackburn to the east side of the intersection and set up my little command post and casualty collection point where we could work on casualties in relative safety. I remember seeing a small parked car facing east and one facing north. These made for good fighting positions and gave us a little cover. Moore was still trying to reach the command group when the medics told me that we needed to get Blackburn the hell out of there or he was going to die. I tried calling Captain Steele on my handheld Motorola radio. This was a backup radio that really wasn't very powerful; in urban or built-up areas, radio waves don't always make it up and over buildings to the other receiving radio. I finally got a hold of First Lieutenant Larry Perino, who was located with the commander and would act as a relay. I mentally told myself to be calm and to speak clearly and distinctly, as this was a somewhat stressful situation and I didn't want to be spastic on the net for everyone to hear. Of course when I spoke he couldn't hear me, so I yelled louder into the handset. The connection probably wasn't very good, so the more I yelled and got pissed off, the less the man on the other end could hear. His response to me was to tell me to calm down.

By this time I was ready to become uncorked. Finally the word came back to me that no one on the objective could move to our position for the evacuation, so we would have to move him to their position instead. Time was critical for Ranger Blackburn. We had been under steady fire from the Somalis almost since we inserted. I never looked at my watch, so I have no idea how long we were there, but it seemed like an eternity. I called Sergeant Joyce. Casey was there in an instant for my instructions. I wanted him to take an aid-and-litter team and move Blackburn down to the objective for an immediate evacuation back to the hospital at the airfield. Good had Blackburn stabilized and all ready to go.

We had a collapsible stretcher that we carried with us during missions. We always had to have the ability to move a wounded soldier, and a stretcher or litter was much easier than the fireman's carry. The problem is that stretchers are somewhat bulky and, though necessary, are another piece of gear that some Ranger has to figure out how to carry. Deadweight is deadweight, and unconscious people are just that. It takes several men to carry one wounded Ranger. If you add in the weight of the equipment the wounded is carrying and the fact that there are about ten thousand Somalis shooting at you, a seemingly simple task becomes exponentially more difficult. Sergeant Joyce had to deal with all of these dilemmas, and bless him, he did.

Sergeant Joyce gathered a few litter bearers and began his movement toward the objective. One of the men who went with him was our forward observer, Staff Sergeant Jeff (Mac) McLaughlin. Mac's primary job was to direct the fire from the Black Hawks and Little Birds that flew overhead cover. In a nutshell, Mac would mark our position with a small multicolored piece of nylon called a VS-17 panel. One side is orange and the other is red. The panel is placed in a prominent position so that the pilots and crew can spot you from above. Mac also had a radio to talk directly to the pilots and alert them of any fire missions we needed from them. The MH-60s had come to our help several times already. The crew chiefs engaged the enemy militia with their miniguns in a ferocious display of firepower. Just when the enemy fire would hit high tide, one of the Black Hawks would slide through the air over our position, open up, and quiet things down. It was Mac's job to control these precious assets. At this point in the fight, I could have used the firepower of every man on the chalk, but we had to evacuate Blackburn, so Mac jumped in and helped. Rangers Joyce, McLaughlin, Good, and another medic took the litter and headed down the road to the objective.

Our hands were getting pretty full about this time. I don't remember exactly when I took my first shot, but I do remember that it was a very easy and natural decision to make. Specialist Dave Diemer was my light machine gunner. He carried the M-249 SAW, which was a little smaller than Snodgrass's M-60 machine gun. Unlike the 7.62 mm M-60, Dave's SAW was 5.56 mm, the same caliber as our rifles. Still the SAW is a fully automatic machine gun, and Dave had become a master of his weapon. One of the armorers back at the airfield had done some work to Dave's gun and mounted a pistol grip under the barrel. He was happy with this nifty accoutrement and demonstrated great poise and talent during the battle. Specialist Diemer was fighting the enemy to the east of our position and was steadily engaged. There was an abandoned vehicle in the middle of the road a few blocks east of us that the Somalis used as a fighting position. The Somalis would run from the corner of a building to the car, fire at us, then dart across the street to the other side and fire some more. They seemed to love this daring game of chicken.

I had been watching Diemer fight the entire afternoon. He was lying prone behind the right rear tire of another car we used to shield Blackburn. The windows of this car had been shot out and the body of the car was riddled with bullet holes. Most of the tires had been shot out as well. As I knelt behind the trunk next to Diemer, the last of what was left of the rear window exploded over us after a burst of gunfire. We ducked down as low as we could and then, when the shooting stopped, scanned for the enemy. There was a Somali about a block away behind the corner of a building. He would hug the corner and spray at us with his weapon before retreating to safety. I saw this guy and waited for him to turn the corner. As soon as he did, I engaged. So did Specialist Diemer, First Sergeant Harris, and Ranger Berendsen. *Low tide in the Black Sea.* Unfortunately, there were a hell of a lot more Somalis to take this guy's place.

Sergeant Jim Telscher was running the fight on the west side of the street. He had been the first Ranger from our helicopter to get his feet on the ground. Telscher was one of those men who just had an innate knowledge and understanding of Rangering. He picked up on new techniques and mastered them in short order. Telscher knew demolitions very well and had weaponry down to a science. Peers, leaders, and subordinates liked working with Jim. He was a stand-up guy with a great sense of humor and wit. There was nothing bad I could say about Sergeant Telscher, and I was glad that he was one of my men. Jim had Specialist Kevin Snodgrass and Sergeant Scott Galentine with him. They, too, were using the abandoned vehicles for cover from the Somali fire.

Every so often a Black Hawk would slide through the air to our position and let loose a long solid burst from its miniguns. It was exhilarating to see, hear, and feel the power of these machines. I thought surely the Somalis would stay away from our perimeter after a lesson in ballistics from Sikorsky. But they wouldn't stop, not on this day. It was shoot-an-American day, and they were all ready to participate. I think my feelings of sheer incredulity were as powerful as the personal fear I had inside. It was unbelievable to me that so many people would willingly walk down the street to join the fight.

Despite the intensity of the firefight, it was reassuring for me to see the men in action. It is true that battle will turn a boy into a man in seconds. The sight of these brave men taking the fight right back to the thug militia stirred one of the most powerful emotions I could ever have imagined. If I was scared then, watching these warriors execute their drill certainly made me feel much braver and more confident.

Private Berendsen took a round in his arm. He was across the street from me, on the south side facing east, when he was shot. Berendsen was my grenadier and had been gainfully employed all afternoon. I saw him just after he was hit and his eyes were as big as silver dollars. It was hard to tell how bad it was from across the street, but when he made it to my position I saw immediately that he would be okay. He was coherent and focused on the same intersection where he had taken fire. In fact, he didn't seem overly concerned about his wound. While I was putting the dressing on his arm, he kept fidgeting with the breech of his M-203 grenade launcher with his other hand. To this day I have no idea what the hell I was thinking, but, in a fit of frustration, I opened his breech for him. As I continued bandaging his arm, Berendsen fired a high-explosive round. The round sailed through the air toward the corner of the building where the firing originated. It was a moment of beauty. The round impacted and we heard no more firing. Low tide in the Black Sea, again.

Berendsen had done well. I turned to check the west side of the street just as Sergeant Galentine was shot in the hand. Again, the time trick suspended all other events at that second, and all I saw was Scott's hand turn red as the round hit. He had been shot in his thumb. It didn't look life-threatening, but it seemed pretty bad from my position. As he moved across the street to my position, I could see that his thumb was almost completely severed. Scott wasn't saying a word, and Berendsen and I were afraid he might be going into shock. All I could think to do was bandage the thumb right back in place. Berendsen was supporting him as I bandaged his hand. "Keep your hand above your heart," Berendsen kept saying. Scott seemed to be doing okay, so we started back to the fight.

About ten seconds later I saw Sergeant Telscher working on Snodgrass. Our machine gunner had been hit, but Telscher was right there taking care of the situation. Things were rapidly getting worse at our position. A few moments later Moore, the RTO, called out to me that the word had come across the command net that we would be ready to collapse on the objective and head back to the airfield in a few minutes. What a relief. I figured the mission went as planned at the target and we must have captured the precious cargo. We would have plenty to discuss once we returned to the hangar. Even though we were still engaged by the Somalis, we felt pretty good about getting ready to pack up and head home. I was anxious to hear what the other leaders had to say about the fight on their side of the battlefield. I didn't know if any of them had even been in a fight.

I do not know if Dave Diemer called me by my rank or by my name— I don't know how he even got my attention during the fighting—but as I was planning our movement back to the target building, Diemer told me that a helicopter had crashed. What helicopter, where? All Dave could do was point down the street to our east. A few blocks away I could see a big pile of rubble. No way was that a Black Hawk. I told Diemer to check his sector of fire. Having an enemy force between friendly elements is a very bad situation. Fratricide is one of the worst things that a soldier can commit. It is literally a self-inflicted wound.

He was still engaged, but I could see that his sector of fire was nowhere near the crash site. I still couldn't believe that it was one of our helicopters in that street. I had no idea who it was or how it happened. But the fact was there was a friendly helo down that road to our east. Moore confirmed from his radio that a helicopter had gone down and that the task force was to move to the crash site and set up a perimeter. Our only problem was that we were still being engaged from three sides, and most important, we had enemy to the east, between us and the crash. I acknowledged to Captain Steele that we had received his transmission and that I understood that we would all link up at the crash site. The question to me was how: left, right, straight? Any of the choices was bad at the moment. We didn't have that many charges to blow holes in buildings, and we certainly couldn't walk straight down into the shooting gallery. We would have to figure out another way to get there.

Out of nowhere, and much to our relief, the ground convoy started to move from the objective toward us. Lieutenant Colonel Danny Mc-Knight, our battalion commander, was walking up the road behind the door of his Humvee, using it as a shield. I was never so happy to see those men as I was right then. Like the Black Hawks, the Humvees were heavily armed, but with M-2 .50 caliber machine guns or MK-19 40 mm grenade launchers. The convoy was creeping forward to our intersection ever so slowly. As it moved to the intersection it too became engaged by the Somalis. I tried to point out the direction of the incoming fire to the gunner on the top of the lead Humvee as they approached us. Apparently he didn't need any help from me, and I watched him lay a heavy burst from his .50 caliber to the north. I remember the gunner crouching deep down in the turret almost underneath the gun as he fired so as not to expose his head above the sights of the big machine gun.

Of all the sensations I remember from that day in battle, the most prominent memory was the noise. From the moment my feet touched the ground, every sound in the city seemed amplified. It did not help that I hadn't worn my hearing protection that day. I had been so worried about being able to hear the pilots on the headset that I did not even think to put in my earplugs. That certainly was a pretty stupid move. The sounds from that machine gun were so loud it made my teeth hurt. Even though it physically hurt to watch him shoot, I did feel much better about our security and certainly felt a hell of a lot safer.

I linked up with Lieutenant Colonel McKnight and gave him our status. At this point we had one litter-urgent casualty who had been evacuated by ground and three walking wounded, Galentine, Berendsen, and Snodgrass. As McKnight reiterated that we needed to move to the crash site, I looked south and saw Sergeant Dan Schilling, USAF, pulling security across the road from us. The friendly faces were blessings and morale boosters. I told McKnight that I understood the order to move to the crash site and that we were trying to figure out how we were going to get there. He told us that the convoy was heading to the crash site and for us to climb on board. That was a much better option than any of the other thoughts that I had at the time. We began breaking down our position and started to load onto the convoy.

We picked up everything that was at our location, even the fast ropes that were cut away from the helicopter. We definitely didn't want the Somalis to get any of our equipment after we left. However, the biggest concern for me as the leader was knowing where my men were so that I could coordinate for the fight ahead and, even more important, so that I would not leave anyone behind. As the fifth stanza of the Ranger Creed states: "I will never leave a fallen comrade to fall into the hands of the enemy." Wounded or not, we would make sure that we had everyone, and it was my responsibility as the leader to make sure that happened. The problem was that we could not all load onto the same vehicle. I had no idea onto which Humvee or truck my men had loaded, only that there were no longer any Rangers on the street at our blocking position. Satisfied that we had all our men, I turned to climb onto a cargo Humvee only to find the whole convoy already moving forward. A few loud yells and some choice words got the driver's attention, and he stopped so that I could climb on board. As I stepped onto the top of the left rear tire of this Humvee, I remember looking down and seeing pieces of green plastic smashed into the street. I didn't know exactly what it was, but I remember thinking: *How the hell did a plastic coffee cup get smashed way the hell out here in the middle of Mogadishu?* I did not give it another thought and climbed on board. We were in a race against time to get to the crash before the Somalis.

I took one last look around as we started to pull away from the blocking position. The crash site was due east of our location, so I figured that we could drive a block north, make the first right, drive a few blocks, take another right, and we would wind up right at the crash site. Unfortunately, Mogadishu is not quite set up on a grid system the way, for example, Manhattan is—in Somalia the roads and streets are not uniform by any standard. Maybe this quick detour wouldn't be quite so easy.

When I climbed onto the Humvee, I tried to sit with my legs over the side and my body facing the street. That way I could pull security and at least see what the hell was going on. Unfortunately, we all piled into the cargo area and landed in a big heap. I was the last on top, and when the vehicle started to move I lost my balance. That was one of the scariest moments of the day for me. My feet were hanging over the side of the Humvee and I was flat on my back. I could not sit up because of the weight of the body armor and all the other equipment I had on. I could not see where we were going, and I certainly could not shoot. All I could do was hang on as we raced through the streets of the city. I had absolutely no control whatsoever. I kept thinking that I was going to get shot, and it pissed me off that I would not even have the chance to return fire at the bastard. But I knew we were heading toward the crash site as planned and that we would be there soon.

How long were we driving? It seemed like an hour. We raced through the streets. I thought, *Shit, I had just been looking at it two seconds ago.* I could see it from our blocking position; Diemer had pointed it out to me. Why weren't we there yet? The truth of the matter is that I have no idea why we could not drive straight to the crash. I do know that easy tasks become very difficult when performed under fire, and driving is no different—and the poor shape of the Mogadishu streets was no help. The lack of good radio communication also factored into the equation.

Then we stopped, although I did not know why. Whatever the reason, this was the time to get off the vehicle and pull security. Just like when we were getting ready to insert and were stalled in the air, sitting in a stationary target was not a good idea. The convoy was halted on some street that obviously was not the crash site. We all dismounted and quickly moved to the front of the vehicle and found cover. We were at a four-way intersection again. The obvious problem with these intersections was that it gave the enemy three directions from which to fire at us. Plus, adding in the houses and multiple-story buildings, there was an awful lot of ground to cover and not nearly enough men to do it. But that is the drill, and of course you have to do the best you can.

We started to receive gunfire again but I felt much safer off the vehicle and on the ground. Diemer and I were on the left side of the lead vehicle, and Sergeant Telscher and Sergeant Joyce were on the right, each of us pulling security to the front and the left or right. Engaging the enemy was not difficult, and unfortunately there were plenty of opportunities to do it. There was no doubt about it—they were not about to give up. But then again, neither were we. I pictured all these Somalis pulling their old AK-47s off the mantel, running down the road to take a few shots at the Americans, and then running home to Mom before dinner. They would shoot out of windows, around corners, over walls, from everywhere.

I figured that the convoy had stopped to do a map check. We should have been at the crash site by now but after my earlier experience at the blocking position, I certainly was not critical of whoever was making the decisions. Everything is more difficult when people are shooting at you. I kept thinking that any moment now we would get back on the Humvees and go pick up the men at the crash.

The next thing I knew, I was kneeling behind a Humvee with a wounded Ranger on the ground, his head resting on my knees. One of my team leaders, Sergeant Casey Joyce, had been shot. He had been with Telscher across the street from me and was engaging the enemy down the road to the right when he was hit. Unfortunately, as Casey had been engaging the enemy to the right of the vehicles, he had been hit by a bullet from the unprotected side. Despite the Kevlar vest he was wearing, the round entered his body right under his arm where it was not covered by the vest. This was the first life-threatening gunshot wound I had ever seen. The wound was small, almost the size of my pinky nail. So small, in fact, that I almost overlooked it as we tried to assess its severity. Jim and I followed the first aid procedures just as we had been taught. It's going to be okay; its going to be fine, I told myself. Casey did not seem to be in any pain, and he did not move or make any sound; he just looked up at me. As I tried to reassure him, Jim and I frantically worked on the wound to his chest. I had no idea what was happening around us until the senior medic bent over and checked Casey's vital signs. He already knew. He checked the vital signs and told us to put the litter on the vehicle. I don't think it registered with me that one of my men had just been killed. Nothing in my training had prepared me for that. There is nothing that can replicate that feeling of loss. But the reality of the events all around me kicked back in. We loaded back onto the vehicles and began the process of turning the convoy around to head *back* in the direction from which we came.

After making sure that there were no Rangers left on the street, I turned to get on board another Humvee. There was no way that I was going to pile onto that cargo Humvee again and be in the same position as last time. My guess was that we were heading back toward the crash site, and again I was thinking it must be close. I quickly climbed into the back of a Humvee and found myself right on top of a wounded Ranger. We were moving now, and I was face-to-face with him. He was bleeding pretty badly around his neck and face. All I could say as I lay there was, "Hang in there, you'll be okay." Someone started screaming and yelling at me. It was Sergeant Chris Schlief, the machine gunner in the back. He was kneeling, and when I jumped in I had landed across his ankle and lower leg. It did not register at first what he was yelling about. I thought he might have been shot also. Then I realized that I was on his leg—and that the Ranger I was talking to was dead. I was lying on one of our fallen comrades. It was another of those sick doses of reality that we all would experience that day.

The sound of metal being torn apart was deafening. Much like the sound of a burst from miniguns, you know that something real bad had just happened when you hear it. We had just driven through an ambush and some vehicles were hit by small-arms fire and rocket-propelled grenades (RPGs). It was so loud that it hurt. I saw a Humvee behind us swerve and pass us on the right as we came to a screeching halt just past an intersection. There were soldiers wounded and lying in the street. One of our Humvees had been hit by a rocket, and the men riding in the back had been literally blown out of the vehicle. Several of us immediately jumped from the convoy to help the wounded. As I started to climb out from the back of my Humvee, I watched as a Somali pipe grenade landed between one of our wounded Rangers and my vehicle. It looked like one of those old World War II potato mashers that the Germans used. Regardless of who made it, it was going to hurt. There was no place to go. The vehicle was stopped, and there was this grenade right in front of me. I tucked in my head and waited behind the tailgate. A couple of seconds later there was a puff of white smoke, and that was it. It was a dud. What a lucky bastard.

We began to take care of the wounded, but the bad news was that we were still pretty much in the kill zone. All we could do was move the wounded to a good vehicle, police all our equipment, and get ready to move again. Most of the men in the vehicles were engaging the enemy, while those on the ground attended to the wounded. We began to take heavy gunfire from down a street. In one of those vivid moments, I watched Sergeant Aaron Weaver appear out of nowhere and toss a grenade with the grace and accuracy of a Nolan Ryan fast ball. It was awesome. Like Berendsen's one-handed M-203 shot back at the blocking position, Weaver threw that grenade with all the confidence of a major leaguer, and the grenade sailed right in the direction of the firing. The grenade detonated a few seconds later, buying us some time to load our casualties onto the remaining vehicles.

How many Rangers were wounded? I had no idea. All I knew was that we were taking fire from every direction and were in a fight for our lives. We had lost a vehicle or two in the ambush. In concert, all the Rangers on the ground were taking care of business. Watching men like Weaver jump into the mix was so reassuring to us all. We were reacting to the events all around us and doing, like the old Shaker adage, "the next thing." In this case, the next thing was taking care of our casualties, policing all our men and equipment, and fighting the enemy with all our might, though not always in that order.

It wasn't too long after we began moving again when we ran into yet another ambush. Again, the wretched sound of metal crashing through metal slapped me back to the moment. We stopped and had to begin another round of fighting, aiding the wounded, and policing the battlefield. Many times I have remembered the events of the day like a bad movie in slow motion viewed frame by painful frame. But in each of these frames, there were so many moments of incredible individual courage that they offset any of the intended results of the enemy actions. In an ambush, the goal is to kill all the people in the kill zone, or at least to render them incapable of fighting anymore. The Somalis were getting a lesson from this task force. While we tended to our wounded we also delivered the fury of the best that America had. We would not be stopped, not now.

When we started up again, I found myself in the rear right seat on a Humvee. It was much better for me because at least I could fire back at the enemy as we drove, but apparently Humvees were not built for passengers over six feet tall. I'm six-four, and for me it was worse than being in the cheap seats of a commercial airplane. The body armor, the web gear, and of course the weapon made movement inside the vehicle difficult at best. Even with the window down, it was hard to move my weapon around to engage the Somalis.

The Somali battle drill was very simple. They would race down both sides of the street, turn toward the center, and start pulling the trigger, waiting for us to drive through the wall of bullets. *Macabre* would be the adjective that best describes this tactic. There was no way of telling how many of their own people they killed. I could only focus on the right side of the street, and I knew that the Rangers on the other side of the vehicle were doing the same. The only person that I remember being in the vehicle with me was Sergeant Marc Luhman. He was sitting in the front passenger seat, riding shotgun. As we raced down the street, we were following an unwritten rule: pull the trigger faster than the bad guy. With the window down, I had to contort my body in order to get a good shot. Because I wanted to engage the enemy to the front, I decided that I would open the door and lean out. That way I was not restricted by the door frame and would have more room to traverse my barrel. Plus, being a right-handed shooter, it would give me more room. Good initiative, bad judgment.

The roar of the big Humvee engine made it sound like we were doing about ninety miles per hour. In actuality, it was quite a bit slower, as we could watch Somalis running on the sides of the street actually getting ahead of us. As I looked to the right something caught the corner of my eye. There was a vehicle parked along the street ahead of us. I had just enough time for it to register when I yanked the door closed before it was taken off by the obstacle. That was a close call. I could just imagine the door catching the parked car and snapping off not only my barrel but my arm between the door and the frame.

I was back to the open-window engagement technique. There was no way to fight like that, so I turned myself around halfway and knelt on the seat. It was easier to twist my upper body to the left and shoot out of the window.

I had started the day with thirteen magazines of ammunition—390 rounds of 5.56 mm ball ammunition at my disposal. Now I was running low. I just could not believe how many armed Somalis there were. If nothing else, the Somalis should have learned that we would not back down from a fight, especially this one. For everything that the Somalis threw at us, we gave it back to them in spades.

We drove toward a Somali man in the street. Oddly, this person, whoever he was, was walking toward us. He was either pretty stupid, brave, or arrogant, I thought. I put my front sight post on his body and was ready to pull the trigger. But I couldn't see his hands. He was covered with the local garb and shuffled along the street, hunched over, clutching a shawl or similar piece of cloth over his head and shoulders. We were getting close to him. The last thing any of us wanted was to miss a target only to have him turn around and shoot one of our Rangers. We were almost alongside, and damned if he wasn't still walking toward us. *Come on, buddy, let me see your hands.* I couldn't see his hands. *Damn it.* No hands, no weapon. Nothing—it was too late. We were past him and he was still walking. For the three or four seconds this scene took, I had my barrel leveled right on his chest.

In an instant he was forgotten and we were right back in the thick of the fight. There seemed to be endless crowds of Somalis along the street shooting at us. Time was playing havoc with my mind. How long had we been in the city? How long had we been driving to the crash site? How many vehicles had we lost? I had no answer to any of these questions—all I knew was that we were still moving and the enemy was still shooting, and that was about all I needed to worry about. Luhman and I were shouting to each other from the front seat to the back. I am sure it was nothing more than reassuring babble that probably made us both feel better. The next thing I knew, our Humvee stopped. In a second it was turned around and heading back in the direction from which we had come. I could not believe it. We were heading right *back* into the fire.

In my vague mental picture of Mogadishu, I knew that the ocean was east and the desert was west. Luhman made the announcement that the convoy was heading back to the airfield. He must have heard it on the radio. This made the prospect of driving back through that street a little more appealing, but not much. As quickly as we had turned around, we were right back in the fight. Same position, same enemy, just a different side of the street. It was a fight for survival, to say the least. Just as before, all I was focusing on was guns. No faces, no men, no women, no children—just guns.

We headed toward the same Somali that we drove past before. He had crossed the road and was still walking along, all hunched over. What a lucky guy. The same thoughts crossed my mind. Where was his weapon? In an instant we were next to him, and a second after that we were past him and he was gone. *No time to worry about him now,* I thought. We were heading back to the airfield. I knew we had quite a few wounded who needed medical attention. There was no telling what our casualty list looked like.

Luhman yelled out that he was hit. I was still facing the rear of the Humvee, so I couldn't see what had happened to him. I was yelling for his status in between shots. There was nothing, no response. Finally, Luhman yelled out he was okay. What a relief. He said a few obscenities about the Somali who shot him, but nothing more. An instant later, it seemed, we crested a hill and saw the ocean in the distance. The ocean meant the airfield, and the airfield meant safety.

In the exact same moment that we crested that hill, the Somalis on the streets took on a new appearance as well. All of a sudden there were fewer of them. And the streets seemed to be as wide as U.S. highways. Instead of gunfire and explosions, there was quiet. It was eerie yet peaceful. We had made it through the city; we had made it through the fight. We were heading back to safety. We were heading home.

We became more anxious the closer we drew to the airfield. There were many wounded in the vehicles behind us and they would need immediate medical attention. As we pulled up to the gate, expecting to drive through, we were halted. Now what? Why had we stopped? There was a United States Army Humvee in front of us blocking our advance. Why wouldn't they move? Didn't they know we had wounded? I started to come unglued. I had had enough. I threw the door open, took off my Kevlar helmet, and ran up to the other vehicle's front passenger door. I remember screaming at the top of my lungs for them to move the vehicle. I could see all the medical staff at the tents a hundred yards away from us. Every second counted, and no one was moving fast enough for me. I must have sounded like a lunatic. After a moment or two, the Humvee moved and our convoy was free to drive through. The soldiers in the other Humvee were there to protect us—they were doing their jobs. But in the moment I lost my cool.

We made it to the aid station, and the medics began to do their jobs. I was trying to tell them the status of our soldiers. The more I spoke, the more frustrated I became. The more frustrated I was, the more upset I became, until finally I was a babbling idiot. My BDU trousers were completely soaked in blood, and the medics kept trying to take care of me. I couldn't believe it. Why wouldn't they listen to me? Couldn't they see that they needed to work on the men? In my hysteria I failed to see just how good the medics were. They were making sure that they did not miss anyone. They were on target and doing their jobs with the same intensity and enthusiasm that every Ranger took to the fight.

As I watched them unloading our wounded I began to feel tears well up. I couldn't help it. All the images of the past few hours were starting to come to the front of my mind. The faces now had names, and of course I knew them all. I found myself eye to eye with a medic. He was saying something, but it didn't make sense. He was asking my name. He didn't ask my rank, he asked my name. That seemed very unmilitary to me. It was so odd to me at the time that I couldn't think of anything to say other than to answer "Matt" through my tears. He said, "Matt, you can't cry. Your men can't see you cry. Do it someplace else." With that, I stopped. Just like that, the tears stopped and I went back about my way. I needed to check on the men.

I went inside the triage area and saw the wounded men. There were a lot of them. I found Scott Galentine. He was on a litter, and I knelt down to give him a comforting word. He asked about his buddy Casey Joyce. I felt the tears again and managed to say, "He is home in heaven."

That was it. I had just been over to the morgue. Someone had asked me to go identify the body, and I did. Like a robot I'd walked inside, looked down, said a prayer, and walked out.

I walked from the triage area back to the hangar. I saw Telscher. Everyone was trying to figure out not only what had just happened, but what was happening right then in the city and what was going to happen next. I told Jim to get a status of the men we had remaining and to reload ammo. I went to find someone in command for guidance. I checked over my list. I had one KIA and several wounded. From my chalk: Blackburn, Snodgrass, Galentine, Rodriguez, Berendsen, McLaughlin. Who wasn't wounded? Telscher, Moore, Diemer, Harris, and I were the only ones without a scratch. I did not know where the first sergeant was, so I headed toward the Joint Operations Center, the JOC. The first person I ran into was our battalion commander, Lieutenant Colonel McKnight. The thing I remember most about our exchange was that he was very calm as he spoke to me. He asked my status and I told him that there were only a few of us from Chalk Four left and that we were reloading our ammunition. He matter-of-factly told me that almost everyone from the hangar had just left to head back to the city. Lieutenant Colonel McKnight went on to say that there was very little security on the JOC and hangar and that it might be a good idea to get my few men on the perimeter.

I didn't know the big picture, only that we obviously were not done yet and that we were still in for a fight. I found the first sergeant and confirmed our status while Sergeant Telscher got the rest of the men from Chalk Four situated and organized. It must have been yeoman's work, but Jim was a solid young man and handled it with grace and efficiency. We spread our men out along the perimeter and filled the vacancies as best we could.

I went into the JOC to get what information I could. As best I could determine, the situation was that members of the task force had made it to the crash site. The quick reaction force from the 10th Mountain Division was trying to conduct a link-up with our men in the city, and we had launched another convoy of Rangers to help. Unfortunately, the rest of the news was bad. A second helicopter had been shot down sometime during the fight, and we had another downed crew in the city.

I was numb. Everyone who had a weapon and an American flag on their sleeve was called into the fight. Our cooks and our mechanics grabbed their weapons and jumped on the vehicles to help the cause. There was, however, a certain calm inside the operations center. The officers inside were nothing but professional and decisive from what I could see. It was very reassuring to me as a young leader to see them in action, to see the other side of combat, to see the side that no one sees or even bothers to mention. I must have looked a mess standing in the door of the operations center, covered in blood from the waist down. One of the officers of the task force approached me, looked down at my pants, and very calmly asked if any of that was my blood. "No, sir, it is not mine," I said. I could see the pain in his eyes for the soldiers who'd lost the blood that stained my clothes. He gave me a sympathetic look and a very fatherly nod, then moved back inside to attend to the matters at hand. Somehow I knew we would be okay—we had to be. It was just a matter of time.

My immediate concern was that the Somalis would eventually realize that we were shorthanded at the airfield and turn their attention toward us. If they attacked, it would be an even bigger fight than we had just seen. If they overwhelmed our base at the airfield, it would be certain death for us all. I made the rounds of the perimeter and checked on the men. I tried to give them all the information I could so that they knew what was going on in the city. Each man felt the same regardless of rank: fear, pain, anger, and unbelievable dedication to his duty. Everyone understood that we were not out of the woods yet, not by a long shot. With the relief of being out of the battle came the realization that all our buddies were still out there, still fighting, still living the Ranger Creed. Every half hour or so I checked in with the communications center to hear the progress of the rescue convoy. Each report was the same: we were almost there.

It was pitch black outside, and periodically we saw the helicopters touching down at the airfield to refuel and rearm their guns and rockets. There didn't seem to be as much fighting going on in the darkness, at least from what I could gather from the radio transmissions. The dreaded attack on the airfield never materialized, and early on the morning of October 4 the remaining men of Task Force Ranger made it out of the city. As the exhausted men made their way back to the hangar, it was a mixture of joy and sadness. The joy of seeing each and every Ranger walk back through the wire was tempered by the duty to inform them who had been wounded and who was dead. I assumed that at least the men who had been at the crash site had been informed, but they hadn't. The Second Platoon had one Ranger killed in action, Sergeant Casey Joyce. He was one of my two team leaders. It was a shock to Lieutenant DiTomasso when I told him the news. He had been with the other half of the platoon at the crash site and knew nothing of our situation. Sixteen members of Task Force Ranger had been killed, more than seventy wounded, and one pilot, Chief Warrant Officer Mike Durant, had been captured.

Every Ranger saw the battle from a different perspective, and each Ranger took the news differently. The only thing that everyone was in agreement on was that we now had a new mission: we had to find Chief Durant and bring him back to safety. As we dealt with our frustrations and our grief we tried to piece together just how this all happened. I was talking to some of the Air Force combat controllers who had been on the convoy, and I mentioned the lone Somali walking down the street during the fight. Someone from a vehicle that had been behind me said he'd seen the same thing. He said that he'd been going to take the shot but didn't because he couldn't see a weapon. In one sitting several men described that same scene. I thought that spoke volumes about the professionalism of the task force. We were warriors and we were fighting for our lives, but we lived by a creed and were guided by an ethic that set us apart from those we fought.

When I found some of the crew of Super 67 I was thankful that they made it out okay. They were the best, and though shaken by the capture of Durant, they were still ready to get back into the mix with a vengeance. We truly were one team. The crew chief reached into his pocket and pulled out a pair of goggles. They were mine. When the strap broke before the insertion I had thrown them on the floor of the *Texas Express*. He'd picked them up and saved them for me. It was a small thing, but it made me smile. How ironic that of all the things to say after a battle, he would turn to me, hand over a piece of broken equipment, and say, "By the way, good job following directions—you pulled the entire headset out of the helicopter when you roped in." Sure enough, when I placed the headset on the seat behind me, the wire had gotten caught on my web gear and had followed me down the rope into the city. Those smashed bits of green plastic on the street were the remains of the headset earpieces. All I could do was shrug.

Because of the large number of casualties, reinforcements from the States were inbound immediately: more Special Forces, more Rangers, AC-130 gunships to fly twenty-four hours a day. Yes, the next fight was going to be brutal. The gloves were off, and you could feel the animosity in that disgusting air.

On October 6 we held a memorial service for our fallen comrades. The entire task force gathered to pay respects. All the officers gave thoughtful eulogies. The final speaker of the afternoon was the task force commander, Major General William F. Garrison. Standing at the lectern next to the display of inverted rifles, boots, and headgear, the general recited extemporaneously the battle speech from Shakespeare's *Henry V.* Never in my life had I heard such inspiring words of commitment in the face of overwhelming odds.

"Whoever does not have the stomach for this fight, let him depart, give him money to speed his departure since we wish not to die in that man's company." Tears were streaming down my cheeks before he finished with "we few, we happy few, we band of brothers."

Later that evening, after two months of worthless mortar attacks from the Somalis, one round made it over the protective barriers and landed in the front of the hangar. We lost another brave operator, with several more wounded. Fear was transformed into pure rage. We promised ourselves that the next battle would be a bad day for Aidid.

We would find out much later that there were forces far above my pay grade working to solve this situation on the Horn of Africa. Our mission changed now from a snatch mission to a recovery operation for our captive pilot. We had seen pictures on CNN of Chief Durant being held prisoner somewhere in the city. This was fuel to our fire. Pissed off as we were about our situation and the unbelievably cruel and thoughtless pictures that had been aired on television, we went about rehearsing for our next operation.

Diplomacy won the day, and Ambassador Robert Oakley was called to pass a message from President Bill Clinton to Aidid. Ambassador Oakley gave Aidid an ultimatum, and within a few days Durant was released. Jim Telscher, Dave Diemer, and a few other Rangers were sent to the hospital to provide security and escort Chief Durant back to the airfield. When he arrived the chief was transferred to the belly of a waiting C-130 and flown straight to Germany. Seeing Chief Durant on that stretcher moving toward the aircraft was an inexplicably proud moment for me. I knew that the events of the past month would be studied and discussed ad nauseam. Some would call it a victory, and some would yell defeat. Historians and pundits would certainly decide sometime down the road. I could care less what the naysayers would conclude; they had not been there and fought with us. As I watched Chief Durant move up that ramp, after all that had happened and all that we had been through, the only things that made any sense to me were our mottos: "Night stalkers don't quit" and "Rangers lead the way."

SUA SPONTE:
OF THEIR OWN ACCORD

Raleigh Cash

Raleigh Cash was a twenty-two-year-old sergeant on the rescue convoy for Task Force Ranger. He was the primary forward observer for Third Platoon, Bravo Company, Third Battalion, 75th Ranger Regiment. Forward observers are responsible for directing fire support assets during a Ranger mission. The vehicle convoy was assigned to assist in the blocking positions and to exfiltrate the Rangers as well as the prisoners.

I was the primary forward observer for the vehicle convoy, which consisted of eight vehicles. The alternate or backup forward observer was my RTO, or radio telephone operator, Private First Class Tory Carlson. We were one team. Sergeant Jeff McLaughlin and Specialist Joe Thomas were another team, as were Sergeant Mike Goodale and Private First Class Jeff Young. We also had Sergeant Chris Huneke as our mission tactical air controller. He was an Air Force member of the task force. Chris was a little different from the combat controllers in that he made a living controlling fast movers.

On Saturday, October 2, we were out at the shooting range having a good time. I remember it was a gorgeous weekend. Not a cloud in the sky. Tory and I had done our PT, our physical training, by running around the airfield earlier that day. When we ran around the airfield, we were required to have a weapon with us at all times, so we either got really good at going on morning runs carrying a 9 mm pistol, or we strapped on a CAR-15 or M-16 and felt it bang against our backs the whole way. That morning Carlson carried his CAR-15 with him so I didn't have to carry the 9 mm.

To pass the time, we'd sit on our bunks and read books or listen to a Walkman. We each had a Walkman, and we shared the three tapes that we had. I had a mixed Metallica tape. I remember Carlson had a Red Hot Chili Peppers tape and another tape that he'd borrowed from someone else. We pretty much wore out the Chili Peppers and Metallica tapes, playing them over and over and over. It got to the point where we knew every word to every song, every guitar riff and drumbeat, and we'd be dancing around, having fun to pass the time.

Carlson was known for his dramatic ability. We'd make him read stories to us. Whatever magazine was around, somebody would give it to Carlson and have him read the letters that people wrote in. Carlson would read it in his best newscaster voice. He'd have a huge audience sitting around listening to him. He was up there reading with his hand outstretched, speaking like he was a well-known actor in some theatrical production.

That evening our standard game of Risk was being played. Sergeant Watson was probably winning. He usually won. The best thing about the Risk games was that they gave us a break from the monotony of hangar life. We were competitive and there was no rank in a Risk game. Everybody could be who they were, could yell and scream at each other, could punch each other, even tackle each other. We got to be ourselves and let off some steam. We didn't have to think about being a Ranger or being a private or sergeant first class or platoon sergeant. We didn't have to think about anything other than the game we were playing, and there were no holds barred.

I was slated to go on the resupply detail the next morning. We were supposed to link up with an eighteen-wheeler and fill it up with water so we could have our two-minute showers in the morning. After a workout, it was a nice thing to be able to pop in the shower for two or three minutes and cool off. We would take turns on resupply. The vehicle convoys would split up into eight Humvees. Carlson would be the forward observer for his four vehicles, and I would be the forward observer for my four vehicles. Carlson rode with the platoon sergeant,

Sergeant First Class Bob Gallagher, and I rode with the platoon leader, Lieutenant Larry Moores.

October 3 was a beautiful sunny day, like most of the days there. Carlson and I went and ran our PT. We were both trying to get our six-pack abs going so that we could show them off when we got home in the wintertime and everyone else was putting on their layer of fat. We were pushing ourselves to get in the best shape of our lives.

Afterward, the plan was to go to the beach. It turned out that there was a detail needed to go do some cleanup of the connexes that we'd just set up. We put these connexes or boxcars in front of the hangar and filled them up with sandbags so we wouldn't be as exposed to direct fire from Somali thugs passing by. I was instructed to assign one of my men out of the headquarters section. Headquarters section is made up of the communications section, the supply section, the forward observers, and medics. Basically, it was all the people who had jobs other than the infantrymen. I sent Carlson.

I was getting ready to go out the door and link up with the platoon leader and hop on our vehicles to go to resupply when First Sergeant Glenn Harris, the ranking sergeant of the entire company, came over and asked where some of these guys were. I had to tell him I didn't know. And, rightly so, I had to go find them.

I found Carlson in the hangar watching TV. I'd given him instructions to be at a certain place at a certain time, and instead he was in watching TV. I yelled at him a little bit—I guess you could call it constructive coaching to a point—and I made him do some push-ups.

"Do you know what today is?" I asked him. It was the birthday of the regiment—the day that marked the formation of the modern-day 75th Ranger Regiment, and also the same day that the Third Ranger Battalion had been formed. Of course, he told me he didn't know. I told him to think about it, and he still didn't know. So now I was doubly mad. That was going to be his reprieve—if he'd known what the day was, I was going to let him off the hook. But since he wasn't at his detail cleaning and he didn't know the significance of October 3, I made him do some push-ups. And I turned and walked out.

That's the last time I spoke with him until October 4.

•　　　•　　　•

We first heard the code word, *Irene*, over the radio while we were out on resupply. Specialist Milliman and I were on top of the tank trailer, filling her up. We immediately cleaned up without even finishing the resupply. It might have taken us about an hour and a half to get back to the hangar. We could hear some information over the net, but it was pretty garbled and hard to make out.

As soon as we got back, we heard on the radio that Sergeant Wilson had been hit. This was maybe three o'clock in the afternoon. We didn't know how bad he was hit, or anything else for that matter. I just got a cold feeling: *Oh, shit, somebody got hit this time.*

We were all a little worried for Sergeant Wilson, and we were listening to the radio. We all wanted to ask questions, but we didn't want to get in the way of the guys who were in the middle of this mission— actually in the *middle* of it. The volume of fire over the radio was audible. You could hear the utter confusion: "What's going on? Where's this vehicle? Where? Where's so-and-so? Where's Chalk Four? Where's the vehicle convoy?" Things were getting answered in order, so we knew that everybody was figuring out who was supposed to be where and what was going on. That made us feel a little bit better.

We were told that we were going to button up and head out. The task force had captured the two enemy soldiers that they had intended to take. I'd be heading out with my vehicle convoy, the same four vehicles that had gone out to fill the water resupply. We each grabbed some extra ammo and some IVs because we didn't know if anybody else had been hit. We packed for the worst. I hopped in the Humvee, and the first thing I heard was Sergeant Weaver yelling over the radio. You could hear a horrendous amount of fire going on in the background.

When we were sitting around stockpiling and getting our equipment sorted out, I heard Mike Kurth on the radio saying the first Black Hawk helicopter had gone down. I just remember him saying: "There's a Black Hawk down . . . a Black Hawk going down . . . a Black Hawk down in the city." Everybody just kind of looked at each other. We'd been thinking that these guys were finishing up and that they were on their way back to the airfield with a few casualties, and now a Black Hawk had just gone down. Our whole mission changed entirely. Now it wasn't just a snatch and grab; now we had to go in and get those guys out of the downed helicopters.

After we heard that the first Black Hawk had gone down, we decided that we were going to need a lot more ammunition. We were going to need a lot more IVs. We were going to need a lot more of everything.

We were scrambling to get as much ammunition as possible. I grabbed two crates of 5.56 ammo in case we ran into any of our guys so we could resupply them. Also, my turret gunner and I grabbed a couple more boxes of .50 caliber ammo for his heavy machine gun. We figured we were in this for the long haul and that things were going to get really crazy.

I'd made a decision not to wear my back plate because I had to carry a radio on my back the whole time. On my hip I carried a Sabre radio, which is like a walkie-talkie. I also carried a UHF radio as backup to talk to the helicopters. I kept that radio on the helo common net. In addition to the radio equipment that I carried, I also carried a CAR-15-203. The CAR-15 is a shortened version of an M-16 rifle. It has a shorter barrel and a collapsible butt stock. A 40 mm grenade launcher mounted underneath it makes it a "203." I also carried a shotgun, a sawed-off Remington 870 that I would use for breaching doors, two hand grenades, an ammo pouch full of flash-bangs for crowd control, and a standard load of 210 bullets for my rifle. In my web gear I carried some machine gun ammunition. My web gear held three ammo pouches, a first aid kit, and NVGs, or night vision goggles. On this particular day I also carried about 100 or 150 rounds of SAW ammunition. Everybody tried to carry a little bit extra. Just in case.

I can't tell you when the second Black Hawk went down, but it didn't seem like it was that long after the first. We knew that the guys on the streets had split up and that they had started going to the downed choppers. Sergeant Struecker had been directed to leave the scene of the original assault in order to evacuate Blackburn.

When Struecker's convoy pulled in, we ran forward to help unload the wounded. Sergeant Pilla had been killed on the way back in. I went over to help them carry Pilla's body over to the medical tent, where the medics were starting to set up triage.

I heard Sergeant Struecker instruct some of the guys to go clean out the Humvee. I walked back toward the Humvee and saw him talking to Specialist Brad Thomas. Brad was visibly shaken. He and Pilla were very close friends. I heard Sergeant Struecker consoling him, and after a short discussion we all knew we were going back out.

I was looking at all these guys who had just come in from the initial assault with some of the wounded, looking like they had just gone through hell. I then realized that those same guys were going to go *back out*. I'll tell you, I wanted nothing to do with it. I was scared to death.

Right then Dale Sizemore came running up to me. "Who's on the back of your vehicle?" he shouted.

"Velasco."

"Well, I'm going out."

I looked at him. "Dale, you got a cast on your arm. You *can't* go out."

He said, "Fine, I'll cut it off," and he ran back in the hangar. I was thinking I hated to be so short with him, but he'd be more of a liability with that cast on. He ran back to the hangar and apparently cut his cast off. I don't know where he got his uniform or helmet or body armor because it was six sizes too big for the guy, but he came running back up to me and said, "Sergeant Cash, I'm going out."

I pointed to the back of the vehicle, and he hopped in with his SAW. I was impressed. Very impressed.

Once we were loaded up, Sergeant Struecker led us back out in a convoy. I was in the second vehicle with Lieutenant Moores. Our Ranger cooks had grabbed their weapons and jumped in along with us because we all knew we were in the middle of a hornet's nest. Basically every free body we had was hopping on the vehicles. Everyone is a Ranger first.

As soon as we got through the gate, we were ambushed. We were getting small-arms fire from the left and from the right. Specialist Eastabrooks from the lead vehicle had his pinky shot off in that initial engagement. We got a little farther on into the city and we were ambushed a second time. Basically, they'd shoot RPGs at us as soon as the first vehicle passed, and then open up with small-arms fire. When I noticed we were receiving fire, I started screaming, "Action left! Action left!" meaning that I saw enemy to the left.

My turret gunner, Pat Lepre, immediately started engaging with his .50 caliber heavy machine gun. Somalis were running over a wall, shooting through the doorways at us, just tearing it up and making a mess as we drove along. I was engaging targets with my CAR-15 and my 203. We were trying to get through the city to the big trucks carrying the prisoners.

Every time we were on a mission in the city, the Somalis would get the word out and all the locals would run out into the middle of the street, grab a bunch of tires or whatever else they could find, and build a roadblock to mark what was going on. I think they also wanted to keep us from where we were attempting to go. We ran into one of those roadblocks and were trying to navigate our way around it, receiving fire the whole time. A roadblock would cover the entire street—like a giant speed bump made of rubber and wood or any type of debris the Somalis could pull out into the street. They'd build them up till they were about three feet high. Then they'd set it on fire. All we'd see would be the flames and the black smoke from the burning rubber.

Lieutenant Moores was trying to talk to the commander to figure out which way we needed to go. Behind him sat Major Nixon, who was in the right rear seat. I sat in the left rear seat behind Milliman, and in the back was Specialist Velasco, our RTO. Velasco had just graduated from Ranger School. I was talking to the Little Birds, trying to find out if there were any near us that could give us better directions. I had access to what was called the helo common, or the helicopter common net, where all the helicopters talk among themselves to coordinate airspace. Obviously, the Little Birds were tied up with what they were doing—supporting the men from the initial assault.

When I did get directions from the helicopter, I would tell Lieutenant Moores, who would tell Sergeant Struecker, who was up in the lead vehicle; but by the time it got to him, it was too late—we had missed the turn. We'd get turned around and have to drive right back through an area we'd just received fire from. I'd yell to take the left, and the lead vehicle would miss it. I can't tell you how many times we did this. It seemed like a hundred.

At this point I just sat back in my seat in the Humvee and turned the world off for a second. I thought: *You know what? I'm going to die. I don't think anybody's going to make it out of this.* I figured that if I got hit in an extremity—an arm or a leg—it would hurt like hell, but the doctor would fix me up and I'd be okay. And if I got hit in the head, I'd just die and it'd be over. So all I really had to fear was the pain of getting hit in an arm or a leg or something, because if I got hit in the face or the head, I just wouldn't know. So I made my peace with God. I said: *Well, you know—this is it. I've got to do the best I can. I'll do everything that's in my power to make sure that my Ranger buddies and I get all of our boys back to the hangar.* And as soon as I made that peace with God and decided that the only thing I really had to be scared of was the pain of getting shot in an arm or a leg, I became calm. Or more calm, I should say—I wasn't exactly a smooth operator.

By now it was around 1700 hours. My side of the vehicle was getting hit pretty hard. Our driver, Milliman, was driving with his right hand, with his left hand holding his M-16 out the window, shooting as best he could. I was sitting behind him trying to cover him by engaging as many targets as possible in front of the vehicle or beside him. My point of fire was the front and left of the vehicle, with Specialist Lepre, our turret gunner, taking the rear.

Lepre was on full autopilot. I don't know how to explain it any better. It did not appear to me that Lepre had any concern whatsoever that he was in an exposed position. As our turret gunner, he would take out targets left and right without even thinking about it. He would engage, rotate, engage, rotate.

The rounds were flying, and the side of our vehicle got peppered hard. I remember my door getting hit; I looked down and I saw a hole in it. It scared me. Was I hit? I'd never been shot before. I looked down and saw the hole in the door, and I was thanking God that *that* day was the day we'd put doors on the Humvee. Those doors had saved my knee.

We turned around and around until we finally linked up with the rest of the convoy, which was on its way to the airfield. There was some sporadic fire, but nothing too major. I tried to spot some targets for Lepre. Specialist Velasco jumped out to check all the radios in the convoy to make sure everybody was still up, because we were having a few commo problems. I kept trying to link up with Carlson to find out what was going on—to see if he knew something or was in a better position than any of the other guys on the ground.

With my radio on helo common, I was able to talk directly to the Little Birds. I had the fire's common net—which was how the forward observers would communicate if the Sabre radio—the walkie-talkie—didn't work. Each chalk had a fire support specialist with them. The fire support guys would talk back and forth between each other to figure out where the friendlies were, where the enemy was, and who was the closest forward observer in position to direct the Little Birds. I could also tune to the command frequency, which is what the senior officer, Major Nixon, and all the platoon leaders were using to coordinate with the command and control of the battle. I knew pretty much at any given point where most people were, where most of the fighting was, who was engaging as well as who was *not* engaged, and who needed fire support. If you knew that somebody wasn't using the Little Birds, you would call the fire support officer (FSO) and ask for permission to use that asset. We use what's called "silence is consent." If the RSO said nothing, then that was consent. If he didn't want you to use that asset, he'd break in and tell you no. But if you heard somebody using the Little Birds, you wouldn't cut in unless you were in a worse position. Usually you would wait until you heard "End of mission" over the radio. As soon as "end of mission" came up, then you could pretty much grab that asset and rock and roll.

As I hopped out of the vehicle we received a couple of bursts. Lepre was engaging a target to my front left. Sizemore was still in the back of my vehicle. I yelled out a target to Sizemore, and he yelled, "Where?" Sizemore had his SAW. I pointed out a Somali in a tree. My rifle was equipped mostly with tracers because my primary function was to indicate targets for the Little Birds. I popped a couple of tracer rounds in the tree, where this guy was shooting at us. Sizemore ripped into him with his SAW. The guy fell down, along with half the tree.

Sizemore turned around and asked me: "Is that it? Did I get him?"

"You took half the tree down," I said. "That's it. You got him, Sizemore."

•   •   •

When we linked up with the ground convoy on National Road, they were facing one direction and we were alongside facing the other. We got the word that we were going to escort them back to the hangar. I ran back to a few vehicles to get them turned around, and in that narrow street it seemed like Milliman had to do a fifteen-point turn to get going.

Then we started receiving more fire. Lepre began shooting again. That's when a Somali jumped out from behind one of the stone walls and shot an RPG at the vehicle in front of us. Milliman slammed into the back of the stopped Humvee. All of us got smashed up inside, bouncing our heads off things. I remember looking at my strangely oriented pinky and thinking it might be broken. I grabbed some electrical tape off my web gear and taped it up in case it started swelling. I then went back to pulling security on the vehicle.

The RPG blew a lot of sand into our vehicle, and it was hazy for a second. I couldn't tell if we were being fired at or not. I couldn't really hear anything—my ears were ringing. Then it cleared up and we started moving again. We had to drive some crazy crisscross pattern back toward the hangar—*turn left here, turn right here*—to avoid the burning roadblocks and piles of debris. We started receiving fire again, and this time they were shooting from the windows, from the alleyways, the doors, everywhere. I could hear the alleyways erupting like crazy as we were going past them. We were picking off onesies and twosies as best we could, discriminating among those who had a weapon and those who didn't. We were still following the rules of engagement as written. But as we were driving farther it was getting crazier; more and more people were coming out. I was seeing more and more weapons and fewer and fewer civilians until it seemed we were engaging everybody. There were so many of them. I recall hitting another roadblock and having to back up to go around it. Finally, as we got closer to the airfield, the fire began letting up a little bit. The vehicles in front of us were still firing sporadically, engaging targets as best they could. I think at this point the very front of the convoy was getting hit hard, but by the time we got to their position, it was only sporadic fire.

I remember pulling back into the airfield and it was like we had crossed an imaginary line to safety. As soon as we crossed that line, everything stopped and it was quiet. It went from crazy noise and shooting and RPGs blowing up all around us and people yelling out directions and orders to—*nothing*. You could hear some chatter on the radio, but it was like only background noise.

We dismounted and headed back toward the hangar and started to look around, to get a situation update. Who'd been hit? Who'd gotten wounded? Had we lost anybody? We unloaded some of the wounded from the initial assault and tried to clean up the vehicles a little bit. Sergeant Struecker directed some of the guys in the platoon to change out tires on the Humvees because some were shredded to nothing. We began cleaning up our weapons as best we could, running rods and patches through our rifle barrels to get all the carbon buildup cleaned out. We loaded extra ammunition—as much as we could get on the vehicles—and IVs, anything we could think of, because we still had guys left out on the street.

I asked someone, "Where's Carlson?" because I'd heard he'd been hit. I knew he'd been part of that original assault convoy with Struecker, so I thought he might know. Sergeant Struecker put his arm around me and said that he was sorry, but he thought Carlson had been killed. It broke my heart.

I also heard that my Ranger buddy Mike Goodale had been hurt and that Jeff McLaughlin had been wounded, along with Bill Powell and Jim Lechner. Those were all the fire support guys. I was extremely worried because we really didn't know how bad any of these guys had been hit.

Before every mission, Mike Goodale and I would walk over and meet each other halfway just as we were getting ready to board. We really didn't say anything. We'd just shake each other's hands. *This could be the last time that I see you. I just want you to know.*

I helped the guys who were changing the tires and hosing out the back of the Humvees, getting all the debris and mess out. We reloaded ammunition for the .50 caliber machine guns and the Mark 19 40 mm grenade launchers, small-arms ammunition, more grenades, and shotgun rounds. Next, Velasco checked every radio on every vehicle to make sure they were good. We had to reset some of the frequencies in a couple of the vehicles. Then we went over and made sure that the guys who were operating the radios or who could possibly end up operating radios understood what frequencies we were using and what station each frequency represented: command, the Little Birds, and so on. I took a cheat sheet and wrote down what frequency set each of these frequencies would go in. Preset one was Command One; preset two was that particular chalk or platoon. With a SINCGARS radio you could have up to twenty presets, so you could change channels to talk to different people. You could also set it up to scan all of those frequencies so that when somebody talked on one of those frequencies, you could hear that. It was a lot easier than with the old radios, because you didn't have to constantly switch back and forth between preset one and preset two. You could scan all these frequencies, and as long as you keyed the hand mike or squeezed or pressed the talk button within one second, it would automatically go to that channel and let you talk back. That came in extremely handy.

Around sunset we found out that we were going to be going back into the city but that this time we were going with the Pakistani and Malaysian peacekeepers. The Malaysians had APCs, or armored personnel carriers, and the Pakistanis had tanks we could use to help get the guys out. We also found out that there were elements from the 10th Mountain Division who were going to come over and augment us. We got everything fitted up and drove over to the docks. Because of the different types of radios involved, there was a huge communication problem between the task force and the 10th Mountain Division. It proved to be a tremendous task to get this convoy organized and ready to go. We were at the hangar for an hour or so, and then we drove over to the shipping yard where the Somalis conducted their barge trade. We linked up with the 10th Mountain Division outside under the stars.

We had to wait another couple of hours for the Pakistanis and the Malaysians to show. Then it felt like another three or four hours for the coordination effort to be completed. Once you'd been out there in the fighting, the way I had, you knew what our guys were going through. They didn't have hours. I was getting more and more frustrated with the amount of time it was taking to get all this coordination completed. I was voicing my anxiety and frustration when a lieutenant from the 10th Mountain Division came over and wanted to know what the problem was. I told him that some of my friends were out there dying. He told me to calm down. I'd just heard the report on the radio that one of my friends *was* bleeding to death—that they were out of IVs. In desperation they were cutting the tops of the IV bags and refilling them with water. And, of course, I wasn't there. And then it came through over the radio that we'd just lost Smith. At that point, I was crushed.

We were all listening to the reports from the streets, wondering when we'd be able to go back in when we finally started moving. It was late at night. Everybody was tired. Right before we'd left the hangar, I'd taken some leftover Copenhagen that my mom and dad had sent me. Out of a log of ten rolls, I probably had four or five of them left. I gave the tobacco to the guys. They were tired, and they needed something. Even if it was just the idea that Copenhagen might keep them awake until we got moving, that was enough. As our vehicle convoy finally began to move, anxiety flooded my mind again: *What the hell's going on? Where are we going? Are we going to be okay when we get there? Are all those tires going to be in the way? Do I have the right equipment? Is so-and-so dead? Is so-and-so wounded? How bad? Did we bring all the stuff we need?* I'm sure these things were going through everybody's mind.

Pretty soon we hit another roadblock. Right away, we had to turn around. We started receiving sporadic small-arms fire, and as we turned around it started picking up intensity until it sounded like a heavy-metal drum solo.

We found out later that all the men waiting for exfiltration could hear us getting close and then drive past them. They said that as we approached, the volume of fire would increase but then it would go away. What they didn't know was that we couldn't get to them. There were roadblocks at almost every intersection. Basically we were a moving firefight, pretty much a nonstop engagement, all night long. There were times when it would slow down or we would go through an area and it would seem like nothing was happening, but for the most part, it was continuous. It seemed like every Somali in the city was drawn to us. They would chew khat, a cocainelike stimulant, and get hyped up. Their fear would be pushed down—like an eighteen-year-old kid who feels invincible after drinking beer. They thought no harm could be done to them.

We had lost at least one APC. When we drove by it all you could see was a burned-out hull. Fog began to roll in—it may have been compounded by the smoke from the APC and the smoke from the tires burning all night long. At any rate, the vehicle behind us lost sight of us. We heard on the radio that they could no longer make visual contact with us, and so they didn't know which route to follow, whether or not we were still there or if we had made a turn somewhere. They were probably no more than a hundred yards behind us. I told Velasco to check the radios to make sure that they were okay and to give them a signal that we were just in front of them. It seemed as though we'd checked the radios a lot already, but redundancy is the key to success. The more often you checked your weapon and made sure that it was functioning properly, the less of a chance there was that it would malfunction when you needed it most. A radio is as important as a rifle—especially to a Ranger.

We got to a point where we stopped next to an alleyway, midway between the two crash sites, and waited for the helicopters to report the best path for us to get to them. There were some members of the 10th Mountain Division unit there that had linked up with us earlier that night. I walked over to the squad leader or whoever he was and asked him to pull security down this alleyway because we had received sporadic fire from it.

I checked in with Lieutenant Moores to see what was going on and give him the information I had. I then headed back to the position where the alley was to find nobody guarding it. I walked over to Specialist Sizemore and told him that we had to do it. I took the left side and he the right side. I poked my head around the corner. It looked clear. I put on my night vision goggles and saw what I thought was some movement, but I couldn't be sure, so I took a couple of steps down the alleyway, and that's when I saw someone walk around the corner. I raised my rifle and told him to halt: "*Ka hanaga joogo ama waa gubane*—stop or I will shoot." The guy froze for a second. I'm sure he wasn't expecting me to butcher his language that way, but I think he got the gist of it. He raised his rifle at me. I shot him. I lobbed two or three grenades down the end of the alleyway to clear it out. Sizemore peeked around the corner and couldn't see anybody else. I went back to the squad leader and told him he needed to maintain security in the alleyway. He said he'd take care of it.

For the two hours that we sat there, we received some sniper fire—little bursts here and there—but nothing too major. During this time I went to see how everybody was doing, making sure they had water and such—water being most important. I just kept talking to the guys, giving them whatever information I had because knowledge is power and at this point any Ranger might have to step up and be the leader. Information needed to be given down to the lowest-ranking man so he knew or at least had an idea of what was going on. All the time I was frustrated with how long it was taking.

When we started moving again, we split in half—part of the group went north and the other south toward the crash sites, as well as the buildings sheltering the stranded chalks from the assault. Again, this seemed to take a while.

Almost immediately we began receiving more fire. I happened to be over by one of the Pakistani tanks when it let off a round from the main gun. I don't think I'd ever heard anything that loud. That sound can wake the dead. And then I heard the dual machine guns on the APCs just tearing up the night sky, tearing up anything that moved. More RPGs were flying in.

I used my tracers to locate targets for the turret gunner and some of the guys with the machine guns and the SAWs. This teamwork functioned pretty well. If I couldn't hit a target then I'd mark it for the guy with the heavy stuff, and he'd take it out. As this went on we began hearing reports that they were having problems getting one of the bodies out of one of the Black Hawks. They were trying to cut out the console. I remember hearing a report from the CSAR (combat search and rescue) team that there was a delay and they were working on it.

As it got later and later into the night and earlier and earlier into the morning, the fire started decreasing in volume and turned back into kind of potshots, a couple of bursts of machine gun fire, AK-47 fire here and there. It wasn't as intense, so it felt like a break to us. I attributed the decreasing fire to the khat wearing off.

All during the night we listened to Joe Thomas and his Little Bird doing gun run after gun run after gun run. The Little Birds are small helicopters, painted black. The pilot and the copilot kept their ammunition and extra fuel tank behind their seats. They had 7.62 mm miniguns on both the left and right sides, in addition to two pods of 2.75-inch rockets. Their targeting system was crude but effective. After taking a couple of practice runs, and figuring out exactly where the bullets were hitting in relation to the windscreen in front of them, they'd take out a grease pencil and put a little X there on the glass and that would be their gun sight. These guys hit exactly where you told them to, using nothing but a little X on the windscreen.

Monday morning, October 4. As dawn was breaking, the firing began picking up again. We knew the Somalis were waking up and starting to chew khat, getting hyped for a new day of shooting. By now we'd arrived at the critical intersection of Marehan Road and the alleyway where most of the stranded chalks were located. The CSAR team had finished extraction of the pilot's body. We'd loaded up a lot of the men onto the vehicles, but there wasn't much room left. I told Specialist Milliman to back up our vehicle to get close to some of the guys who were running from their positions. We filled up the back of our Humvee. There must have been four or five guys in the back, maybe six. They jumped in, and grabbed some of the Kevlar that we had lying back there for added protection in case we hit a mine. While we stopped and the guys were hopping in, I started organizing who would shoot where— who had what. Everybody seemed to be working well together. As the ranking NCO, I was in charge of my vehicle.

I looked around and began to see the damage to the vehicles around us, to the city, the streets themselves, the buildings, and the bodies of the dead—the casualties taken by our opposition. There were quite a few on the ground in various positions around the vehicles. We found out that many of the Somalis had been a lot closer to us than we would have liked to believe. All night we'd been engaging targets that we could only guess at how close they were. Now, during the day, we could *see* them. Some bodies were as close as four or five meters away. In the night we'd fired at muzzle flashes or outlines of bodies; now we were seeing the result. The utter destruction to the city and the sheer number of Somalis that had been taken out by our fire power was mind-numbing. As we pulled forward, it seemed like the city erupted on us again. Maybe they knew that we were leaving. The vehicles in front of us were shooting down alleyways, shooting everything that posed a threat.

The sun was coming up, and the sky had that beautiful reddish-orange glow it gets before turning to blue. We continued to drive, and then, like the abrupt ending of a spring shower, the noise just stopped. It was around eight in the morning. The sun had been up a couple of hours. It was as though we'd crossed a line that marked the exit point of the battle, and then all at once you could hear on the radio all the guys yelling at all the different vehicles: "Cease fire! Cease fire! Cease fire!"

The "Paki Stadium" was the closest safe area to the Bakara market where we could link up and assess our casualties. It was an old soccer stadium the Pakistani soldiers now controlled. We pulled in and immediately began taking a head count of who was there, who was wounded, and who had been killed in action. I started frantically looking for the forward observers. I expected to either find Tory Carlson's body or be told that he had been transported elsewhere. But I couldn't find him or anyone who knew what had happened to him.

I found Mike Goodale lying facedown on a stretcher. He was pasty white and shivering. I didn't know how badly he'd been wounded, so I started talking to him. "Hey, Mike, how're you doing, Ranger buddy? Are you all right?" He told me he'd been hit in the ass. I think he was trying to lighten it up for me. He'd gotten shot in the back of the thigh, and the exit wound was the buttocks. Mike and I were talking, but it was obvious to me that he'd lost some blood and was looking pretty pale. I rushed over to one of the Pakistanis who were walking around with glasses and clean towels and trays of water, as though they were *waiters* or something. I snagged a blanket from one of those guys and laid it over Goodale to keep him warm, and then continued looking for the rest of my Ranger buddies. I found McLaughlin, who'd been hit in the hand. It was all wrapped up in this giant cast—it looked like he had a club for a hand. He was okay. They were all dazed from the painkillers the docs had given them.

I found out that Jeff Young had twisted his ankle and gotten some shrapnel in his leg. I found Bill Powell, who'd also been shot, but he was doing okay. I didn't see Lieutenant Lechner, although I later found out he had been hit in the shin. Joe Thomas and I finally linked up, and we gave each other a big hug and looked in each other's eyes. That look pretty much said everything. We stayed there while the helicopters took turns ferrying everybody from the stadium back to the hangar. We got back in our vehicles and drove back through the city. We took the long way around so as to avoid the Somalis, but we still had to drive through the city to get back to the hangar.

When I finally got back to the airfield it was almost three in the afternoon. After seeing some of the wounded guys and shaking hands, I headed for the hangar. Specialist Kevin Snodgrass came over to me and pointed me to Carlson. I couldn't believe it. He was alive! I ran over to him. He was lying on a cot, all drugged up on morphine or whatever, but he was being his typical Tory Carlson self—half smiling, enjoying life, running the pretty nurses around. I told him I'd thought he was dead. He said, "No, Cash, I'm fine. I got shot but I'll be okay." That's when one of the nurses came over smiling and said, "Hey, Tory, here's the soda you wanted." It just seemed like he always had that effect on people. He could make anybody smile.

My area was three bunks down from one of my Ranger buddies who had been killed. When I saw his empty bunk, that's when it really hit me. That's when I knew that I was never going to see some of those guys again. I walked around, as did some of the other guys, staring at the empty cots. I can't describe the feelings—the anger and the sadness all mixed up together, the pain that I felt in my stomach and my head, and the sadness that was in my heart. I found Sergeant Weaver sitting on his bunk, and I walked over to him and sat down next to him and we started talking a little bit, and then we both started crying. So much adrenaline had been going through us for so long, and it needed an outlet. I felt as if I'd just done a four-hundred-mile road march. Every muscle in my body ached; every ounce of me was in pain. I had never felt muscle fatigue at this level. My mind, my body—everything—was just completely spent.

All I thought about was that I never wanted to go back out into that city. I wanted to go home. I wanted to have nothing to do with this place again.

Somebody said that CNN was on. After every mission we'd go turn on CNN and watch. I got up and wandered over to where the TV was, and the first thing I saw was a dead body being dragged through the streets of Mogadishu. All the guys—pretty much without saying anything— just got up and walked back to their bunks. I thought it was tasteless that the media would show a dead body being dragged through the streets. Everything changed once we saw that video. We all took it very personally. I started cleaning up my rifle, reloading magazines with bullets, and then I walked out to my vehicle. I started cleaning it up and getting ready to go because I knew we were going back again.

That's when we heard that Mike Durant had been captured. That was another slap in the face because so many had died to make sure no one was left behind. My resolve immediately hardened and I knew what I was there to do: to complete the mission we'd been sent there to accomplish, at all costs. *Let's fix this place. Let's not leave until our job is done.* But we were redeployed before we could complete the mission.

We were Airborne Rangers. We knew that we had been sent to do a job and that the job was dangerous. Granted, we had taken some casualties, but we were all ready to put our lives on the line again and again and again, until we'd completed the mission. We had a job to do, but we were pulled out.

Later that night I remember wondering why my right shoulder was in so much pain. I walked over and I was talking with Pat Lepre, my turret gunner, trying to make sense of what we'd just been through. I told him that my right shoulder was really hurting, and Lepre looked at me and laughed. I asked him why and he said, "Raleigh, when I would ask for a new case of .50 caliber ammo, you'd grab it with your right hand and shove it right back up to me one-handed. Those things are pretty heavy." With all the adrenaline going through my body, I was lifting these fifty-pound cases up like they were egg cartons.

• • •

One of the hardest things to deal with after the battle was packing up for the guys who were killed in action and the guys who were wounded—packing up their equipment, putting it in duffel bags, and sending it home. Some of those guys were still getting mail. With the empty bunks, it was a very solemn place. In letters I'd written home I kept telling my parents not to worry about me. I wrote that they'd hear if I was wounded or killed. They wouldn't hear anything if I was fine. I had to keep stressing to them: no news is good news. A couple of days after the battle I sat down and wrote a letter to my parents. Reading the letter again, I can see the anger and the hostility I felt toward Somalia and the way things had gone for us. I stressed to my parents the importance of what we were doing and that I was very happy being a Ranger—that I was proud of what I had done.

On October 5, an AC-130 Spectre gunship came back in country. Because of all the casualties we had taken, for a brief period I was the fire support officer and Joe Thomas was the new fire support NCO. We set about making plans as to how we would utilize the Spectre gunship as another fire support platform and the AC-130 guys offered to give Joe Thomas and me a ride and get familiar with this powerful asset.

We jumped at the chance. Joe and I boarded the AC-130 and took off. We talked with the pilot, the copilot, the targeting officer, and all the other crew members. As we flew over the city they told us that they had to zero their guns.

One of the things you do when you go on a Spectre gunship as a forward observer is to try to get a shell casing or "brass" from the 105 mm howitzer on board. A 105 mm shell casing is quite a coveted item. Knowing that they needed to zero their guns, we asked the pilot if we could get a couple—one for each of us, maybe one for each of the wounded guys on the FO team. At first they told us they would not be firing the howitzer while they were over there unless they really needed to. Joe and I told him we understood. After a moment the pilot said, "Screw it. After what you guys went through, let's go get you some shell casings." So he flew out over the ocean and fired a smoke flare to train their guns onto and fired a few rounds for us. They generated enough shell casings for us and every one of the wounded FOs on the team.

Their primary mission that day was to fly over Mogadishu looking for any information that would either help get Durant back more quickly or quell an attack on the airfield. As we were flying around, one of the crew saw a flash. Its profile looked just like the launch of a SAM, a surface-to-air missile. As soon as they saw the flash, the AC-130 started evasive action, sinking and diving, continually dumping chaff and flares—trying to confuse the missile and keep it from hitting us. I'm sitting there thinking, *Oh, great. I just made it through October third and fourth unscathed, and now I'm going to die on an AC-130 joyride.*

What the targeting officer saw turned out to have been the glint off some metal or glass—something with the same visual signature as a SAM. We all got a pretty good laugh about that after the fact, after we all calmed down a bit. The pilot decided to take us down. I guess he figured out that Joe and I didn't really want to be up there anymore. We landed, grabbed our brass, and thanked everybody for the wild ride we'd gotten to go on.

When we got back to the States, our old regimental commander General Grange greeted each and every Ranger as we were walking off the ramp of the aircraft. Grange had just relinquished his command in July 1993 and was a Ranger icon. It was a great thing to see him standing there on the ramp as we exited, shaking our hands and telling us he was proud of us, that he was sorry for our loss, and that he wished he could have been there with us. When I shook General Grange's hand, I looked him in the eye and said: "We're still your Rangers, sir," and then moved on.

Then we hopped on another plane and flew home to Fort Benning. I didn't have anybody waiting for me at Fort Benning, then again, a lot of the guys didn't. Many of the out-of-town families couldn't make it on such short notice. They had a band playing for us as we walked into the hangar. We just wanted to come home to the barracks and try to unwind somehow.

After the formation broke up, the man who had raised me in the

Ranger battalion, Staff Sergeant Kevin Stewart, walked over and gave me a big hug. Kevin was a Panama vet and had ridden me and Mike Goodale really hard in the past. He'd gotten us into shape and taught us everything we needed to know, and I can safely say that because of that man I'm here today. I believe that he's one of the reasons I'm still alive. He helped train me to be the best that I could be: to be an Airborne Ranger NCO. I owe Sergeant Stewart a debt of gratitude that I can never truly express to him. I was so proud that I'd gotten to do what he trained me to do, and come through it. You could tell he was proud of what we'd done. He also knew the Rangers who had been killed.

In May or June of 1993 Bravo Company had gone over to Thailand to do some training. We had been deployed there for about a month. It was miserably hot, but we got to do a lot of live firing—that is, mock missions.

One day while we were there, the forward observers went to hang out with the Thai Rangers to trade some gifts. I think we gave them some jump wings or some extra braids, and the Thai Rangers gave each of us a little Thai medallion. They said that as long as a man was wearing this medallion it would protect him and that the only way someone could hurt him while he was wearing it was with a knife.

I wore my medallion every day on a shoestring around my neck. I wore it on October 3, and Joe Thomas wore his. Of all the forward observers, Joe Thomas and I were the only ones who didn't get hit. All the other forward observers, McLaughlin, Young, Carlson, Goodale, Lechner, and Powell, were wounded. I believed in that medallion symbol so much that I decided to have it tattooed on the small of my back. That symbol is with me now for the rest of my life.

During the battle, I didn't recall my ears ringing at all. I can't believe it, because I know how many guys experienced some hearing loss because of the noise. Everyone's body deals with things a different way. But I will say that for the next six months to a year, it seemed like my senses were extremely heightened. I was more aware of my surroundings and everything going on around me, whether it was my depth perception, my peripheral vision, my sense of smell, or my sense of hearing. Everything was fine-tuned, and it took a while for that to go away.

I remember Mike Goodale and I were driving around Fort Benning after he came off convalescence sometime in mid-November. It was gray and overcast in Georgia but still warm. We were driving down Range Road, and apparently somebody was having some weapons training with heavy machine guns. As we were driving down the road in my Jeep Cherokee, we heard the machine gun fire—it didn't matter that all the windows were up and the radio was on. The next thing I knew, I was lying on top of Mike, who'd leaned over so far that his face was underneath the dashboard. The jeep careened back and forth, and we looked at each other and started to laugh. Here we were back in the States, where we were no longer in harm's way, but we were still ducking bullets.

THROUGH MY EYES

Mike Kurth

Mike Kurth was a radio and telephone operator on October 3 and 4. Though the Texas native was an infantryman, his assigned duty was to carry the portable radios and provide the communications link between the command center at the airfield and the Rangers operating in the city. Often required to do multiple tasks at once, Specialist Kurth was the critical link between the leaders on the ground and arguably one of the most important members of the combat unit. He was twenty-two years old.

It was a beautiful day that morning. The sun was shining, and an ocean breeze kept a few of the light, fluffy clouds rolling across the sky. The coastline surrounding Mogadishu was actually quite scenic; parts of the beach were covered with black rock, with small gaps where you could see the ocean water running beneath. The rest of the beach was spectacular—you could almost picture yourself at a resort down in Mexico. But then you'd do an about-face and realize you were in Mogadishu, Somalia—a city filled with dilapidated, bullet-ridden buildings, no sewer system, and no electricity. The only things the Somalis had multitudes of—drugs, weapons, and lots of time on their hands—didn't make our job any easier.

We had been in Mogadishu for about six weeks. We were making some progress, capturing some key personnel, but it had been some time since we had been on a mission. The longer it was between missions, the more anxious we were.

Sunday was our down day—there wasn't a first call, we didn't have a timeline to follow, and the only thing on the agenda was getting the weekly haircut. As for me, all I had planned for Sunday, October 3, was to sleep in as long as I could, play a little volleyball and a couple of games of Risk, and maybe do a little reading. As I remember, it was a pretty standard Sunday: guys taking trips down to the beach, lots of board and card games in the hangar, and the Ping-Pong table in constant use. I was there by the volleyball court, directly in front of our hangar, pounding the crap out of the white ball.

I had been playing for pretty much the entire day except for lunch and my after-lunch nap. Sergeant Joyce woke me from my nap asking for a haircut. I told him it was way too early for me to start giving haircuts. I told him that I *knew* as soon as I started in with the scissors everyone was going to start getting in line, and I'd be stuck there for a good couple of hours giving haircuts while there was still daylight burning. (I happened to be one of the handful of guys you would trust to give you a haircut in Bravo Company!) So I told him I was going to play volleyball for little while longer and that I would give him a haircut before chow.

I guess it was around 1430 hours when we all noticed the key leaders heading into the Joint Operations Center. Fifteen minutes later the officers all came pouring out of the JOC, and First Sergeant Harris sounded off with our favorite words, "Get it on," which meant we were good to go. Most of the time this wouldn't amount to much. We would gear up and sit on the end of our bunks and wait for the word to head out to the birds. If we received the word, we would move out to the birds, load up, get cramped in, and wait to take off. Sometimes we took off, sometimes we didn't.

I was the platoon radio telephone operator (RTO), so I was responsible for all the radios. I made my way over to First Lieutenant Perino's bunk. I checked to make sure that his batteries were at full strength, that his radio was on the right frequency, and that he had his backup frequencies already programmed. His equipment checked out, so I went to check my radio. I was also good to go. After getting on all my gear, I heard my chalk leader, Sergeant First Class Watson, call the squad leaders and myself into the briefing room to give us information on the mission. Evidently, several of Aidid's top lieutenants had been spotted. They were in a building across the street from the Olympic Hotel, in the middle of the Bakara Market.

We had all heard about the Bakara Market before. It was dead in the center of Aidid's territory—which meant that everyone who lived in that area supported Aidid. On all of our previous missions we had dealt with only a few bad guys at a time. We'd gone in and done our jobs in the midst of a lot of curious onlookers. In that sense, we'd just been practicing riot control. This was going to be a lot different. We all knew it without talking about it. Everyone in the Bakara Market would either have a weapon or the ability to get a weapon. Watson told us that we could very well see some action on this one. I don't think anyone knew what to say to that. We knew the drill.

The plan was for the D-boys (Delta Force) to go in first and hit the building. Once they were inside, the four Ranger chalks were to fast-rope in, each one on its respective corner. Our chalk was going to be a little different; we would be roping down in the middle of the block. There were some power lines at the intersection that hindered the helicopter from dropping us directly on the corner, so when we hit the ground, we knew we'd have to run fifteen or twenty meters to the corner in order to set up our positions. After Delta secured the building and captured the personnel, we would be there to extract them all. They would call for the five-ton trucks that the Ranger ground convoy would escort on the drive up National Road. The enemy detainees would be loaded onto one of the five-ton trucks, and the Ranger chalks would be loaded up on the rest of the vehicles. This was the game plan. I thought: *Wait a minute, that doesn't sound right.* "Sergeant Watson, we're not taking the birds back out? We're riding on trucks back to the hangar? On five-tons?"

"That's right, Kurth, there are no landing zones for the Black Hawks that are close enough—so we are going to have to ride out on the five-tons."

On every other mission we had roped in and then set up an LZ: a landing zone for the 60s to come in and lift us out of enemy territory. After the birds picked us up, the mission would be pretty much over, although everyone was still ready for something to go wrong every time we got on board the aircraft. For the most part, though, it was always a pretty quiet ride back to the hangar.

This time we all knew we'd be roping down into a bad neighborhood and that everyone was going to have to complete the extraction in vehicles on the ground—subject to ambush and enemy fire. We'd been told we'd have the escort service of the Black Hawks and Little Birds. But this was still unsettling. To this day, I don't know precisely why I didn't like the idea of being extracted by the five-tons—whether it made the mission more risky or was simply having to confront something new. But whatever it was, I felt it.

I'd been under enemy fire before—most of us had taken fire. When it comes to being a target, I've always liked the theory that the smaller you are, the better. I've always been comfortable on my feet. But to be trapped in a truck deep in enemy territory, inching along in a convoy— nothing about it sounded good. Those five-tons were awfully big targets and didn't provide much cover; the Humvees, at least, had some ballistic protection.

Sergeant Watson pointed to a map, highlighting a street none of us had been down, marking the route back to the airfield. We stood there, nobody saying much. "Any questions?" he asked. There were none. That map pretty much said it all.

I went back to my cot to get a quick drink of water and recheck my equipment. I grabbed the drink because I wasn't going to be carrying any water with me on the mission. I had extra ammo pouches on my LCE (load-carrying equipment) but I had filled them with RTO extras, like extra batteries for radios and NODs (night optical devices), and different types of chem-lites, used to help set up the landing zones for the birds. Under normal circumstances, this would have been okay, but since we were basically conducting riot control on most of these missions, we also had another arsenal of weapons—nonlethal munitions. We each carried flash-bangs, which do exactly that: they generate a big flash of light followed by a big bang. We also had plastic hand grenades that were filled with plastic pellets. Some of the guys carried a CAR-15 with a shotgun attached to it, and we all carried both lethal and non-lethal rounds. After a couple of missions with my loaded-down butt pack filled with a two-quart canteen, a large IV, spare batteries for my

SINCGARS radio, and some small field dressings, I knew something had to go. On October 3, I eliminated the canteen.

Less than a minute to flight and I had all my gear squared away—all my grenades properly secured with the pins butterflied so they would be less likely to come out of the spoon. All my magazines were good. I got to the front of the hangar and ran into Joyce. He was on his way to his bird—he was on Chalk Four—but was still concerned about getting his haircut.

"Don't worry, I'll square you away as soon as we're done," I told him. "You guys be careful out there. I'll see you when I get back."

"You too. See you!" Joyce replied.

As I made my way past the Humvees I saw Pilla loading up his gear. "Hey, Pilla, watch your ass out there today, and don't keep us waiting!"

"Whatever, dude. See you in about an hour." He grinned and gave me one of his famous mugs—his special sneer.

I did my last commo check with Command, then got on the bird. Watson got the word over the bird's headset. I heard him shout: "It's a go, we're taking off!"

The birds revved up. I got that weird feeling of excitement, nervousness, and anxiousness, like always. It was a mini adrenaline rush. After being in Somalia for a month and a half, I'd learned to keep those emotions in check, otherwise you have all that energy without much of an outlet, especially if the mission gets scrubbed. When we were airborne, I felt more comfortable. There is something to be said for being part of a large air assault package armed to the teeth. From where I sat, I could see all the Black Hawks and Little Birds in formation over the ocean—a pretty amazing sight, all that airpower.

We didn't stay over the water for too long before we headed inland. It was all part of the flight plan they'd briefed us on. Once we were over land, I started to watch the ground to see if I could actually tell the difference between the Bakara Market and the rest of the city. From where I sat, I couldn't tell where the enemy territory began. It took me by surprise when Sergeant Watson gave us the one-minute warning. I could see the Olympic Hotel in the background. We were getting close.

At the one-minute mark, I would always go through in my head what I was going to do as soon as I got off the rope. I always thought that if I did that a few times in my head, it would be easier for me to do what I needed to on the ground. Sometimes you can land pretty hard and get dazed. That can create a little hesitation that you want to avoid if you possibly can. Hesitation at the bottom of the rope can get someone hurt real quick. For this mission I knew I was going to hit the ground and roll toward the building once clear of the rope. That was my one thought: to get to the building and go left toward our corner. Once I made it to the corner, I'd hook a right, find cover, and call in the first situational report, or sit-rep.

Sergeant Watson gave us the thirty-second call. *Okay*, I thought, *cinch up my gloves, put on my goggles, and double-check my weapon to make sure it's still on safe. All set and good to go.* We had already started slowing down, and the pilots were getting ready to flare. I could look out the door gunner's window and see our objective, which was across the street from the Olympic Hotel. It looked just like it did in the aerial photographs.

Right then the bird flared, and everything disappeared. I couldn't see five feet outside the door. I couldn't make out the ground or even the buildings. I was beginning to wonder how in the world the pilots could fly in those conditions without hitting anything. I looked outside the front windshield of the bird and saw nothing but dust. I was sitting next to Private First Class Floyd, and we looked at each other with complete amazement. We were both completely dumbfounded. We'd had brownouts before, but nothing like what we were witnessing. The first thing that popped into my head was, *This can't be good.* I was hoping the pilots knew where the power lines were.

As if the visuals weren't bad enough, the audio wasn't exactly spreading out a welcome mat for us into Bakara Market. Almost immediately we were greeted with incoming fire *way* too early in the mission. On the other missions, when we'd rope in, the only firing we heard, if any, was the D-boys over toward the objective. Not this day. As soon as we started to flare, you could already hear the AK-47s firing. They seemed to be firing at a pretty consistent rate, too, which was understandable, considering that there weren't too many Rangers yet on the ground ahead of us able to return fire.

Finally Sergeant Watson gave us the sign and the ropes were kicked out. I assumed that they hit the ground but I couldn't tell from where I was sitting. Once the ropes went out, normally I would start looking for possible threats to our position. I always tried to get some sort of feel about the area before we hit the ground. I was trying to see where the shots were coming from, but there was simply too much dust. The only thing I could do was listen. It sounded like most of our problems were going to come from directly across from our blocking position on the Olympic Hotel side of the street.

It was my turn to get on the rope. After I went, Floyd would go, to be followed by Sergeant Watson. But when I got up to get to the rope, I was hung up on something. I was only about six inches from the rope but couldn't pry myself loose. It seemed like I was stuck there for a while. Floyd was there, trying to help, but it was taking too long, so I told him to move ahead and go. We were wasting precious time—time that we didn't have. Sergeant Watson had already noticed that I was having trouble getting loose, so he came over and yanked me around. That did it. I made it to the rope and went down, with Watson hot on my tail. I got on and off that rope as quickly as I could. Our bird had already been stationary long enough, and the last thing I wanted was for someone to draw a bead on it and shoot it out of the sky because I'd gotten tangled up.

I hit the ground running. Sergeant Watson and I made our way to the building and then darted up to and around the corner. By the time we got there two squad leaders, Sergeants Boorn and Hulst, were setting up fields of fire for their guys. I took a position just off the corner across the street from the objective building. I called into Higher and told them that Chalk Three was in position with all personnel accounted for.

The traffic on the radio started to pick up. Someone in Chalk Four had fallen and was in pretty bad shape. They were saying that as soon as they got him stable he needed to get back to the airport immediately. It turned out to be Private Todd Blackburn, a young Ranger from Florida. It dawned on me that I'd almost taken a leap out of that bird myself. In trying to get free I could have easily lost my balance.

We had been on the ground only a minute or two, and everything was going according to plan except for the Blackburn casualty at Chalk Four. I remember looking across the street and noticing this frail little Somali man standing on the corner of the objective building. It looked like he was begging for something. Sergeant Boren was over there motioning, trying to get him to leave the area, but the old guy wasn't having anything to do with that. He kept pleading his case to stay. The entire time I was watching Boren deal with this guy, I kept thinking: *What is this guy doing and why does he want to stay?* It didn't make sense. The old guy looked very distraught and saddened, but there was no way Boren was able to understand what he wanted—at that point we all just wanted him gone. Finally, Boren pushed him off. It looked like he was going to leave, but as he turned to go, our eyes met. He started to make his way across the street toward me. He took about three steps before I was up on my feet advancing toward him with my weapon up to my cheek and my nonfiring hand waving him away. He ended up giving me a puzzled look and then turned around and walked off. I guess he'd thought an African American Ranger might be more sympathetic.

I went back to my position and continued to monitor the radio and pull security. The firing was light and sporadic. I was right next to Sergeant Ramaglia. We had gone through RIP (Ranger Indoctrination Program) together. We were facing down the street toward Chalk One's position—that's where the other part of First Platoon was, along with the command element. There wasn't too much going on that we could see. We saw Willie and Goodale taking cover behind a car, engaging targets about every thirty seconds. The only thing Ramaglia and I had in front of us was a big group of bystanders—maybe twenty or thirty strong—about two or three blocks away. They didn't appear to hold weapons and they weren't making any aggressive moves toward us. To our rear, it was a little more active. Occasionally Private First Class Neathery would rattle off a burst, and someone else would take a few pot shots here and there.

Over the radio they came up with a plan to evac Blackburn. Once the ground convoy arrived, the plan was to load him on a Humvee and, escorted by another Humvee, take him back to the hangar. The rest of the convoy would stay and continue on with the mission. They said the convoy was about ten minutes out. Sergeant Watson was across the street by the entrance getting a sit-rep from the D-boys. The building was secure, and they were just finishing up flex-cuffing the prisoners. We'd be ready to move out in five minutes.

The crowds were starting to get a little bit bigger, but at our end they were still keeping their distance. The volume of fire seemed to be getting more intense the longer we stayed. But we knew the convoy was on their way with the big guns: .50 cals and MK-19 grenade launchers. A few more minutes and we would load up the prisoners, get ourselves up on the five-tons alongside them, and move out to the airfield. Then Boren got hit.

You could hear the convoy firing their guns from blocks away as they rolled toward our position. They hadn't arrived more than a few seconds before one of the .50 cals cut loose again, and everyone at the blocking position, including the Delta boys, started cheering. Staff Sergent Boren wasn't wounded too badly. He'd caught a ricochet round in the neck, and it had just barely grazed him. They slapped a field dressing on him and he was fine.

Our first priority once the convoy arrived was to get Blackburn loaded up and back to the airfield. The next task was to load the enemy prisoners of war onto the five-tons. I must have counted anywhere from fifteen to twenty prisoners. I'd been sitting there with Ramaglia, still pulling security, and I noticed one of the Black Hawks circling a little lower than normal. It was weird, because it looked like it was drifting somewhat. They were just about finished loading the bad guys when I saw the bird go down. At first I thought the pilot was doing some strange maneuver in order for one of the snipers on board to get a clean shot at someone. But the bird continued to spin and kept losing altitude. After almost a full turn, the bird completely disappeared behind the buildings. I couldn't hear the crash, but I knew what had just happened.

I was on the radio as soon as I saw it disappear: "All stations be advised—we have a bird down, we have a Black Hawk down." I had no idea if anyone else at the other blocking positions had witnessed this or not. The sooner Higher Command knew about it, the better. I made the initial radio call to let everyone else know what had just happened.

Radio traffic became very intense, almost frantic. We all knew what a bird going down meant. About a week earlier, a 10th Mountain Division helicopter had been shot down and no one had been able to get to them in time.

Traffic on the ground became increasingly frantic; it seemed everyone in the Bakara Market was trying to find the crash site. The enemy was converging from all over the city.

The company's commanding officer (CO), Captain Steele, was trying to find out if anyone had a visual on the downed bird. I reported that we did not but that I knew the general location of the crash site. Chalk Two said that they were pretty close to the site. First Lieutenant DiTomasso said that they were maybe a couple of blocks away. Steele wanted to know if that meant DiTomasso could make it to the site and take steps to secure it. DiTomasso said he could. He informed Steele that he was going to take a small group to the site and secure it until either we arrived or the CSAR bird arrived.

Over at my position things were starting to heat up. The .50 cals and MK-19s were firing at a real consistent rate, and the guys at the blocking position were returning fire more often than before. I was keeping an eye on the mob down the street. Only a few had weapons. They weren't using them—they were just carrying them around. Ramaglia and I happened to notice this one particular guy wearing dark pants and a white shirt. Before the bird went down, we'd seen this guy making his way back and forth across the street. Now we could see him making another trip, crossing toward the area where the Black Hawk had gone down. Ramaglia and I decided that if he showed his face one more time, we'd eliminate the threat. We had a helicopter down. No telling what would happen next.

The Command had been trying to formulate a plan to get the chalks and the convoy over to the crash site. Chalks Three and Four would move down to and link up with Chalks One and Two, respectively. We would make our way to the crash site in two elements, proceeding on two parallel roads. Everyone had checked in and was ready to move except Chalk Four—Command wasn't able to reach them at all. The CO asked me if I could raise them on the net from where I was.

I tried several times and got nothing. The RTO for Chalk Four was

Specialist Moore. I told the CO that Moore was unreachable, so he asked if we could get a visual to see if they were still there. Sergeant Watson told someone to stick a head around the corner to see if Chalk Four was still there. The visual was affirmative. The CO wanted a couple of guys to go to their position and relay the plan so we could all move out. But as soon as the men turned the corner, that side of the building erupted. We laid down suppressive fire, but to no avail—we were going to have to link up with them another way.

By this time a call came through that Lieutenant DiTomasso had arrived at the crash site. As soon as they arrived, we received word that one crew member was KIA and a Ranger had been wounded. About a minute later we heard, "Another man hit!" And not long after that: "Another man down!"

We started moving in single columns on either side of the street at a slow but deliberate pace. Walking, pulling security, and communicating on the radio all at once presented a bit of a challenge. I had to drop my head from time to time to monitor the radio. Yet I needed to keep my head up to watch where I was going and pull security. I always figured that it would be just my luck that someone would pop out and take a shot just as I got a call over the radio.

I looked toward the lead part of our formation and could see the five-ton making a left turn to head toward the crash site. That's when I noticed one of our guys up ahead get hit; it seemed like he took a round in the leg. It didn't look too bad since he was able to scramble to some cover with a little help. The convoy was still in the vicinity of the Olympic Hotel, and I heard Captain Steele tell them to send the wounded Ranger down to where Chalk One was positioned, and that the Humvees would evac him back to the airfield.

We were just about to the point where I'd seen the Ranger get hit in the leg. Our forward movement was very slow. The Somalis were running to figure out how to make their way toward us. We were all set up in good positions, so we were able to hold them off. Neathery and I were hanging back a little more than normal; we were waiting for a better position so that Neathery could cover the entire street. The Somalis were coming out of the woodwork, all with the same goal—to make it to the crash site before we got there.

I squeezed off a couple bursts. I heard Neathery fire a burst, so I got up and ran back to him and covered his rear. I had just turned around to cover Neathery when he fired, his muzzle right next to my left ear. The last thing Sergeant Watson wanted was a radio telephone operator who couldn't hear.

Our chalk was pretty much intact. The only casualty was Sergeant Boren, and he was walking wounded. I looked ahead at the next corner, and the battle going on there was incredibly fierce. I looked to our rear and saw a small road—more like an alley than anything else. If we had continued on the major road, we would have gone straight into the alley, but instead, in order to get closer to the crash site, we'd taken a left. I noticed that the road we were on had a slight elevation to it, which gave us a slight advantage, but at the same time it was crowned, so it was hard to get a really clear field of vision all the way across the street.

Our chalk and part of the CO's chalk were all within about a block of each other. We were in a kind of a U-shaped courtyard. To our rear was a house with a small patio, and to our front was a pretty large intersection. The fiercest part of the battle was taking place there. The volume of fire had grown so intense that it had been a little while since anyone had crossed the street. In our immediate area the major threat was coming from a small road that veered away from the crash site—somehow the enemy had managed to backtrack away from us and had found small alleys to make their way down the road that led to our chalk. We were between them and the crash site, but we didn't know exactly how close our position was to it.

I looked up at the next corner just in time to see a Ranger cross the street. How he managed to make it across without getting hit, I have no idea, because it sounded like the Somalis were laying down a wall of lead. One of the operators was getting ready to cross the intersection. He was about four or five feet from the actual corner and just about to make a break for it when *bam!* He took a round right into the helmet! They didn't wear K-pots like us; they wore small black skateboard helmets that didn't offer as much protection against rounds or shrapnel. His head snapped back and I saw a red mist spray out the back. The mist of blood covered the wall behind him. He crumpled to the ground. I couldn't believe what I had just seen. And yet as soon as he hit the ground another operator stepped up to try to pull him to safety. He didn't take more than two steps before he was hit also. Fortunately, the round only grazed him and he was able to pull the wounded man to safety. I jumped on the radio and told the CO that we needed an aerial medevac ASAP. The CO acknowledged my request but said it probably wasn't going to happen due to the volume of fire.

I relayed, "This guy has a serious head injury, and if we don't get him out right now, he's probably not going to make it."

"Negative. The area is still too hot for the birds to land."

I asked if the ground convoy could get down here to take him back to the airfield. The CO said that the ground convoy had sustained too many injuries trying to get to our position and had returned to the airfield and were waiting to link up with the 10th Mountain quick reaction force. Once that happened, they would come and get us out.

Now we were waiting on them to reinforce with ground troops. I was getting ready to yell the sit-rep to Sergeant Watson, and then I froze. No, I needed to tell Watson face-to-face. I got someone to watch Neathery's back and said that I had to go and talk to the sergeant.

I worked my way over to Watson and told him. We were in this little courtyard area that he was using as his command post—only about fifteen to twenty meters beyond the position Neathery and I had been holding. He told me to stay put while he went out to disseminate the info to the rest of the guys. I could hear him yelling out to Sergeants Thomas, Hulst, and Ramaglia, "Hey, conserve your ammo—we might be here a while. The convoy has to be reinforced before they can come and get us." That was smooth, I thought. He'd told them exactly what was going on, and morale was still intact.

Throughout the whole mission Sergeant Watson didn't really change a whole lot. He was still Watson—same tone of voice, same demeanor, and same sense of humor. You looked at him and you could have sworn we were at Fort Benning, doing a routine live-fire exercise. Even at times like this he was still good for a laugh. You always kind of gauged yourself by your leaders. If they appeared to be worried or upset, so were you. If they were confident, that made you feel confident. I'd known as soon as I got the news that things were going to get worse before they got better. But I watched Sergeant Watson and saw how he kept everyone focused on the task at hand. I remember a burst of rounds hitting just above his head. His eyes got big, he raised his eyebrows, and his mouth looked like it was getting ready to drink a Coke through a straw: "Ooh, the bastards are getting close!" Then it was back to business. We had to hold our position until the convoy arrived, whenever that was going to be.

As we sat there waiting for the convoy I kept an eye on the doors that led to the little courtyard. No telling what was on the other side. Sergeant Watson said it had already been cleared, but who's to say that the Somalis wouldn't eventually make their way through them to get to us? After about fifteen or twenty minutes, Watson told me that he wanted me to go across the street to strengthen the positions over there. I looked across the street so that I knew exactly where I was going to run. The last thing I wanted to do was get halfway there and then try to figure out where I wanted to go. I wasn't planning on giving them time to get off any extra shots. I took a couple of deep breaths and then made a break for it.

As soon as I got in the street I could hear the volume of fire pick up. All around my feet the ground was taking a beating. The rounds kept getting closer and closer, and the volume of fire was growing at the same time. I couldn't believe it. It seemed that I stepped out into the street and all hell broke loose. I had made it only about ten or twelve feet across the street. The fire was so intense I thought that if I took one more step I'd get tagged for sure. Just then I noticed a small pile of rocks in the middle of the street, and I ended up half diving, half falling behind this pile of stones. I figured I would wait there a few seconds till our guys gained enough fire superiority to force the other guys' heads down so I could make it all the way across.

The next few seconds seemed to drag on forever; I couldn't have been behind that pile of rocks longer than fifteen to twenty seconds. I could hear Watson yelling to the guys to get the volume of fire up so I could get across the street. I glanced at my watch: 5:10 p.m. We didn't have much daylight left. There was no way the convoy was going to make it to us before the sun went down.

I wasn't feeling very confident. We were completely outnumbered on streets we didn't know shit about, and we had to wait until the convoy came to get us. The way we were stacking up casualties, the only stories that were going to be told about us after today would be the ones told by the pilots flying over us. No way were we going to make it out of there in one piece. Just then a few more rounds peppered the ground around me and threw some more Mogadishu dirt in my face. I almost lost it.

I thought if I just got up and ran until I got hit, I wouldn't have to worry about anything—I could sit it out in the CCP (casualty collection point). *I have all this gear on. I have a helmet, and I have a vest. If I get hit with all this gear on, I'll live, and if I get hit in a vital place, I won't even see or feel it coming. So I might as well go down swinging. If I make it through this, I'm getting out as soon as my enlistment is up—go home, get a nine to five.* Then it dawned on me: *That's a bunch of bullshit, a coward's way out,* I told myself. *What the hell kind of thinking is that? Who's going to stick around and show the new guys what's what? More than half of the guys who taught me what I know were Panama vets, and they didn't hightail it when they got back. They stayed and taught others what they'd learned. Do what you're supposed to do, do what's right, and if your number comes up, it comes up, and there's nothing you can do about it.* That was when I decided I was going to reenlist.

There was a small lull in the enemy fire, so I decided to make a break for it. From here on out, it was just do the job, complete the mission, and don't think about the consequences. Everything I had been taught and trained to do kicked in. It made doing my job a lot easier.

Once I made it across the street, it was like I was in a different world. There were only a handful of us over there. Collett was in the street on the SAW behind a pile of rocks that were pretty similar to the ones I'd been using earlier, only his pile was a little bigger than mine was. He was covering a small trail that came directly from our rear. The Somalis were using it as one of the avenues of approach to get to the site. To Collett's left, about four or five feet away, was Neathery on the M-60. Sergeant Keni Thomas was to the rear of Collett and Neathery, watching the other direction. Ramaglia was watching the alley, and so was Young. As close as the groups were within our chalk, it was as though we were in a different world. We were all doing what needed to be done—what we had been trained to do. When we were back training at Fort Benning or anywhere else, we always took it seriously. If a squad leader went down, the senior team leader stepped up and took his place. Same thing if a team leader went down—the senior team member would step up and take charge. All that hard training was paying off right now, and I barely realized it. Sua sponte: of their own accord—the official motto of the Rangers.

I thought back to the time right before I'd gotten on the helicopter, when we all knew we were going into a bad part of town. In the back of my mind I had known it could get dicey, but then again, I'd thought, how bad could it get?

I went back to watching the alley. There wasn't any activity, but it still needed to be guarded in case the Somalis found a way to get back. Then I heard Neathery get hit behind me. I glanced back and saw him clutching his arm. Someone called for Doc Strauss to take care of him. In the meantime, I heard someone tell Errico to get on the M-60. I could hear Doc working on Neathery behind me, telling him that he was fine and he'd be okay. Errico screamed out that he had been hit. I looked back and saw him rolling away from the gun, clutching both his biceps.

I went over to Errico and knelt beside his left side. I noticed a small entry wound in his BDU sleeve, but there was only a little blood visible. He asked me how bad it was. I looked right at him and told him it wasn't that bad and that he was going to live. Neathery seemed to be doing okay. I told Errico to hang in there and we would be getting out soon, even though under the circumstances I had no idea when that might be. *How in the hell did we get ourselves in a situation where we have to wait for the QRF to get us out?*

As I was applying pressure to Errico's wound, something clicked. Neathery and Errico had both been hit in the same place. Some guy had the M-60 locked in! I looked up and saw Keni on the gun firing away. I told him, "Be careful. Someone has a bead on that gun." I'm not sure he heard me, but I bet he noticed the same pattern. There was one guy he couldn't hit with the M-60, so he lobbed a grenade at him. It didn't get him, though, because he was still popping off rounds. Doc Strauss came over and began working on Errico. I went back to watching my alley, but I could hear Keni asking Watson for more frag grenades. I could hear Watson yell back at him to use the light antitank weapon. Keni looked stumped. Watson shouted, "The LAW on your back!" I saw Keni look over his shoulder and shake his head. In all the commotion he'd completely forgotten he was hauling around a LAW. Keni fired it off. There was no more fire. It went quiet for a little bit, but it wasn't long before someone else was over in that area sending rounds our way. I looked at the vacated M-60 and noticed rounds kicking up dust all around it.

I asked Collett if the M-60 was covering anything that he couldn't cover with his SAW, but he said no, that he pretty much had everything covered. I looked back at the 60. If Collett had everything covered, why be redundant? You'd wind up putting guys in the CCP faster than Doc could fix them up. That M-60 was no longer an effective weapon—it was just a definite trip to the CCP for anyone who got on it. I was all for pulling the 60 back at that moment. It might not have been doing us any good, but why leave it there to get destroyed by enemy fire? I started low-crawling up to the machine gun. As I got within arm's reach, I grabbed it and I began pulling it back. But as soon as it moved an inch, the Somalis opened up on it. The entire time this was going on we were all concealed behind this paper-thin tin shack. At any point in time, we *knew* the Somalis could rake through that wall and just create chaos for us. Once I got the M-60 out of harm's way, I noticed that my watch was gone. I looked around for it because I knew it was in this small area. I finally located it just short of the M-60's old position. I'd had that watch since I was in RIP—that watch had been all around the world with me. I don't know why, but I didn't want to leave my watch in that godforsaken place. I started crawling my way back up to where my watch was, and we made it back unscathed. I remember thinking, *If I get shot while going back to get my watch, I'm kicking my own ass!*

Doc Strauss called me over to help with Errico's wound. The round had entered through his bicep and had pretty much blown out the back of his arm. Errico was a pretty stout guy to begin with—he wasn't fat by any means, but he was hefty. Normally I wouldn't have been able to put my hands around one of his arms, but now when I grabbed his arm I knew that round had done some damage. It was all Doc and I could do to contain his wound and get it dressed properly. I looked at Errico and could tell that he had seen the look on my face. I tried to reassure him as best I could.

Just as Doc was finishing with Errico, there was a weird movement that caught my eye. I looked up and noticed a smoke trail. *What the hell is that from?* I followed the smoke trail to its source—an old-time pineapple grenade! It had hit the ground and rolled right up to Collett's position. As soon as I saw it I yelled, "Grenade!" We all started scattering like crazy, rolling away as fast as we could, trying to get out of harm's way. The grenade had landed so close to us it wasn't possible for us to get up and run, so that's why we were rolling. I had gone about four or five feet and was completely up against the tin shack. I couldn't get any farther away from the grenade's position, though I knew there was a chance that most of us were still within range. I positioned myself so that my K-pot was aimed directly at the grenade. My thinking was that if any shrapnel came my way, the Kevlar helmet would catch most of it. I put my arms between my chest and the ground to protect them from any shrapnel. That instant it felt like someone punted the earth directly into my chest. The next thing I knew, I was coughing and spitting up dirt. It dawned on me that I was still alive. I started to do a roll call: "Doc, you good?"

"Yeah!"

"Neathery?"

"I'm all right."

"Errico?"

"I'm good."

"Ramaglia?"

"Good."

I had saved Collett for last. I didn't think there was a chance in hell he had made it. The grenade had landed just a few inches in front of the pile of rocks that he was using as cover. I didn't want to call his name for fear of not getting a response, but I went ahead and did it anyway. "Collett!"

There was a brief silence and then a little bit of coughing and then Collett answered, "Yeah, I'm good," in his usual laid-back tone.

Doc and I finished working on Errico, and then he went over to patch up Young. Young had been the one the farthest away, and he'd caught some shrapnel in the foot. Grenades blow up and out. We had been so close that this one had blown right over us.

Since the M-60's position was deemed too risky, it just sat up against the tin shack. I continued to pull security. If the Somalis were able to find their way to this little alley and find us off guard, they could really put us in a bad way. Doc finished up with Young. It was starting to get dark. Under normal circumstances we would have looked to this as an advantage. We were used to operating under the cover of darkness, but today was anything but normal. I don't know about anyone else, but I hadn't thought to bring my NODs on this mission. We'd left in broad daylight, and it just didn't seem to make any sense.

Thomas was the go-between for us and the rest of our chalk. He told us as soon as it was dark, he would start shuttling the casualties inside the house that they had taken over. After about ten minutes, Thomas came and got Neathery and guided him into the house. There was a porch in the front, made out of tin. Earlier, Thomas had kicked out the corner of the tin wall so that he could get in and out more easily. I was lying there pulling security on that side of the house and Thomas came busting through the wall, scaring the shit out of me. Next Thomas came back to get Errico and pulled him into the safe house. By the time Thomas made it back to me it was pretty dark.

Once I got inside the house I felt a great sense of relief. The house had already been secured before we got inside, so we were pretty much just sitting tight until the convoy arrived. It turned out that the CO and part of Chalk One had been positioned here since we made that left turn toward the crash site.

We settled into the main living area of the house, our makeshift fortress. It wasn't that spacious—maybe a ten-by-twelve-foot room. Sergeant Watson told me to sit tight. The house had an unusual setup to it. I was sitting in the living room, but every other room was connected to it. I noticed three doors in the room, so I guessed two bedrooms and a kitchen. As you walked into the house, one door was directly in front of you on the back wall. The second door was just to the left on the wall perpendicular to the other wall. The third door was across the room on the opposite wall. Watson had told me to sit tight near the left and back walls close to the two doors. When I looked around the room, there wasn't much furniture that I could make out. But I noticed the silhouettes of guys sitting or lying on the floor. It was pretty quiet in the room—no sound other than the murmuring of the CO's radio and the shuffling of some of the guys moving around. That's all you heard.

I heard a voice whisper, "Hey, who's that?" It was Private First Class Hawley.

I whispered back to him, "It's Kurth." I wasn't going to answer him in a regular voice. I was sure the Somalis knew we had moved our position, but they might not know where.

"Hey, what's up, Specialist? You get hit?"

"No," I said. "You?"

"No."

"Who else is here from Chalk One?"

"Me and Sergeant Goodale that I know of—everyone else made it across the street."

"Who all got hit?"

"Lieutenant Lechner got hit in the shin pretty bad. You know Sergeant Fillmore?"

"Yeah."

"He got hit in the head, he's KIA. The Delta medic got hit in the neck pulling Fillmore back, but he's okay. He's in the CCP working on casualties."

"Anyone else?"

"Oh, yeah. Goodale got hit too." Hawley then asked me about Chalk Three.

"Sergeant Boren got grazed by a round in the neck but he's okay. Errico and Neathery both took rounds in the arm manning the M-60. Strauss and Young caught some shrapnel. I heard there's a couple of KIAs at the crash site, the crew, but they also have a ton of WIAs."

Hawley wanted to know how much longer it was going to be before the convoy got here. I told him that I wasn't sure; the only thing that had come over the radio was that our guys were going to be linking up with the 10th Mountain and then they would be coming to get us. Just as I said this, Captain Steele announced that the Malaysians would also be linking up and they would be using light armored vehicles to extract the casualties and us. That was welcome news, but I could only imagine just how long it would take to coordinate this. *Probably forever,* I thought. *We've already been coordinating with the 10th Mountain for three hours now, and we're in the same army, speaking the same language.*

Sergeant Watson came back and told me to move into the CCP. I guessed he wanted more room for the other guys coming in off the street. I made my way back into the CCP, and you could tell there was a definite stench inside the room. The house itself had an odd odor to it, just like anyone's house has a certain scent to it. But the CCP had this thick, pungent, lingering stench. The smell was hard to place but seemed familiar, which was kind of weird because I had never been in a real-world CCP before. It was kind of a sweet, musky scent. Then I remembered: During the third phase of Ranger School at Fort Bliss, Texas, Joyce and I had noticed that we developed an odd smell, kind of like spoiled meat. One of the medics from Second Battalion told us that we were actually burning muscle instead of fat, due to the fact that our fat content was so low. To this day I don't know if that's true or not—all I know is that's what the smell in the CCP reminded me of. I picked out a spot in the CCP and had a seat. Neathery was sitting next to me, and Errico was next to him.

"How are you doing, Neathery?"

"I'm okay."

Errico wasn't so positive.

I asked him what was wrong.

"I'm thirsty. Do you have any water?"

"Sorry, I didn't bring any out with me. I didn't think we'd be out here this long," I said.

"Yeah, you and me both."

I started to shift around and my foot slipped in something that I thought was oil, but it wasn't oil. The moonlight coming through the window was reflecting on the floor, and I could see that the whole floor was covered with it. I didn't touch it with my bare hands, but I knew what it was: I was slipping in someone else's blood. The CCP was pretty quiet. The medic went about his business; the only thing barely audible was the breathing. Needless to say, there was a lot of tension in the air, a mixture of fear and uncertainty.

This was nothing like a CCP back in the States. Stateside we would sit in the CCP and bitch about the cheating OPFOR (opposing force) and how they manipulated their MILES (military integrated laser engagement system) to inflect casualties on us. The OPFOR were pros at using the gear to their benefit. They would hide behind bushes that were thick enough to deflect our lasers, when you knew one 5.56 mm ball would shred right through in a real-world situation. Whenever I had made it to the CCP during our annual evaluations, I would always sit back and try to imagine what it would be like if all the casualties were real. I'd thought that I had a clear picture of what it would be like. But no matter how hard you try you can never imagine how it's going to be, and maybe that's for the best.

I'm not sure why Sergeant Watson had me move to another room, but sitting in a CCP and *not* being wounded was starting to make me feel guilty. I was sure there was some resentment. *Why is he in here when he's not hurt?* Probably nobody thought about it in that way, but that's how I felt. So when it came time for me to move, I was all for it. I got into the other room, and there were a couple of other guys in there already. The only wounded guy was Sergeant Goodale, Chalk One's FO. He was relaying fire missions from another FO to the Little Birds. Apparently another FO had eyes on the action but couldn't get a communication link to the birds, so he was using Goodale to relay the missions. That was pretty motivating to see—a guy who was laid out on his stomach wounded but still doing his job.

"Hey, Goodale, it's Kurth. You all right?"

"Yeah, I'm fine, but one of those bastards got me!"

"Where did you get hit?"

"You don't want to know." He was bandaged up pretty good, with his butt in the air. I couldn't help it. I had to put my head down and take a chuckle or two to myself, quietly.

"Fuck you, Kurth!"

"Dude, I'm sorry, I couldn't help it."

"Yeah, yeah, I know." It sounds heartless to laugh at a guy who literally took one for the team, but I didn't mean it that way. All the FOs in the company and I had a history.

The second reason I always gave the FOs a hard time was that every two or three weeks there'd be another FO on profile—meaning not 100 percent capable of doing the job physically. They were never on profile for anything major—just sprained ankles or swollen knees or something. Even while on profile, these guys would still go to the field and do what they could. So I nicknamed them the FOOPs (FOs on profile). They didn't care for that too much, but there wasn't a whole lot they could say about it.

It was quiet, so I asked Goodale if his wound was bad. He said no, that the bullet had gone in and out—no veins or arteries, just your basic flesh wound. I remembered that during Operation Just Cause in Panama in 1989 there was an FO in Bravo Company who had been wounded in combat in a manner similar to Goodale—he had caught some shrapnel from a grenade. I asked, real serious, "Hey, Goodale, how come any time we're anywhere there's action, there's always some forward observer, taking it in the ass?"

"Kurth, that's *low*."

I couldn't believe I had just said that. I had always been one of the company's jokesters and comedians; still, this was a first—cracking on your comrade while he was wounded and still carrying out his orders. The room stayed pretty quiet afterward, but as weird as this sounds, I actually think it did us some good. As for myself, I know I hadn't laughed or cracked a smile in the past eight hours. For those few short moments, when I was razzing Goodale and making jokes, we kind of forgot about what was going on around us.

"Hey, Goodale?"

"Yeah?"

"Sorry, man."

"That's cool," he said. "I'm good."

It had been dark now for a couple of hours. The firing had died down to sporadic bursts ever since the sun went down. Then out of nowhere the guys outside started laying down some serious heat. The only thing I could think of was that the Somalis had finally decided to make an advance toward our position. The firing went on for about thirty to forty-five seconds. Then our guns went silent. I could still make out the sound of the Somalis firing their AK-47s. *That can't be a good sign.* I was beginning to wonder if they had taken over our outside positions, but the firing wasn't close enough for that to happen. In the background I could hear the dull, rapid clapping of the Little Birds getting closer to us. Since we'd been in the house, I'd heard the helicopter traffic overhead, but it was always at a distance. They had been flying in circles around our positions much like they had done at the objective building. One thing I hadn't noticed was that their circles had been getting smaller and smaller—which meant the Somalis were getting closer, both to us and to the crash site.

Crash site. I had completely forgotten that we weren't even to the crash site yet. I had heard Captain Steele tell Higher Command over the radio that we were about fifty meters to the south of it. This doesn't sound like much, but, given the situation, fifty meters meant you were in a totally different world. Just a few hours ago, fifteen to twenty feet in the middle of a dusty road felt to me like a different planet.

I could hear the Little Birds come screaming in for a gun run. They always started out slowly with their miniguns, then they kicked it into high gear and polished off the mission with a few 2.75-inch rockets. Whoever it was that wanted into our little house party was quickly screened and rejected by the doorman, the crews of Task Force 160th. It felt like a big brother was here to bail us out. After the Little Bird mission, Goodale said, "Oh, *yeah*—those boys came to play." I thought, *Hell, we* all *came to play—we just didn't know how high the stakes were going to be.*

Ever since we'd gotten into the house, radio traffic was pretty much nonexistent. Every so often the C2 (command and control) bird would jump down onto our net to tell us about enemy movement going on around us. They mostly pointed out one or two individuals at a time, nothing too major. They gave our guys a heads-up before the enemy got to us.

Some more time passed, with not much going on, before the C2 bird passed along to us that we had a group of about twenty to thirty Somalis heading our way from the east, some armed with RPGs. I looked over at the east wall and noticed that there were no doors or windows we could shoot from. One huge blind spot was staring us in the face with the enemy on their way in from the other side. I looked back over at the leaders, and I could tell that's what they were discussing. Someone suggested blowing a hole in the wall so we would be able to defend ourselves. I don't know why, but I didn't really care too much for that plan. Finally they decided they were going to stronghold the positions to the east with a few more guys. One of the D-boys and Sergeant Watson went out to scout for more positions. After they got back they grabbed a couple guys and lined up by the front door, getting ready to move out. As soon as they took off, our guys started laying down fire to cover them, and the Somalis returned it with a vengeance. The firing didn't go on for too long—no more than a couple of minutes. It died down, and I figured our guys were set. The CO told us that the mob was now moving in at a faster speed. I guess that little firefight got their juices going. We moved away from the east wall just in case they got off an RPG and hit it. I was back to my original spot in the living area again. The house was quiet, real quiet. I was thinking this was the calm before the storm. We knew what was coming, but at the same time we didn't, and that is not a great feeling to have. The worst thing about it was that I was in the house. I wasn't outside, where I could maneuver, find a better position. We just waited to take it. Then came the sweet sound of vengeance on its way: the Little Birds.

As per standard operating procedure, they started off with a long burst from the miniguns, then followed with about three or four rockets. The burst was pretty long this time, and they actually gave them a few more rockets than normal. That only meant that the enemy threat was larger than in the past. I could tell they hadn't gotten close to overrunning us yet because the Little Birds were still off at a short distance. Still, that fire was getting a lot closer than we would have liked. I heard the Little Birds fly overhead after they were done with their run, and the CO passed down that the targets had been neutralized. I shook my head and thought: *Neutralized. Yeah, they got neutralized all right.*

We still kept our positions fortified just in case, but Sergeant Watson let us know that they were going to be rotating us out from time to time. Everything was pretty quiet inside and outside the house. Occasionally there would be some sporadic gunfire, but not much else. The CO got a call over the radio—Higher Command told him that they wanted us to link up with a chalk that was a few meters shy of the crash site. He passed that information on to us, and immediately you could feel the apprehension in the air. For me it was utter amazement: *They want us to pick up and move? Are they out of their minds?*

I looked around at all the able bodies we had and then looked over at the casualties. We were at about 65 percent strength. I figured that for us to get ourselves, the casualties, and all our equipment over to Chalk One, it was going to take at least two or three trips. That's without taking any more casualties while we were making those trips back and forth. Somehow I didn't think that was going to happen. Not only were we going to have guys carrying litters and equipment, we were going to need guys already in place to cover their movement. The idea of us moving to the crash site was *not* a good one. By the time we got everyone and everything there, we weren't going to have any able bodies left to protect the crash site. So what would be the point? Sure, we would all be consolidated into one giant CCP, but the CO had to see that this would be disastrous.

The leaders were in another powwow. The CO, Watson, and one of the Delta sergeants were all going over options. After much discussion, I heard the sergeant speak up and tell the CO it might not be the best idea to move. He told the CO that we had a lot of wounded and for some of them their condition could deteriorate during the move. Sergeant Watson agreed that the move was a pretty big risk. The CO was standing firm, though: "Higher wants us to consolidate. They want us to be one collective force instead of a couple of smaller separated groups."

"We're fortified here, sir. We've got visuals or know exactly where the other guys are. I think we need to sit tight and wait for the convoy to arrive."

Captain Steele told him: "Higher wants us to consolidate. We're going to consolidate!"

"I think we're better off here, sir!" You could tell that the sergeant was getting a little hot under the collar at this point.

I was sitting there watching and could see a really big pissing contest taking shape between a Ranger captain and a D-boy sergeant first class, though they were keeping their voices pretty low. After that, I couldn't tell what was being said, but it was getting pretty heated. Finally the meeting broke up, but I could tell by the operator's demeanor he was not happy.

I began to get ready to move. I wasn't a happy camper either at this point. I could not believe that we were actually going through with this! I began to wonder what kind of shape we were going to be in once we actually got to the crash site. If we sustained too many casualties, we were going to be in a bad way if the Somalis mounted any sort of large force. With all the casualties that we had and the ones that were already with Chalk One, there were a lot of people unable to protect themselves. It was becoming a little too morbid to think about.

I could see the sergeant making his way back over to the CO. I guess he was making one last plea to the CO about the move. It was not nearly as heated as it had been the last time, but after a few minutes I heard the CO get on the radio. He was telling Higher that he thought it would be in our best interest if we stayed where we were. After he was done on the radio he told us, "All right, men. We're staying put."

The mood in the room was a lot more relaxed now that we weren't moving out to the crash site. Those few moments when we thought we were going to hit the streets again, you could smell the anxiety in the air. Now it was back to more of the same: sporadic gunfire, a CCP full of casualties, and a bunch of guys wondering when they were going to be getting out of this hellhole. Sergeant Watson was getting ready to rotate the guys that were outside back into the house to give them a break. Watson pulled Siegler and put him outside at one of the positions. He had been on guard duty watching the family, so Watson told me it was my turn to watch the family.

The entire time we had been there, I knew we were in somebody's house—I just wasn't aware that those somebodys were still inside, in one of the other rooms. I had only been focusing on our situation and how much trouble we were in. But now something changed. It was pretty dark in the room, but I could make out silhouettes: a mother, a father, and their small infant.

I sat there watching the family. They weren't much of a threat. They had already been searched and flex-cuffed—with their hands in front so that the mother could still hold her baby. They were scared to death, and I can't say that I blamed them. I was scared to death, too, and I was the one who was armed and guarding them.

Inside that room, I couldn't help but wonder what they were thinking. Here we were, a bunch of Americans who had forced our way into their house and taken it over. Don't get me wrong—I had absolutely no problem with that whatsoever. We do what we have to do. But I'll tell you this: if I were sitting at home playing Nintendo and a bunch of foreign soldiers busted in and took over and I couldn't communicate with them, well, I don't know how I'd react.

I noticed the baby getting restless and moving about. It had started to cry some, and the mother began rocking it nervously back and forth. It wasn't working, and the baby was crying louder. The mother was trying to shush the baby as much as she could, but it wouldn't stop. Even the father was trying to keep the baby quiet at this point. I could hear the mother start to weep, and I was thinking, *Why is the mom crying? Okay, so the kid's crying; he'll shut up eventually, nothing to cry over.* Then it hit me like a ton of bricks. These people thought we might do something to them or their kid if he didn't stop. I started to feel bad for the parents; they were getting more and more scared as the baby continued to cry. There was no way for me to tell them that no harm was going to come to them, that we would be out of there as soon as we could. I wanted to tell them that we didn't want to be there any more than they wanted us there. Finally the baby stopped crying. I guess it went back to sleep.

I just sat there and wondered when the hell we were going to leave. Guarding this family was really wearing on my nerves, but then again everything was wearing on my nerves. The only thing that was going to make me happy was a convoy of APCs sitting outside the front door.

I was wondering how the other chalks were doing and how they were holding up. I thought about the convoy and how bad they had gotten it earlier. They must have really taken a beating. I was starting to get a little tired by this point, not so much physically as mentally. I had been thinking hard about everything since before we got on the bird, and it was starting to catch up with me now. I wanted to sit there and zone out and not think about anything until the convoy got there.

Just then the CO said that they were almost done with the coordination and that they would be disseminating the plan and moving out within the hour. Thank God. Someone came to relieve me. I was glad to give up my shift. Something about guarding a family bound up in their own home brought a little too much reality into the situation for me.

Sergeant Atwater, the CO's RTO, asked me if I had any extra batteries, as his were beginning to die out. I said I had extras in my rucksack, and told Hawley I'd be back in a minute. I hadn't even gotten up on one knee when a Somali opened up on the house and rounds peppered the wall just above my head. The burst wasn't even over before I slammed myself into the floor sideways so that the radio didn't come crashing into the back of my K-pot and crush my nose, which had happened on many occasions throughout my RTO career. I was lying on the floor scared shitless and not moving, trying to catch my breath. My initial thought was how in the hell that Somali had seen me move around inside the house. That's when I heard Hawley yell, "Kurth's hit! Kurth's hit!"

How does he know I'm hit? Did my blood splatter him? Am I hit? It had happened so fast, I hadn't even checked myself out. I gave myself a once-over and piped up, "Negative! Negative, I'm good." I could hear the Delta medic make his way back through the CCP. I'm sure he was relieved—one less casualty for him to worry about.

Hawley was dumbfounded. "Holy shit, Specialist, you hit the floor so fast I thought for sure you got hit!"

I moved up toward the front of the house about two feet, on my belly this time. I was right behind a small concrete divide that was about a foot and a half tall, so I made that my new home. Hawley demanded that he wanted to move up with me. I couldn't say that I blamed him. Hawley was sitting next to me. "Damn, Specialist, I've never seen anyone move that fast before!"

"Yeah, me neither," I told him. I had heard about survival instinct, but I had never experienced it. I guess that was it. I know for a fact that no matter how many times I practiced or how hard I tried I would never be able to match that speed for the rest of my life. The CO passed along the news that the convoy would be moving out in about twenty minutes. After my little run-in with Mr. 7.62 mm, that was good news to hear.

Next I was told to head back to the CCP and help with the evacuation of the casualties. Once again I low-crawled back to the CCP. It was pretty much the same scene as before—the only thing different was everyone was a lot thirstier this time. Someone had passed a couple of canteens outside to one of the positions. Apparently they'd found a rain barrel full of water. They had filled the canteens up with water and put in the iodine tablets, but they still had to wait for the iodine to do its job before they could drink the water. The only day it had rained while we were in country was sometime back in August, our first night in Somalia, so that rainwater had been sitting there more than a month.

I remember the night it had rained, because Goodale and I were on guard duty that night watching the helicopters. I remembered telling Goodale, "Wouldn't you know—this is just like Nevada." We had gone to Nevada for a few weeks and had spent almost the entire time there without any rain. Out of the three weeks scheduled in Nevada we'd only had one night out in the field. I'll give you one guess what happened—four hours of rain. I remember Goodale sitting there that night looking as miserable as I felt, saying, "That rain god's a pussy."

When the canteen of Somali rainwater reached me, I passed it on to the guys who really needed it. Lieutenant Lechner, wounded in the leg, had been draining IVs like a Boston native draining pints on St. Patrick's Day. This meant that a lot of the less severely wounded guys weren't getting IVs like they should. They were more dehydrated than I was.

I was beginning to wonder how the evac plan was going to work—who was going to do what, who was going out first, who was going to get the extra equipment, and so on. Moving casualties was always a crucial time because your security was lessened, although we figured we weren't going to have to worry too much about security because the 10th Mountain would be taking care of that. We did need to be organized, though. The evac needed to take place as quickly as possible so we could get the hell out of there.

I asked the medic how many casualties we had, and he told me the number. I can't remember how many it was, but it was higher than I'd thought. Then he added, "And one KIA." That kind of threw me off.

Lieutenant Lechner was the only one who would need to be carried out on a stretcher; Goodale said he just needed some help to the APC. It didn't take too long to get the order of the casualties down. I figured out who was going to help whom get out to the vehicles. I made sure we had enough guys to carry out all the extra equipment. After we formulated a plan, we all went over it a few times so we'd know exactly what to do when the vehicles showed up. Now all we had to do was sit and wait, and we all had that one down.

Just then Sergeant Watson came into the CCP to check up on everyone. I told him that we already had the evac plan put together and that everyone knew what to do. He asked if everything was accounted for—personnel and equipment—and if the OOM (order of movement) was set. I told him we had it covered.

I knew that there was some activity still going on outside because the Little Birds hadn't stopped their gun runs all night. We sat and waited for the arriving convoy. I figured it would probably be about thirty to forty-five minutes before they actually got to us. That was on the generous side. I knew the Somalis weren't just going to lie down and let the convoy pick us up and go home. We still had a little more time on our hands. Another half hour passed before the CO told us that the convoy was getting ready to move out in about twenty minutes.

Twenty minutes? They said they were moving out in twenty minutes thirty minutes ago! This is absolutely crazy! You could tell that the mood in the house had definitely taken a turn for the worse. You could hear the grumbling and moaning under everyone's breath. Of course we were going to hang in there—what else were we going to do, stage a walkout? But it was really beginning to wear on me. We weren't totally helpless, not by a long shot. We were still able to fend off the Somalis and keep them at bay throughout the night. But, as a consolidated force, we were depending on the convoy to come get us. Sure, we could have fought our way out—if there was no convoy at all and if there were no other options open to us. But it would have been catastrophic—no telling how many guys would have been wounded or killed.

The medic made it known to Sergeant Watson that he was running really low on supplies. He said that he would be able to sustain the CCP for a little while longer, but after that some of the men would begin to deteriorate. We were also beginning to run low on ammo, especially SAW and M-60 ammo. Sergeant Watson went to the CO to see if we could arrange for some sort of aerial resupply. I heard the CO say that the convoy was on its way and couldn't we hold on? But as we'd learn later, they hadn't even left yet and they still had to fight their way to our area and then find us in the dark. If we didn't get a resupply before the convoy got there, there might not be any of us left when they arrived. Watson came back to us and said the CO was going to see what he could do. I was sitting there thinking about all the different events that had transpired in my little world that day: the beautiful weather we had had that day and how those kind of days were very few and far between, that it was Sunday, our day off, and while we'd been sitting around all week waiting for something to come down the line, the moment we got a little time for ourselves, the call had come.

Fifteen or twenty minutes later the CO told us that one of the Black Hawks was going to fly over our position and drop off a resupply. The Black Hawk was going to fly over the alley between us and Chalk One. Sergeant Watson said that would be fine, as he'd posted some guys in the alley earlier. Right before the Black Hawk got there we heard the door gunner open up with his minigun on cyclic and chew through a ton of rounds. Our guys on the ground had also opened up on the So-malis. The Black Hawk wasn't there very long before it took off again.

When Sergeant Watson returned with the supplies, it was a big lift for everyone in the house. It wasn't a ground convoy to get us out, but it was some sort of a physical connection to the outside world, some-thing other than a voice coming through a hand mike. It gave us a little hope—as bad as things were, if we were still able to get resupplied, we could hold out until the convoy got here, no matter how long it took.

About half an hour after the resupply the CO told us that the convoy was en route to our location and that their ETA was about forty-five minutes. Earlier that day it had taken the Ranger convoy about twenty-five minutes to get to the objective building, and that had been in the daylight, before all hell broke loose.

We went over the evac plan again just so everyone remembered their part, and everyone did. That was when Sergeant Watson said that CSAR couldn't get one of the pilots out of the wreckage. They needed some special tools that the convoy was bringing with them. Once the convoy arrived they were going to use those tools to get the pilot out and then we would all be leaving. He told us to get ourselves ready to evac as soon as the convoy arrived. The anxiety in the room was pretty intense. We were all ready to leave this house. Rangers are never really happy holing up at defensive perimeters; we'd rather be on the move.

Another thirty or so minutes passed, and we began to hear some intense firing pretty far off in the distance. The CO said that it was the ground convoy taking fire. That was the convoy? They sounded pretty far off to me, but hey, at least we could hear them. It was kind of weird listening to the firefight, because you could hear them fight street by street. The firing would get real intense and then die down, escalate again and then fade once more, like an audio seesaw. Earlier in the day the Ranger convoy had made it only a block or two before they had to turn around and find a different route. These guys sounded like they were on a pretty direct route heading toward our location. The closer the convoy got to us the more intense the firing became. You could also tell that their movement had slowed down a little bit because of resistance from the Somalis.

The convoy firefight only seemed to excite the Somalis camped outside our door. They fired off a few rounds here and there to say they were still nearby and didn't plan on leaving. Then something strange began to happen. The convoy firefight seemed to be moving away from us. Were they lost? Had they taken too many casualties to continue? After another minute or two, there was nothing—nothing on the net from the convoy, nothing in our area. Nobody knew what was going on. If they couldn't get to us with the Malaysian APCs, how in the hell were we supposed to fight our way out with all these casualties?

As soon as the convoy disappeared, the CO reported that the convoy was going to have to use a different route to get to us due to all the roadblocks. If they were having that much trouble that far out, there was no telling what the convoy was going to encounter when they got closer in.

There was some more sporadic gunfire outside and then nothing again. I'm sure the D-boys had been in similar situations before, but I hadn't. It was almost an hour later when we finally heard the convoy making their way back to us. It sounded like they were about the same distance away as before. Even though they were firing back at the Somalis, there was no way for me to know just how the firefight was going. I knew those guys were going to take some casualties on the way in. I just hoped that the number was as low as possible. The firing was still very intense, maybe more so than the first time, and just like the first time, they got closer and closer and then turned away.

That creepy but familiar aura fell over the house again—a worn-down, tired, scared, pissed, but still hopeful feeling that blanketed all of us.

Sergeant Watson was changing out the positions outside again. I was sitting there wishing I didn't have that freaking radio on my back. But the fact remained that I did have it, and because of that I was stuck inside, not outside doing something more useful.

Again we were told that the convoy had run into more roadblocks but that they were still trying to make their way to us. We all had pretty much figured out what that meant at that time; we just wanted to hear that they hadn't turned around and gone back to the airfield. I started to think about what we would do if we were told that the convoy couldn't get to us. It wasn't a pretty thought.

I remembered that in those few short seconds right before the grenade went off, I hadn't been scared; my life hadn't flashed before my eyes or anything like that at all. I remembered feeling a weird sense of acceptance, as though I'd known there was absolutely nothing that could be done. I figured if I could get back to that feeling, the time would pass by a lot easier. Besides, if we were going to have to fight our way out, I was going to need that feeling, but I was going to need it in a different way. I did not want to die, but I could face the possibility, and there was nothing to be done about it. Same as before: *just do the job*. It wasn't a new thought, but then again we had a lot of time on our hands to think about a lot of things.

I could still hear the Little Birds doing their gun runs. The convoy sounded like it was actually making some good headway. It seemed to be getting closer to us than before. The firing was still pretty intense at times—it would die off some the closer they got, then it would pick back up again, just as before.

The convoy must have hit a big pocket of resistance, because suddenly it sounded like all hell broke loose. It went on for about three minutes, and that all too familiar sound of pulling back returned. It didn't affect me as much this time as it had earlier. I couldn't tell if it was because I was becoming numb to the situation or because I was starting to come to terms with what was going to happen if they couldn't get to us. I was worried about the convoy and the well-being of the guys in it, but I was also concerned about how we were going to make it out in one piece. I was sitting there, waiting for the call to tell us that we were on our own—that we were going to have to fight our way to the convoy.

About forty-five minutes later we heard the convoy make yet another attempt to reach us. They were making headway again and getting much closer than they had on the previous trips. Finally the CO told us that the convoy had the Olympic Hotel in sight. All sorts of firing was going on: you heard the Somalis, the APCs, and the Little Birds, all of them, ripping off rounds. We went over our evac plan one more time; everyone was set to go. Everyone was shuffling around, getting their gear together, preparing to move out.

Once the convoy reached the Olympic Hotel, you could hear a massive increase in the firefight. The way the convoy responded meant they were *not* going to be denied this time. They were definitely on the warpath. Those gun runs were like the baying of some great bloodhound that had just found a fresh trail.

Sergeant Watson told the guys to put out new infrared chem-lites, because that's what the convoy would be looking for when they got close. The firing outside started to die down a bit. It was still sporadic, but so was the convoy's return fire. The Somalis seemed to have decided that they'd had enough. It was almost as if they were waiting to take their best shot at us from somewhere else down the road.

We could hear the APCs rolling toward us. The CO was giving directions to the convoy, trying to walk them into our location. They weren't too far from making the last turn that would put them right in our lap. Link-ups could sometimes be a little tricky, especially when different units were involved. I knew what our link-up procedures normally were, but I had no idea what kind of plan they had put together for this little escapade. Any miscommunication at all could send them in the wrong direction or down the wrong alley or toward the wrong building.

I heard the CO tell Sergeant Watson to tell the guys outside to keep an eye out for the head of the convoy, because they did have some guys dismounted and on foot. Our men should make sure they had a positive ID before they fired. Next the CO got word that the point man had spotted some IR chem-lites on the road and just outside some houses. They were finally within sight. I'm sure they were just as relieved as we were. After hours of planning and preparation and hours of fighting on the streets with the Somalis, they had finally made it to us. It was a tremendous weight off our shoulders, knowing that they were finally here and that we wouldn't have to fight our way out to them.

I could hear the CO giving these guys information to the best of his ability on exactly where the other chalks were. They were going to have to do that whole link-up procedure again with the other chalks, just as they had done with us, because as close as we were to each other's position, we couldn't see each other.

Sergeant Watson told us that once they linked up with all the elements and had all our positions confirmed, they would bring the rest of the convoy up to us. Then once the vehicles were in place we would load the casualties, load everyone else, and move out. Sounded good.

They had to back one of the APCs right up to the front door of the house so it would be easy for us to load the casualties. The APCs filled up pretty quickly with the wounded. Sergeant Watson told us that they were still working on getting the pilot out of the wreckage. He told us just to hang back in one of the rooms and sit tight. After a little while, he came back into the room and told us it was okay—to get some sleep if we could, that the convoy had the perimeter secure outside the house, and we weren't needed for anything right then.

That was something weird to hear: *get some sleep*. I was completely exhausted, but there were still guys out there pulling security, and we weren't even in a safe zone yet. I didn't even finish that thought before my eyes had shut themselves and I was asleep. The only thing I can think of is that when my brain heard that everything was secure and there was nothing left to do, my mind took its cue to rack out.

I wasn't sure how long I was asleep, but when Sergeant Watson came in and told us it was almost time for us to move out, I got up and walked back out into the living area. I remember I froze in my tracks. I was completely dumbfounded that it was full daylight outside. Good morning, Mogadishu! I started making my way up to the APC. There were about two or three guys in front of me.

Just then Sergeant Watson turned around and said that all the APCs were full—just like that. "It looks like we're taking the Heel-Toe Express, men!"

My stomach felt like one big knot. Not only did the Somalis know where we were, they knew where we wanted to go. On top of that it was broad daylight, and we had to run out! This was un-fucking-believable! We had sat there all night waiting for the convoy to come get us, only to find out that some of us were going to have to walk out *on foot*.

"Whaddaya mean?" I asked Sergeant Watson.

"All the APCs are filled with casualties, and some of the chalks, including the rest of us, are going to walk out beside the APCs and use them as cover. We're going back the same way we came. About four-fifths of a mile past the Olympic Hotel is a secure intersection with more vehicles, and we will load up there."

How in the hell did this happen? I wondered.

Sergeant Watson divided us up, half on one side of the road and the rest on the other. His last words were: "Once the APCs start moving, stay with them and use them as cover! Good luck!"

Fucking-A right, good luck! I ran across the street to get in position to move out. As soon as I got there a Little Bird passed by on a gun run. It was nailing the intersection where Fillmore had been shot. The APCs started creeping forward, and the twenty or so of us who were left moved out with them. When we got to the corner, one of the APCs in front of us had already made the turn. I looked at the turret gunner—and there wasn't one. The APC started to take some AK-47 fire, and I saw the gunner's hand come out from below and just start spraying the area, blind! He didn't even stick his head out to see what he was shooting, and I had to walk behind that! *This just keeps getting better by the moment,* I said to myself.

By the time the APC I was walking next to got to the corner, we were already at a slight jog. By the time we turned the corner we were running. Twenty feet later the APCs were at full tilt, leaving nothing but dust and us behind. There was no slowing those guys down at all; they just put the pedal down and hauled ass out of there. We were going to have to fight our way out of there ourselves. At least we had the casualties loaded on the vehicles. We got to the first street, and there were already some guys there, laying down covering fire. Floyd was there with his SAW. I told him to go, that I had his back.

We were going out with guns blazing! If they were still hanging around by this time, you knew they were up to no good. There were about twenty-five of us out there fighting for our lives. I turned the corner and started laying down some heat. I got about six rounds off and my M-16 jammed. I yelled, "Jam!" as loud as I could about three times and pulled back from the corner. I took a few steps back to fix my weapon. I completely forgot I had traded my M-16 with Keni at some point in the night, and I didn't know he had fired it so much. The carbon buildup caused a double feed, a real nasty one. I couldn't get the rounds out to save my life. I was slamming the butt of my weapon on the ground trying to force the round out, but no luck. Finally the last guy told me to go, so I hauled ass across the street. I made it about halfway down the block before I stopped to try to unjam my weapon again. Nothing was working; those two rounds were so wedged in that I couldn't pry them out. I needed to find someone carrying two weapons and *fast*. I couldn't believe how badly this was going. *It's daylight, there's no room on the APCs, we have to walk out, the APCs leave us, and now I'm running out of this thing naked with no weapon!*

We fought our way out like a bunch of caged dogs that had been beat and tortured all night and then turned loose to seek a little revenge. I could tell the Somalis were firing, but I couldn't see who was doing the shooting. But it wasn't like I could return fire anyway. We didn't need spotters; we needed shooters.

I kept moving to the next street. I got close to the intersection and again tried to clear my weapon. I'm surprised I didn't break the butt stock off trying to get those rounds out of my chamber. Again, no luck.

I made it to the corner. I told the guys to cover me as I crossed the street. I made it, and where were we? Right back where we'd started out

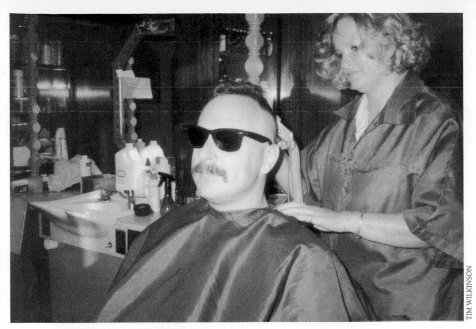

Dan Schilling getting his "Ranger" haircut the day before Task Force Ranger deployed. Note non-regulation mustache.

Raleigh Cash '93

Tim Wilkinson in front of
his helo Super 68

Matt Eversmann before a mission

Dan Schilling inside the hangar.
Left to right: Dan, Tim Wilkinson, and Pat Rogers

Task Force Commanders (confined to stretchers) playing volleyball
against senior enlisted to determine who would serve the troops dinner

The first Task Force Ranger mass formation of all troops

A full moon over the Task Force Ranger compound front gate. Note the lack of rear doors on Hummvee, which did not arrive until the day of the major battle on October 3.

DAN SCHILLING

Combat Controller Dan Schilling and PJs Tim Wilkinson and Scott Fales in front of CSAR helo "Razor's Edge"

RALEIGH CASH

Ranger Fire Support Observers '93. *Squatting; left to right:* Jeff Young and Tory Carlson; *sitting on wall, left to right:* Mike Goodale and Raleigh Cash; *standing, left to right:* Chris Huneke, Joe Thomas, and Jeff McLaughlin

DAN SCHILLING

Dan Schilling on a training flight at Ft. Bragg, N.C., with Task Force 160

JOE THOMAS

Task Force Ranger finishing a day at the range

The Mogadishu coastline

Aerial view of Mogadishu from a profile flight

Aerial view from Super 68

Little birds (MH–6s) and a Blackhawk over Mogadishu

Birds inbound in Mogadishu

Malaysian APC used in the rescue

DAN SCHILLING

Typical Somali roadblock of vehicles and debris strewn across the road. Photo taken on a raid prior to October 3. Notice the helicopter providing overhead cover.

JOHN BELMAN

CSAR Team Members: *Standing, left to right:* Mark Belda, Rob Phipps, Ron Galliette, Mike Collins, Al Lamb, and Pat Rogers; *kneeling, left to right:* Alan Barton and John Belman

Heading back to the hangar in Mogadishu. Waiting to pick up an L7.

Ranger Joe Harosky, Dan Schilling, and Ranger Mike Pringle in front of their Hummvee that led the assault convoy. Note the bullet holes in the windshield.

Dan Schilling in front of the door that saved his life

B Co. Rangers from the CSAR Bird. *Standing, left to right:* John Belman, Ron Galliette, and Alan Barton; *kneeling, left to right:* Mark Belda and Al Lamb

Rangers firing weapons on the range

View of area near the port facilities

DAN SCHILLING

The post-battle memorial service for the first eleven confirmed killed in action, October 5, 1993

RALEIGH CASH

Mobile Aeromedical Staging Facility. *Left to right:* Raleigh Cash, Randy Ramaglia, Mike Kurth, and Mike Goodale at the USAF, MASF

USAF Task Force members with folded flag for return to the unit.
Left to right: Pat Rogers, Jeff Bray, Tim Wilkinson, and Dan Schilling

Mike Durant passing through Task Force Ranger to a C-141 awaiting to take him to Germany

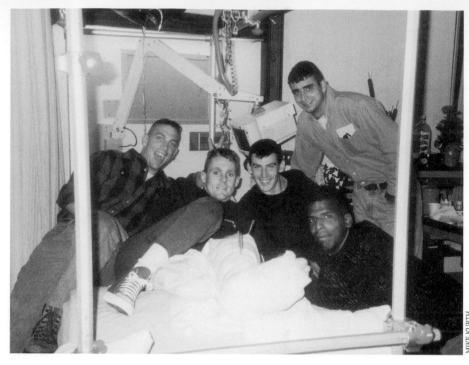

At Walter Reed Hospital, October 24, 1993. *Left to right:* Raleigh Cash, John Burns, Scott Galentine, Brad Thomas (standing), and Mike Kurth

USAF members drinking beers in the van ride home. *Left to right:* Tom Terlikowski, John McGarry, Dan Schilling, and Pat Rogers

the day before. We had made it back to the objective building. I was looking around and there were thousands of expended rounds all over the road. I looked up ahead to the next intersection, and I saw one of the five-tons. It looked like it had taken an RPG. You could tell that it was definitely out of commission—the back was completely shredded, and it was charred all over. *I hope that all happened without any of our guys inside,* I thought. I was hoping that it was just undriveable and they'd all had to abandon it.

Ramaglia, Strauss, and I were at the corner behind the carcass of the five-ton, getting ready to cross the street. The fire intensity had picked up quite a bit. Ramaglia was the first one of us to go across. As soon as he took off, you could hear the Somalis pick up their rate of fire—rounds were going off all around him. Once he got across the street, Doc Strauss made a break for it. You could see the rounds hitting all around him. He made it about two steps into the road, and then there was a huge explosion, with a big cloud of dust and smoke. Doc just disappeared in the cloud. I didn't know what had happened. Floyd looked at me and said, "Doc Strauss blew up!" I looked back over to see if I could see Strauss, so I could go and get him. I was hoping he wasn't in too bad shape so that we could take care of him until we could get to the link-up site. I was terrified of what I was going to see once the smoke cleared. I damn sure didn't want to see pieces of Doc all over the road. When the smoke began to clear, there was Doc, trying to get to his feet. Then he was kind of half running, half stumbling across the street. How he survived, I have no idea.

It was my turn to go. I took a couple of short breaths followed by one deep one. Ramaglia and Strauss had barely escaped. I was just hoping the third time wasn't the charm for the Somalis. I made a break for it. Instantly the street exploded. The rounds weren't nearly as close to me as they'd been the day before, when I'd gotten pinned down, but I still hauled ass. I made it to safety and slammed into the wall. I'd gladly take a brick wall over a 7.62 mm round any day.

I couldn't believe Doc was okay, but he was. A round had hit one of the flash-bangs that was in his ammo pouch, which explained the big explosion. I looked up at Ramaglia, and there was blood on the back of his shoulder, just outside his body armor. He was going about his business, pumping out rounds like nothing had happened. I thought: *When did he get hit? Does he even know he's hit?* I asked him if he was okay, and he said, "Yeah, I'm okay. I just got hit crossing the street."

We were going to have to cross the main road now. The volume of fire was still pretty high, but we all managed to cross without a major incident. Now we were at the steps of the Olympic Hotel, just a few short feet from where we'd roped in the previous day. I had stopped trying to fix my weapon because it was just no use. I knew that I was going to actually have to take it apart in order to get both rounds out of the chamber.

I looked up and saw Staff Sergeant Elliott run by. He had an extra M-16 slung over his shoulder. I ran up to him and told him I needed his weapon. Of course he looked at me like I was crazy. "I need your extra M-16," I told him. "Mine's down. I don't have a weapon." That he understood. He gave me the M-16, so finally I was able to protect myself and my buddies. I found a target and started firing. We made our way about another block and a half to a main intersection. There they had established a link-up site.

On the corner there was a two-story building standing, although the bottom floor was almost a complete shell. In the intersection stood a tank. We started running across. I heard someone say, "We have a sniper in that building," and he pointed right behind us. I glanced back at the building, then heard the tank turret make some adjustments. I was no more than five feet from the tank when it fired. Needless to say, I didn't have any ear protection in. I looked back at the building, and it had been reduced to a pile of rubble. *One way to take care of a sniper.*

When we got to our building, there were about fifteen or twenty of us on the ground floor. Sergeant Watson told us that they were sending more vehicles to come to get us and take us to the stadium with everyone else. *Great,* I thought. *How long is that going to take?* Fortunately, it wasn't too long before those vehicles were on their way. Sergeant Watson was grabbing a few guys, loading them up, and sending them on their merry way. There were only about ten of us left when Watson told Floyd, Elliott, and me to get ready to load the next vehicle. It happened to be an ambulance. I saw a 10th Mountain medic loading a 10th Mountain casualty into the back of it on a stretcher. He was having some trouble getting him in, so I ran out to help him. Once we got him loaded and set into the ambulance, I turned to help Floyd and Elliott get on.

But as they were running toward us, the ambulance took off down the road. I looked to the driver and asked him what the hell he was doing. "Wait for the other guys!" I told him. He just kept driving.

"Where the hell are you going?" I shouted.

"I don't know. I'm just following them," he said, pointing to the vehicle in front of him. *This is just great,* I thought. *I'm in an ambulance with a medic and a guy who has a pretty severe neck wound who is probably bleeding to death. We have room for about three more guys, but we took off because our driver is following the vehicle in front of him and has no idea where he's going.*

I was the only Ranger in the vehicle. I asked the driver if he was going to the stadium. He said he didn't know, that he was just *following.* I got on the radio to try to get hold of someone, to let them know where I was and tell them that I didn't know where I was going. But I couldn't reach anyone.

The back doors on the ambulance kept crashing shut, so I kicked one open and kept it open with my foot. There weren't any targets that I could see, but then again, I could only see out the back of the thing. The people on the street were just watching us go by. They had no weapons and weren't throwing rocks. Obviously, we were out of Bakara Market.

I looked back at the medic working on the casualty. It looked like he had already lost a lot of blood, and the medic was prepping an IV. The IV bag was a small one, and I knew the guy was going to need more fluids than that if he was going to make it.

"Hey, don't you have a bigger IV than that?" I said.

"Why?"

"He's lost a lot of blood. He needs as much as he can get, don't you think?"

"Yeah."

"Hey, I got a big IV on me. Why don't you use that?"

"This will be fine."

"You better stick *now,* because he's not looking so hot."

"Are you a medic?"

"No."

"Combat lifesaver?"

"No." I was getting agitated. "Hey, are you going to stick that guy or what? If you don't want to stick him, I will! Just *do it!*"

It worked. The medic focused and got the IV in and I went back to watching our back. There wasn't a whole lot of activity on the street. I tried again to reach someone on the radio, but I still couldn't get anyone. After about ten minutes we pulled into the stadium. As soon as the vehicle stopped, there were guys there to help unload the casualty, then I jumped out of the ambulance.

It was such a sense of relief just to be in a safe area, surrounded by a big building with guys whose sole purpose was to pull security for us. I couldn't believe it. *I'm finally here, thank God!* But I needed to find the rest of the guys. I looked around, and all I could see were casualties everywhere: guys who could walk around, guys who couldn't and who were strapped to a stretcher, and guys who were completely covered from head to toe—which meant only one thing.

I had no idea that we'd taken that many serious casualties, but here they were, right before my very eyes. It was bad, very bad. I couldn't believe it—the carnage was everywhere. I'd seen this stuff before, but it was in the movies. But this wasn't a movie and my buddies weren't actors. These men were my friends and comrades. I saw Goodale on a stretcher on his stomach with a big bandage on his ass. He didn't look too happy as they were putting him on the helicopter. All the medics were going crazy just trying to keep things moving. I am not actually sure who the guys in the body bags were, but I kept walking. I wanted to find the boys, the Rangers.

When I found my platoon, they were all standing around just as perplexed as I was. I went up to them and dropped all my gear. Someone had some water for me, and I drank it like a madman. "So where's Sergeant Watson?"

"He's around here somewhere."

Watson shouted over: "Hey, men, just stay in this immediate area. We're still trying to get a firm head count; we still have guys coming in." *That's cool,* I thought, *we all made it out.* I started to venture out just a little bit, but not too far—I was still within earshot of the platoon. I saw Sergeant Elliott on the landing zone. It looked like all the dust in the air was getting the better of him. So I asked him, "Hey, Sergeant Elliott, you okay?"

"Yeah," he replied.

"The brownout getting to you?"

"Yeah."

I turned around and started walking away and for some reason I knew that wasn't it. I turned back around and asked him again: "Is everything okay?" Sergeant Elliott was crying a little bit, but he turned around and started to walk away. I thought it might have been from embarrassment. I started to walk off, hoping that it was the rotor wash that brought tears to his eyes. I didn't want to ask him but I did. Then Sizemore began filling me in.

Sizemore had already been crying for some time; I could tell by his eyes. He just kept telling me, over and over, "They're all gone. Ruiz, Smith, Joyce, Pilla, Cavaco, Alphabet—they're all dead."

When I heard Pilla's name, I collapsed. To hear of Pilla and Joyce back to back . . . that was probably the worst news I could have gotten. I knew that there had been pilots killed, and I knew that Fillmore had been killed, and that in itself was saddening. But two of the best friends that I ever had in my entire life were *gone.* I lost it. I thought I'd bought it when the grenade went off; I thought my life was over. Now I had survived, but the only people whom I had let get anywhere near me since I was a child were gone.

Pilla was the one who told me about the Rangers and gave me the inspiration to become one. I'd met Pilla on my flight from Atlanta to Columbus when I first joined the Army. We talked a lot on the twenty-five-minute flight, but once we got to Fort Benning and realized we both had a Ranger contract, we never separated. We met Joyce in the reception station, and we all hung together. Joyce almost didn't make it out of reception because he'd had his wisdom teeth pulled and could barely get out of bed that day. But he did and we all made it to basic together. Pilla and I were in the same platoon at basic. Joyce somehow got separated and was put into a separate platoon, but we were all in the same company. We all graduated from basic together and went on to

Airborne School. We ended up in different companies but went to RIP together. Basic wasn't too hard because I had Pilla with me, and neither was Airborne School. We were all united once we got to RIP—the Three Musketeers back together again. RIP was pretty rough, but we all got through, and we decided to go to Third Battalion, which was right there at Fort Benning, where we all had started.

Eventually, I got up and made my way back to what was left of our platoon. We all looked like shit. There wasn't a happy face to be seen anywhere. I saw some of the other guys in our platoon that were on the other chalk, like Heard and a few others. We all hugged each other and told each other how glad we were to see that everyone was okay. But we were all still in a huge state of shock. Nobody knew what to do or how to act. We just stood around and waited for everyone to get back to the stadium. From there they'd start sending us back to the airfield.

I needed a smoke, but no one around had any cigarettes. I looked up in the stands of the stadium and saw some 10th Mountain guys up there smoking. I walked up to them and asked if I could bum a smoke. The guy looked at me and told me, "Sure, no problem." As I was leaving I heard one of them say, "That guy looks like he's been to hell and back."

I was sitting on the back of a Humvee, finishing my cigarette, and all I wanted to do was to go back to the hangar and play a game of check-ers. That's when it just became too much to take. I realized that I had no one to play checkers with anymore. Pilla, Joyce, and I had had a check-ers tournament going since we had been here in Mogadishu, and now it was over. I just put my head down on the Humvee and started to cry.

Floyd came over to me and asked if I was going to be okay, and I told him I'd be all right. Of course, I didn't really know that. I had just lost my two best friends in one day.

I started to think about their families. I'd met Pilla's family when we'd flown up to Jersey to bring back his car. I'd met Joyce's folks the day we graduated from Ranger School. Joyce had just talked to his wife, Deanna, the night before we'd gone out on this mission. He'd come and told me about it, right after he got off the phone. They had made up over the phone over some sort of misunderstanding, but Joyce was ready to move on from Battalion. He wanted to transfer to a different unit so he could spend more time with Deanna, but he still felt bad about leaving. I told him he had already fulfilled his commitment, and if he thought he needed to leave in order to spend more time with his wife, he had every right to do so.

Sergeant Watson came and told us that we had everyone accounted for and that we would be moving out shortly. We all gathered up our gear and prepared to get on a helicopter. The day before, it had taken two Black Hawks loaded to the gills to drop us down in Bakara Market. Today what was left of our platoon fit on one Black Hawk with room to spare. I was one of the last ones to get on, so I was sitting in the door with my legs dangling out. The helicopter began to lift off. As we were gaining altitude I was able to see the entire stadium. It looked like absolute chaos down there. I was so thankful to be actually on the helicopter and flying out. I don't think I have ever been so grateful about a helicopter ride in my whole life. I thought about the KIAs and began to cry again. I wanted so much for everyone to be able to get back in one piece.

We touched down at the airfield and got off the bird. A couple of the task force guys were there to greet us. Some Humvees were out in front of the hangar. They all looked bad. I don't think I saw one inflated tire among any of them. I stopped and looked at one Humvee that had just been riddled full of bullet holes. I stood there and asked myself how in the world anyone in that vehicle could have made it back.

Sergeant Watson told us to do weapons maintenance, refit and reload, do a once-over of all our gear, and get ready to go back. Go back? I definitely didn't want to go back out there. If I had to, I would, but I was hoping I never had to touch a Mogadishu street again. He told us we were on standby until the convoy made it back to the hangar. If they got into some sort of trouble, we would go in and get them out. I just sat there and hoped to God that they didn't get into any more trouble.

I did some weapons maintenance, and got some more ammo and grenades. As far as my gear was concerned, I was all set to go back out there. But mentally I was drained, emotionally I was hollow, and I was exhausted physically. I went to the back hallway—it's where we usually went to smoke. I lit up a cigarette and just sat there trying to comprehend what in the world had just happened. I couldn't, though. I had no idea what had just taken place. I had no idea just how big this deal was. I knew how lucky I was, but that was about it. I broke down again in the hallway. There wasn't anyone there, so I just sat there and wept. I didn't know what else to do.

After a while, I went back into the hangar and sat down on my cot. I was looking around, and about half the cots were missing. Anyone who had been wounded or killed, their gear had been packed up and their cot had been broken down. I looked across over at where Pilla's cot usually was, and I had a weird feeling come over me. I had never experienced anything like this before, ever.

A few hours went by and the convoy returned without incident. It was a relief to see those guys get back. I went over to Brad Thomas and asked him what had taken them so long to get back. He told me that they had basically skirted around the entire city just to get back to the hangar. I told him I was glad to see him back.

Later on that day we were sitting around watching CNN, getting their version of what had happened. At this point I just wanted to get the hell out of there and go home, but as we watched the TV we saw those dreaded pictures of our task force men being dragged all over the street. I was livid. I couldn't believe that they were doing that to American soldiers! No soldier should be desecrated like that. Seeing that got me in the right frame of mind again. I wasn't scared to go out there anymore. I went back to my cot and started to go over my gear again to double-check everything. I was ready to do whatever it took to get our fallen brothers back here and back to their families. If the Somalis wanted to act like barbarians, well, then they'd get treated like barbarians. I wasn't sure how I was going to react when under fire again, but I knew how I felt right then. That was the only thing that was keeping me going at that point. I was all set to go. I was ready to take out anything that got in my way. Seeing those images on TV changed everything. Come to think about it, the mission changed everything, for everyone.

I was twenty-two years old, and I would never see the world the same way again.

WHAT WAS LEFT BEHIND

John Belman

John Belman was a twenty-six-year-old Ranger sergeant on the Combat Search and Rescue (CSAR) team for Task Force Ranger. The CSAR team consisted of fifteen personnel: three from Air Force Special Tactics, seven from B Company, Third Battalion, 75th Ranger Regiment, and five from the Army's First Special Forces Operational Detachment—Delta. Flying on a 160th SOAR MH-60L Black Hawk alongside the assault and blocking force elements, the team was the sole contingency force on the mission. Should the unthinkable happen and a helicopter go down in the city, the CSAR team would rope in, secure the crash, and rescue any survivors.

Through the initial weeks of deployment in Somalia, the CSAR team had done all its training on its own, flying around, getting the lay of the land, and going over procedures. There was a brief whiff of excitement early on because we'd actually been asked to go in on the ground on a couple of missions in September in order to supplement the assault force. That would mean going in and helping out the Delta Force assaulters, helping them clear rooms, and looking for whoever we were trying to capture. But Delta Force Sergeant Major Tom C., along with Tim Wilkinson and Scott Fales, our Air Force pararescuemen, had strongly objected to this. They knew that if we sent the CSAR force in on the ground, there would be no rescue option available in case a helicopter got shot down, and Task Force Ranger would be left without contingency.

Sergeant Major C. had been on a helicopter himself in Grenada as a member of Delta Force and was shot down in hostile territory. So he knew firsthand the need to have an extremely good combat search and rescue capability. The CSAR search team was a joint unit, which meant that Scott and Tim had access to detailed information from their Air Force colonel, and would pass this on to the rest of the team. We therefore got what intelligence there was before the rest of the Ranger chalks, so we would know pretty quickly what was going on and what the scope of the actions would be.

We weren't expecting too much out of the ordinary to happen because every other mission we'd been on in Somalia had been completed without serious problems for Task Force Ranger, either on the ground or in the air. This meant that search and rescue was not required, which was always a good thing. Anxious as we were to have the opportunity to do our part, we liked the missions that ended with everybody home safe. We all wanted to engage and have an impact on what was going on, but at the same time we knew what that would mean. The nature of search and rescue meant that something had to go very wrong for us to become involved.

We flew in a CSAR Black Hawk, which on a typical mission held fifteen people, jammed in only inches apart. Our contribution to a typical mission would be to sit there eighty feet in the air, all geared up, listening to reports of the mission and watching the Little Birds do their gun runs. From where I sat in the middle of the helicopter, it wasn't that easy to even get a clear glimpse of downtown Mogadishu.

There were nine Black Hawks that flew out of Mogadishu and maybe one spare. Each Black Hawk had its specific number on the side so that people running out to the helo would know which one to go to. Our helicopter was Super 68. The first Black Hawk downed on October 3 was Super 61.

We got the call: Irene. It was our designated one-word signal for mission launch. That Sunday, October 3, we really didn't expect too much. We knew CSAR would be going up in the air along with the other Black Hawks and Little Birds, all in squadron formation. We hoped nothing would happen that would require us to play our part in the mission. We geared up, went out to the helicopters, and got on.

Often these ships had nicknames painted on their sides. Ours was *Razor's Edge*. The pilots and the crew chiefs came up with the names. For the 160th Special Operations Aviation Regiment, the crew chiefs

would act as the chief maintenance personnel for the helos, as well as
the gunners manning the miniguns on each side of the helicopter

The first indication I had that this mission was going to be slightly more
dangerous than any of the others is that we stopped to load the 2.75-
inch rockets on board. I didn't think the Black Hawks normally carried
them, and I remember that sticking a little bit in my mind. I remember
looking out the window, looking over at the helos just ahead of us flying in as sniper cover, thinking, *Boy, they seem to be flying in really close
and really low.* Inside, a Black Hawk is the size of the biggest SUV you
can think of. Outside, once you add the tail and rotors, it's longer than
a bus. This makes it a fairly large target to hit—especially if the helo is
flying around fairly slowly and low enough to provide good sniper
cover. It wouldn't matter that the crew chiefs were manning the miniguns if the Black Hawks were flying low. The Somalis appeared to have
planned for this event by coordinating and getting a volley of RPGs set
up to fire at everything in the sky. Once they figured that out, it was
simple math from that point on. If you're making yourself an easy target, you're gonna get hit.

I knew this was going to be a different kind of mission because the
Little Birds also loaded rockets, which they had not done in any of the
previous missions. Normally we'd be concerned about the collateral
damage to our own forces that an errant rocket could cause. I think I realized then that this might be a more serious mission than those we had
been on in the past. But I didn't really feel very differently about that. I
think we'd all gotten a little complacent. We all thought that since nothing serious had happened before, nothing was going to happen this
time out, regardless of these changes.

With hindsight, our tactics were inappropriate for the environment
we were in, given the amount of fire that the enemy could bring to bear
and the level of coordination that they were capable of. Using Black
Hawks to provide sniper cover was a bad tactic. The risk of these birds
being shot down was simply too great. You can't completely avoid risk,
but you want to balance your risks against the costs involved. Your
strategy should be to solve problems, not to create them.

On CSAR, the team's sole focus is to be prepared for the worst and to get into the right frame of mind. We always knew that if we really got involved in a mission, it would be because things had gone very, very badly.

Even among the best units where there's the most careful planning, sometimes you just don't consider a possibility that becomes critical, and you make inexplicable mistakes. All three of the units involved in Task Force Ranger made the same error in judgment. Nobody thought to pack night vision along except the pilots. The men of Task Force Ranger were the most prepared and best-trained of the entire U.S. military and, really, the world. And still, to a man, we made a judgment call that would, in retrospect, look like a pretty simple mistake.

We proceeded to fly the mission, getting messages relayed to us periodically. A couple of our sniper platform Black Hawks were also flying about, providing cover for the ground forces. Again, it struck me how slowly they were flying. At some point we heard that the ground convoy had taken casualties and that somebody had fallen out of one of the helicopters during the assault. There was a lot of confusion, but it was coming through over the radio that somebody on the convoy had been injured. Right about then we also heard about Blackburn. I don't remember which happened first, but those were two events that had not happened before—immediate and critical casualties. These were the first indications that this mission would be different from all those others.

Then we got the call: "There's a Black Hawk down. Super 61 is down." The reality of the situation hit me. Even though we had prepared time and again for the worst-case scenarios—more, perhaps, than the rest of Task Force Ranger—I knew right away that it was going to be ugly. And it was going to get worse. You just kind of turn cold.

Even if there was no incoming ground fire and there was no battle looming, even if there was *nothing* going on down there, it was going to be bad. A crashed helicopter would mean that undoubtedly you would find people smashed up, people burned up. There were going to be bodies at that crash site, and you just might have to cut them out. I didn't personally know the men in the downed Black Hawk, though I had gone to school with some of the Delta guys

Up there you're concentrating on getting everything just right. I was making sure I had my fast-rope gloves on. You can imagine how it might feel otherwise, sliding down a nylon rope with your bare hands. Some guys followed a procedure of wrapping their gloves with duct tape for reinforcement, wrapping the tape twice around each finger. At this point your training does take over. I checked all my equipment and turned on my Aimpoint sight, which is a battery-operated scope. I usually kept it off to conserve the battery. I was good to go. I know we were all thinking the same thought: *Let's hope nothing more serious happens so that we can get in there and get out of there without losing any more lives.*

Then it was just a question of waiting to get to the crash site. The pilots were being directed by other aircraft to where the Black Hawk had gone down. From the time we got the word, I suppose it was several long minutes until we arrived. We came in on a hover, and the guys on the doors kicked out the ropes and started to go down.

I was one of the last people out of the aircraft. I went down right before Wilkinson and Fales. Alan Barton, who was sitting at the door on the right-hand side of the aircraft, was carrying an M-249 SAW—a light machine gun. In transit, the ropes were coiled and stored in kit bags. To deploy the ropes, the bags were thrown from the helicopter. When Barton threw his fast rope out, one of the bag handles caught on the handle of his weapon, ripping it out of his hands. He flew down the rope, hoping he'd find the weapon on the ground in working order. It was.

Apparently our helicopter was hit with an RPG while I was sliding down, just beneath Tim and Scott. I learned much later that our Black Hawk had to hold the hover while hit. An RPG had taken out part of the main rotor, and the helo was on fire. I remember it was a fairly high fast rope. Once you're on it, you're not on it very long. I'm guessing the drop was about forty or fifty feet, though it was hard to say in all that brown dust. Brownout is typical anytime you have sandy or dusty conditions. The roads in Mogadishu were mostly packed dirt, so with any landing or approach, the brownout completely obscured our vision.

Our pilot held the course—he kept hovering rather than flying away, which would have been anyone's immediate response. He'd been warned by one of the crew chiefs that he still had guys on the ropes, and so he hovered there until we were on the ground. Only then did he cut the ropes and leave. Our Black Hawk was smoking as it headed back to the base, and though the crew survived, they made what was essentially a crash landing.

While the pilots had their worries dodging the RPGs, some of the guys on the fast ropes had thoughts of their own. We had available two types of body armor. One was the new green Ranger body armor with a ceramic plate in the front—these were quite good. But many other folks, myself included, had the older type, quite heavy and colored black. It came with very large ceramic plates to be worn both in front and in back—we called them "turtles." Once on the ground it was great having that protection, but on the ropes they greatly restricted our movement. There was a potential price to pay through the loss of that last bit of extra mobility, particularly if you're exposed to RPG fire and you're trying to get fifteen people out of that helicopter before it gets hit.

I landed in a cloud of dust—there was a lot of junk flying around in the air anytime we'd fast-rope in because of all the trash and refuse backed up from the streets. Though I assume we were taking a good bit of fire once we hit the ground, I didn't notice it at the time because of the sound of the rotor blades and all the dust swirling around. As soon as I got my bearings, I hustled over to the side of a building. Even though we try to stay away from walls because they can act as a channel for bullets, I figured that it was better to stand there and have my back protected than be out in the middle of the road exposed from all directions.

At any rate, I picked up and followed the rest of the team out. Some of us entered a courtyard connected to a network of rooms. Rob Phipps, one of the youngest Rangers out with our team, and I broke in a door and cleared the first room. None of the people inside was armed—they were just a bunch of Somali women and kids. Then I made my way through to the crash site. At this point the dust had settled, so visibility was very good. I rounded a corner, and there was the helicopter. This big, powerful machine, which inspired confidence in us all, was on its side and out of commission, looking extremely out of place. I noticed Scott Fales limping toward me with blood on his leg. Though it seems silly in retrospect, I first thought that he had cut himself on the wreck. But as it turned out, he had been shot.

A Delta sniper who was on Black Hawk 61 when it crashed was lying there, his face severely injured. He was a very brave guy, a very tough guy. Even though his injuries were serious, he was still trying to do his job—defending the crash site—as best he could, but he seemed a little disoriented. I helped set him down behind some cover.

The tail of the Black Hawk was facing west toward the target building in a very narrow alleyway. Ordinarily the CSAR team was supposed to set up four clock positions, first establishing a choke point at the six o'clock position where everyone would come through. This would then allow each subteam within the CSAR team to move out to establish security positions at the twelve, three, and nine o'clock positions. Once we had our four o'clock positions secure, our medics, Tim and Scott and the one Delta force medic, Bob M., would then go look for survivors and conduct an initial assessment of the area so that the Ranger and Delta force personnel could assist them with stretchers, move people forward and consolidate all casualties at the choke point.

But the alleyway was so tight that this devolved instead into twelve o'clock and six o'clock positions. The six o'clock position was on the western side of the crash, under the tail boom, and the twelve o'clock position faced east, near the cockpit.

There were men from the Ranger chalks who had gotten to the crash site before we had: Lieutenant DiTomasso; his RTO, Jason Coleman; Specialist Sean Nelson; Specialist Lance Twombly; and Specialist John Waddell. A few other guys from another chalk ended up showing up as well, John Stebbins and Brian Heard.

I was at the six o'clock position at the choke point, facing west. To my right and to my front were Bill C., the overall CSAR team leader, and Pat Rogers, the combat controller of the CSAR team. John Waddell was an SAW gunner. He was facing east just in front of me. Across the intersection, on the north-south road, were Alan Barton and Scott Nelson. Facing to the east was Lance Twombly. And also facing east on the southern side of the road were Brian Heard and John Stebbins. Over on the other side, at the twelve o'clock position, facing the other direction, were Rob Phipps, Mike Collins, Mark Belda, Al Lamb, Rick W., and Tom C. At some point Lieutenant DiTomasso and Jason Coleman got into the mix there too. The six o'clock position was very tight—not a lot of room there to move and not a lot of cover. Behind me, working on the crash, were Tim Wilkinson and Scott Fales, our pararescuemen, and Bob M., the Delta Force medic.

Once I got my bearings and helped the wounded Delta sniper, Tim and I began to pull out the crew from the wreck. We pulled out one of the crew chiefs, who was wounded, and set him up right behind and to the right of where Pat Rogers and I were situated. With a firefight going on, I needed a good position to shoot from, but there was no space to maneuver, so I had to sit on top of one of the bodies we had also pulled out.

The lane widened up across the intersection from where the Black Hawk had crashed, but there was a big rise in the road, and we were taking fire from farther down the alleyway. There was no room to move, and in order to engage targets with any kind of effectiveness at that distance I had to get some sort of elevation to return fire. In order to provide us with some minimal protection, Tim got the idea of pulling out Kevlar mats that were found around the bottom of the helicopter. We started setting those up around us and around the casualties.

The whole time this was happening we were taking an enormous amount of fire. One time I poked my head out around the corner and a fusillade of bullets hit the wall above my head. While I was sitting there shooting, the wounded crew chief turned to me and said: "They're shooting through it, shooting *through* it." I couldn't figure out what he could be talking about, and I thought he was delirious. What was happening was that the Somalis were shooting right through that Kevlar, because it wasn't designed to withstand the effects of an AK-47. Those high-velocity bullets would just rip right on through. Later on that night, John Waddell repositioned one of those Kevlar mats and he noticed that it was completely peppered with bullets except for an area that had the outline of a person—that person having been *me*. I consider myself very lucky.

• • •

Tim and one of the other medics were hard at work getting the survivors of the crash stabilized while we tried to provide security for them. The volume of fire was deafening. I was scared, but I was focused on the immediate task at hand. I have to say that everyone was doing their job; everyone was doing what he had to do.

I was running out of ammo very quickly. I had already burned through eight magazines of thirty rounds each. I was taking ammunition from people who weren't firing. Tim gave me a magazine, I remember. Then the CSAR team began to take casualties.

The Delta sergeant, Tom C., got shot in the abdomen. I think the guys on the other side of the twelve o'clock position were taking casualties. Whenever we'd try to move anybody, somebody else would get wounded. This presented a particularly acute difficulty because if we couldn't move anybody and we just kept taking casualties and had to remain in that exposed area, then we'd just sit there until we all eventually got picked off. That was the first sense I had that something had to change.

When the helicopter crashed, it had knocked a hole in an adjacent wall, the southern wall of that east-west alleyway. What we tried to do was to get everybody inside into that network of small rooms and courtyards and out of harm's way. But every time we tried to move anyone, someone else would get shot.

The communication nets were absolutely jammed. I could hear Pat Rogers having a real time of it. As a combat controller, his mission was to manage fire support and also to handle communications. You could tell from his face that everything was just a mess. From everything I heard going up to Major General William Garrison back at the base, to the command-and-control helicopters overhead, it seemed as if no one could get anything accomplished. I'm sure they were trying, but it all sounded very confusing.

I could also listen to the internal Ranger net because Lieutenant DiTomasso and his RTO were right behind me. That's about when we got the call from Captain Steele asking if we could move our people to his location. I remember saying to Lieutenant DiTomasso, "No way. We can hardly keep *our* people safe." There wasn't any way we could move anywhere, especially not to where Captain Steele was holed up. Lieutenant DiTomasso obviously agreed with me and relayed that message to Captain Steele. We were in a very difficult situation.

Very soon after we'd inserted, we'd gotten word that another helicopter, a second Black Hawk, had been shot down, and we knew that there was basically nobody available to go get those people. This, coupled with the number of casualties we were taking and knowing that we were all running out of ammunition, made for an increasingly ominous feeling. Once or twice I remember seeing the ground rescue convoy driving one or two blocks down to the west near where the initial target building had been, as if they were coming to us, but then that would be the last glimpse you'd see. I remember thinking: *We're not making it out of this.* More and more people were getting wounded. At one point I looked over at Pat Rogers, saw his arm was bleeding, and said, "Hey, do you know you're *hit?*" And we just started laughing.

John Stebbins and Brian Heard, who was an M-60 gunner, were across the alleyway, facing west, giving and taking a huge amount of fire. All of a sudden I saw Stebbins disappear in a huge puff of smoke and a cloud of dust. *He's down. Goddammit, I have to go run across the alleyway. I have to go get him. I hope I'll be able to get over there and drag him back.* I was figuring he was dead or really badly wounded. Just then, Stebbins popped up and started shooting again. Then *bam*—he disappeared in a cloud of dust *again.* I thought he was dead for sure this time—somebody obviously had a big weapon zeroed in on him, and there was no way anybody could make it out of that alive *twice.* But he popped back up and started firing. Eventually I heard that he did get wounded, but it was a remarkably courageous thing he did there, because he kept the enemy's heavy weapon targeted away from us. He'd never really been on a mission before and never been part of an operational platoon. It was one of those little miracles that happen in a situation like ours.

I remember seeing a Somali woman who kept running into the alleyway in front of us and directing fire for RPG gunners positioned in front of us. We had to determine first whether she was an innocent caught in the cross fire, and so the first couple of times she came out we let it go because we weren't really sure what she was doing. But it quickly became apparent that she was acting as a spotter, or a forward observer, for the Somali gunners, and she was counting on the fact that we wouldn't shoot her. We all were pretty busy shooting at other targets, though at one point I remember asking Captain C., our team leader, what we should do, and he gave the order that we should take her out.

We continued receiving a great deal of enemy fire. We had tremendous difficulty moving the bodies and the wounded into a compound adjacent to the crash. Little Bird gunships would come in pairs, fly in low, and pop up at the last minute, strafing in a direction away from our position, as directed by our combat controller Pat Rogers. They were so good at their jobs that they were able to put down their rounds almost right in front of us and clear a path for some distance. They kept that up all day and all night. That eventually enabled us to move people inside and get everybody consolidated.

I helped Al Lamb carry Mike Collins. He'd been hit in the leg pretty badly. I remember seeing him sometime after the battle, after he'd come back off medical leave. He had a brace around his lower leg to keep the leg in position while it healed because a couple of inches of bone had disintegrated. He wasn't the only one with this type of injury. It was a pretty common effect of the AK-47 rounds.

We were trying to carry Mike in through the doorways in the pitch black. Despite this banging around and his considerable pain, he kept up his spirits and was joking with us. Once we got inside the compound, things got to be a little quieter, and indeed it became a kind of waiting game.

I ended up taking up a position right at the southern edge of our perimeter inside a little courtyard that faced out with a double doorway leading toward an alleyway. Behind me, we'd started to receive casualties in the central room at our CCP (casualty collection point). I believe we had about nineteen people in there at one point. We had medics working on them—nobody seemed to be in critical condition at that time. Then I heard over the radio that Corporal Jamie Smith had died. Jamie was a fellow Ranger who'd been wounded earlier and was being treated by medics in an adjoining compound. He bled to death because they couldn't stem the blood flow from his femoral artery, and evacuation wasn't possible. It turned out that he wasn't all that far from our position—but we'd had no way of knowing that at the time.

We settled in for the long night ahead. All night long the firing continued. Brass from the helicopters' miniguns kept falling on our heads or the tin roofs. Rob Phipps came out once and found me sitting on a bench outside in the dark. We were talking, and all of a sudden it occurred to me that he'd been hit in the foot, and I said "Hey, what am I doing sitting and you're standing?" And we both started laughing at the absurdity.

At one point all of us were out of water. I had a tin of Copenhagen and I was almost out of that, too, but my mouth was so dry I couldn't use it anyway. A couple of people drank the water that was there in the compound. It was dripping out of a small faucet or something, but I wasn't interested in it myself because it was clearly not potable. We had iodine tablets, but it didn't look as though they would be enough to do the trick.

There was a group of Somali women and children in the compound with us. We'd segregated them off into a room and sat them down. We didn't flex-cuff them, but we tried to communicate as best we could that they'd probably be safer inside with us.

Throughout the night it was really just a matter of waiting—and listening to various bits that would come in over the radio; the UN would actually be coming and getting us, that there was actually going to be an effort mounted. We'd heard that a rescue convoy had started out but that they had to turn around and go back. I really didn't have a complete picture of just who was left out on the ground with us because I wasn't sure whether some of the assault forces had made it back to the airfield. None of us had any way of knowing how many other folks were holed up in positions similar to ours, other than those we knew about inside our particular area with the CSAR team and Lieutenant DiTomasso's chalk.

I thought about what it was going to take to get us out. We needed to get going pretty soon, as we were going to have to run out of there with stretchers and we would need the cover of darkness to avoid being cut down by the Somalis. It takes a minimum of two people per stretcher, and realistically, if you're going any distance with any kind of speed, you're going to need probably four people per stretcher. That doesn't leave very many people to provide security. So we figured out how many people we had who were wounded. Some of them were ambulatory, but most of them not. It would be a huge challenge to carry them if we had to go out any distance on foot.

At one point I was sitting there listening to Coleman, DiTomasso's RTO, and it became clear that the UN, in conjunction with Task Force Ranger, had actually mounted an effort to get us. They were sending a convoy. You could hear over the radio the intensity of the fire they were receiving. The closer the convoy got, the louder the firing got, so you could gauge how close they were getting.

As the Task Force Ranger 10th Mountain–UN convoy were getting close, some guys who were holed up nearby began coming through the courtyard we were guarding. Then I heard this voice call out, "Hey, is John Belman here? Has anyone seen John Belman?"

The guy calling out for me was Norm Hooten. He was one of the Delta Force assault team leaders on the force that had gone in on the ground to find the people that we were initially trying to capture. I walked over to the voice and found Norm and we hugged for a moment there. Then he took his team and moved on through all the way down to the crashed helicopter, and that's where he and his team stayed the rest of the night.

Norm and I had originally gone through Ranger School the year before, in September 1992. We had graduated in November of that year. At Fort Benning we had been paired through the course as Ranger buddies. Everybody who shows up at Ranger School has his head shaved and his rank and insignia taken off so that everyone is on the same footing.

We developed a really strong friendship. At Ranger School he eventually wound up telling me what unit he was from, even though that was considered to be a secret. I remember thinking, *Why would anyone in Delta put themselves through Ranger School?* Also in our Ranger platoon were Dominic Pilla and Brad Hallings. Dominic would end up being killed in Somalia in the ground convoy. Brad Hallings was a Delta sniper, the third sniper on the helicopter that Randy Shughart and Gary Gordon were flying on. Randy and Gary went in to go rescue Mike Durant and see if there were any other survivors at the second crash site, and Brad stayed on the helicopter to man one of the miniguns because the crew chief who had previously been manning it had gotten wounded. In the course of providing cover to Shughart and Gordon from his helicopter, Brad was hit by an RPG that took one of his legs off.

Norm was to tell me later that he and his team weren't sure right then who was in the courtyard where we were positioned, whether friend or foe. He had become pretty sure that we were the enemy. As a result, he decided that he was going to use explosives of some sort to make his entry—using a 203 round, for example, which would have wounded several people and probably killed me. But one of the Rangers with him said at the last minute that he thought he'd seen a TacLight. A TacLight is a high-intensity flashlight that we attach to our weapons and use for clearing rooms or to gain more visibility. So Hooten made the judgment call not to breach at that point, because of a single point of light.

I told him later that it actually wasn't a TacLight that the Ranger saw. It just so happened that one of the Somali women had found a flashlight there, and it happened to have batteries, and she'd turned it on.

When the rescue convoy finally got to our position, I remember one of the 10th Mountain vehicles being loaded with water, and I was so happy and grateful to have that first drink. Then we began loading the wounded. One of the first was Mike Collins, and despite how badly his leg was shot up, he was being a trooper. We put him down for a moment, while we waited for some space to be cleared for him in one of the Humvees and we sat there on one knee just sort of scanning the area out of habit, though we were well within the perimeter of the 10th Mountain. Mike was very conversant and relaxed, so much so that when we all got up we almost forgot about Mike—until he reminded us that we couldn't exactly leave him there in the middle of the street.

Next, we had to carry out one of the bodies. There is nothing heavier than a dead body. This guy had started out that day alive and with a family, and now he was another thing we had to find a place for on the vehicles. We hoisted him on top of the APC and tied him down. That was the last time I saw him. From there on in, it was still a waiting game. I still wasn't sure what the whole plan was. I knew there was one remaining body trapped inside a helicopter, but I wasn't entirely sure that this meant that the whole force was staying put. I guess I had the impression that some of the convoy were going to leave immediately with the wounded.

I remember thinking that if I was killed, I wouldn't want anyone to have to die to protect my body. I didn't know what we were actually waiting for, anyway. Coordinating the exfiltrate itself seemed like a logistical nightmare, and I didn't think that we were anywhere near ready to go. But it did lead me to wonder what I would want for myself if I were in that situation. It was a funny thing. We would do anything to get our comrades back—to leave no one behind. But I'd have to say that I wouldn't want any of the guys to come for me at the risk of his own life.

Finally it seemed as though everybody was ready to go. We'd already loaded all of our wounded onto the vehicles, but it became clear that a large part of our force was not going to have a ride back—at least not immediately. We were told to stack up along the street and get ready to run out alongside the convoy.

We were not at a dead sprint, but assumed a quick jog while trying to lay down some suppressive fire. The Malaysian gunners had a vantage point that was ridiculously high, and yet they were shooting straight up into the air anyway. As they were firing their weapons, I remember thinking it was such a waste—that if anybody did get hit, it would just be innocent people.

The Little Birds were working their gun runs again. The sound they make is like the loudest chain saw you could ever imagine, as if someone were just shredding the sky. Their job was to create a protected corridor for us to run through. I don't know how long I ran, but it was a good while and I ended up running out of ammunition halfway through. I didn't really know what I was going to do after that. I didn't even have a bayonet. Luckily, John B., a Delta Force guy whom I didn't really know before then, had an extra magazine, and he threw one to me.

Finally we rounded a corner and met Captain Steele, and other elements of our ground force that had not been at my specific location. There were all sorts of Humvees waiting to pick up some of our people who had been running to make it out of the Bakara Market. I got into one of the last 10th Mountain Humvees. I remember diving into the open roof of this Humvee along with Al Lamb. Considering where I'd come from I thought speed was of the essence.

The ride out was not a lot of fun. We were dodging explosions all along the way. Sitting inside a Humvee really gave me a sense of appreciation for what the guys on the ground convoy had gone through. When you're driving you're essentially a big, slow target with very limited fields of fire to defend yourself. I felt helpless. Our driver kept stopping in the middle of intersections, and I kept saying, "Drive! Drive!" He seemed to keep his cool, even with this crazy Ranger behind him. Then, just when I was thinking we were going to be fine, it became clear that we had been split off from everybody else who appeared to have gone back to the Pakistani stadium. Our Humvee and one or two others had actually started back to the airfield. Had I known that at the time, I probably would have been less alarmed than I was.

Back at the airfield, we dismounted and headed toward the hangar. I heard someone give a shout: "Hey, come back. Come back!" We're thinking, *What could they possibly want from us?* So we turned around and jogged back to where the Humvee sat. *What am I going to do? I have no ammunition. We have only two vehicles—what could we possibly do?*

Apparently what had happened was that another vehicle had split off and gotten lost. We were going back to find this other vehicle. Right when we were getting back on the vehicles to go back out, we got the word that the lost vehicle had made it back into the old port, another one of the United Nations locations.

We finally made it back to the hangar. Colonel McKnight was there to greet us, and he gave me a big hug. His uniform was covered with blood. It was broad daylight, and the first time I really had a chance to look and see that mine was, too. How lucky we had been to make it out of there alive, and how terrible for those who hadn't.

The hangar was almost empty because most of the Rangers were over at the Pakistani stadium and most of the wounded were being flown out to Germany. The hangar would stay pretty empty until reinforcements arrived from Alpha Company, the Third Ranger Battalion, and A Squadron from Delta Force.

As if on autopilot, I began to grab more ammunition and made sure I was ready to go back out again. Suddenly Al Barton came running up to me and crying, telling me about all the guys who had been killed. I guess I thought I'd heard the worst already, seeing guys killed and hearing about Jamie Smith. But I thought somehow they were the only ones that were dead. And then I realized that that wasn't true—not by a long shot. Hearing that Pilla had been killed too, I broke down a little bit and said, "Are we going back out or not? What's going on?" And then I kind of fell asleep. I lay down on my cot and slept for a little bit. You could call it shock.

Later, I walked over to the front of the hangar. Some of the wounded were there, and we sat around and talked for a while. In the aftermath you could really see what had happened. The damage done to the vehicles and to the helicopters was incredible. Out of the eight helicopters we'd had flying that day, five had been hit badly enough to be unflyable. We were lucky not to have lost more than two that day.

At that point I didn't know if we'd succeeded or failed in that particular mission; later I learned that we'd succeeded. But the reality was that Task Force Ranger—and by extension its components: SEAL Team Six, Rangers, Special Tactics, Delta Force, and the 160th Special Operation Aviation Regiment—were among America's finest fighting units and were dealt a major blow. The problem was not that we didn't know what we would be facing. The problem was that we didn't have sufficient force to deal with it. We should have had tanks and armored personnel carriers. We should have been prepared to use the right force at the right time, and our country should have made sure that the target was worth it.

When Alpha Company finally got there on October 5, we immediately felt better about the probability of going out, because Mike Durant was still in captivity and we hadn't recovered the dead at his crash site. We immediately switched into the mind-set that it was time to maybe get Aidid and finish the job. People had already died trying to do this. If it meant enough for the country to have us doing what we did, then it should mean enough for us to finish.

On October 6, we got hit by a mortar attack and lost Delta Force member Matt Rierson. I didn't know him personally, but I remember how he was commemorated at the memorial service afterward. It seemed so unfair to have made it out of that terrible battle all in one piece only to be killed a few days later. After that we trained for a couple of weeks with Alpha Company, until Mike Durant was released from captivity. A Company arrived along with a replacement Delta and Special Tactics contingent. It was clear from the news that Task Force Ranger's role was finished, that a political solution was being sought.

I left on October 22 and landed in Seymour Johnson Air Force Base in North Carolina. I remember one figure standing in the rain all by himself. It was General Grange. He had been the Ranger regimental commander right up until our leaving for Somalia. At his change-of-command speech in front of the Infantry Building at Fort Benning, he said that the thing he regretted most was that he wasn't going to be taking us into combat. At the time it seemed only part of a rousing speech, but after Mogadishu it was clear that he knew that something was going to go down in Somalia and that he felt bad that he wouldn't be there.

We got leave around Veterans Day. I happen to be from Washington, D.C., so I went up there to see my folks. On November 11 I went to the ceremony up at the Tomb of the Unknown Soldier, as President Clinton had asked the wounded from Mogadishu to be there at the place of honor. I just happened to be in the crowd. He asked all the Somalia veterans to stand up, and I did. I was out there in a crowd of people and felt everyone looking at me and wondering: *Who is this guy?*

The Battle of Mogadishu has gotten a lot of attention and has been studied a lot in military circles—but not in civilian forums. I got out of the military in 1995, and at that time, if anybody remembered what had happened in Mogadishu, it was maybe on the order of remembering a bus accident, or maybe something vague that someone had an inkling of, but nothing remarkable, nothing substantial. I would find myself going out on job interviews, and if I had to mention my Army background—although usually I would try to avoid it—I would say: "Do you remember Somalia?" Usually the reaction was a lack of recognition or a reluctance to know about it or talk about something so uncomfortable. Eventually it became something that I didn't want to talk about.

That all changed in 1998, when Mark Bowden published *Black Hawk Down*. I felt very good about that book, although there were some things that I didn't agree with. I didn't think that the friction between the Rangers and the Delta Force guys was really reflective of my own experience there on the ground. We'd all worked together on the CSAR team. We had Rangers, Delta Force troops, Air Force pararescuemen, and combat controllers all working together with no problems at all. But beyond that minor point, I will always be thankful to Mark for recording something so important to me and my comrades. There has been so much in American wars that has never gotten that kind of attention or that kind of focus. I will always be thankful that somebody cared enough to do the story justice.

With the current war on terror, perhaps the story of Mogadishu will fade into the past. But I'm happy with that. I think that we've gotten our story out and that we have had our day. And we have made a difference. Maybe it didn't make a difference at the time. Maybe our mission wasn't a positive thing on its own. I certainly have had my own moments of fearing that it was a waste. But in retrospect I think it has not been a waste. We're beginning to see that the enemies we fought there are the same enemies that we're fighting today. I think we've learned some lessons about combat and about what the country needs to do when our soldiers are in harm's way. And I think that we, the American people, have a much different attitude than we had then and that we've grown up. Twenty years from now, when *Black Hawk Down* and Somalia are just a footnote, we will at least have done that much—and that's all anyone can ask.

BE CAREFUL WHAT YOU WISH FOR

Tim Wilkinson

War is an ugly thing, but not the ugliest of things; the decayed and degraded state of moral and patriotic feeling which thinks nothing worth a war, is worse. A man who has nothing which he cares more about than he does about his personal safety is a miserable creature who has no chance at being free, unless made and kept so by the exertions of better men than himself.
—John Stuart Mill

To every man, there comes in his lifetime that special moment when he is tapped on the shoulder and offered the chance to do a very special thing; unique, and fitted to his talents. What a tragedy, if that moment finds him unprepared and unqualified for the work that would be his finest hour.
—Sir Winston Churchill

Super 68, a Black Hawk MH-60 helicopter with a combat search and rescue (CSAR) team on board, hovered above the battle, ready to go in should a Task Force Ranger team member become isolated or a helo become disabled and crash in the city. One of its crew was Tim Wilkinson, an Air Force pararescueman (PJ), who was two months short of his thirty-fifth birthday. Pararescuemen are rescue specialists trained to find and recover isolated personnel, provide trauma medical care, and escort the person back to friendly control in any environment. Wilkinson had been a PJ nine of his twelve years in the military and had seen everything from combat opera-tions in Panama to civil search-and-rescue recoveries of crash victims in the mountains of Alaska.

Our Black Hawk, known as Super 68, the designated combat search and rescue (CSAR)/SAR Security Team (SST) bird, circled the city in an off-orbit from the target area, trailing the command-and-control (C2) bird. It was approximately 1545 hours on October 3, and we had been in the air for about twenty-five minutes. From our stand-off vantage point, we watched the AH-6 Little Birds maneuver around the vicinity of the target building in low orbits, diving down, zipping between buildings making gun runs on hostile targets with pinpoint accuracy. The larger infil Black Hawks circled around the target area at higher altitudes, their gunners searching for targets.

The personnel on board Super 68 were a mixed bag—a reflection of the composition of Task Force Ranger itself. Her crew came from the Army's premier Special Operations Aviation Regiment, the 160th. The CSAR/SST team in the back consisted of three Air Force Special Tactics operators, including two pararescuemen (PJs) and one combat controller (CCT), and twelve Army personnel—seven Rangers and five from Special Forces. Our job was to perform CSAR in support of any mission Task Force Ranger executed. In the event a helicopter was shot down or personnel became isolated from the main force, we were poised to rapidly respond with a force designed to recover and medically treat any wounded and, if necessary, hold a small chunk of ground for a short period of time until reinforcements could be moved in to assist in the recovery effort.

It was a stiflingly hot Sunday afternoon. But, as they say, it was a dry heat. Even the air blowing through the helo as we flew was hot. This was the seventh assault mission Task Force Ranger had conducted since arriving in country in late August. We had executed the previous missions with varying degrees of success. Some of the targets turned out to be dry holes, while others had provided some measure of success in capturing key individuals identified on the UN's hit list. The mission just prior to this had resulted in the capture of one of the top men on the list, Aidid's finance minister, Osman Atto.

In addition to the actual assault missions, Task Force Ranger conducted at least one and sometimes more familiarization or "fam" flights almost every day—some in daylight, some at night. During these fam flights, the entire air armada would take off from the airport and fly around the city. Many times the ground convoy would also depart the airfield and drive through the city. These maneuvers were done in an effort to desensitize the locals to our manner of conducting operations. In this way the SNA (Somalia National Alliance) never knew if we were launching a mission or just going for a joyride around the Somali countryside.

Throughout all of these operations, whether fam flights or actual target takedowns, Super 68 would fly in trail of the helo formation or in an off-orbit with the C2 bird and watch the operation go down. We were an insurance policy. No one ever wanted to even *think* about using us. The crew and team of Super 68 requested this mission would be no different from the rest, boring and uneventful.

With fifteen of us packed in the back of the helo, it was tight. I mean ugly tight. I weigh around 180 pounds without my kit. With my kit on, I probably dressed out at about 260 pounds, which is about the middle of the road as far as operators go. As big as a Black Hawk helicopter appears sitting on the ramp, one would think it could easily accommodate a crew and fifteen passengers. But in reality, it was like stuffing fifteen guys who don't all get along into a seven-foot-square elevator and having them hang out together for four hours at a shot. Oh, and by the way, six of them have a really bad case of gas.

I was sitting between the two gunners' seats in the middle of the helo on a spare 7.62 mm ammo can in the forward portion of the cargo compartment, facing the rear of the cabin/cargo area. I was wedged in tight but still able to look out the cabin doors on either side of the helicopter. Every now and then, when 68 went into a tight bank, I could catch a quick view of the target area and the Little Birds and Black Hawks circling below.

Sitting across from me along the back wall of the cabin among our Army teammates were Scott Fales and Pat Rogers. Scott, Pat, and I were the Air Force part of the Task Force Ranger CSAR/SST. Scott and I were PJs, Pat a CCT. The three of us had been teammates since shortly after Operation Just Cause in Panama. We had all been in Panama at the same time but assigned to different Air Force units and attached to different operational teams. Scott and I met there in Hangar 3 at Howard Air Force Base shortly after the initial takedown operations. Scott was temporarily augmenting the unit I was assigned to. He and others from my unit parachuted with the Rangers onto Rio Hato. They were in the first-wave assault to take down the airfield.

During Just Cause I had been attached to a SEAL team assigned to conduct raids in and around the capital city. Pat had been attached to the SEAL team that executed the assault on Punta Patilla Airfield and had a rough go of it, taking several casualties. Pat and Scott also did time in the desert during the first Gulf War. All three of us were experienced operators. We were happy to be flying together. With an outstanding aircrew, the formidable Army Ranger and Special Forces security team, we made for a very capable CSAR package for Task Force Ranger.

Most people have no problem understanding what the Army Rangers and Special Forces troops were doing in Task Force Ranger. The same may not be true of the Air Force Special Tactics operators, pararescuemen, and combat controllers. As a matter of fact, the vast majority of people within my own service had no clue as to why we were there and what it was we did. Special Tactics operators have always been content in their quiet professionalism. Despite our participation in every major special operations event from Desert One in Iran and on, our lack of public exposure places us in the aggravating position of having to per-perpetually justify our military worth and utility.

Pararescuemen are rescue specialists. Recovering personnel who are in harm's way is all we do for a living. We are there to save lives. Our motto, "That others may live," is not merely a catchphrase; it is our credo. It is the mind-set and philosophy that govern our professional lives. But we can also shoot and move with the best of them. It takes about eighteen months of training from start to finish to qualify as a PJ. It is a long and arduous path, and only about 15 percent of those who enter the program graduate.

Combat controllers and PJs go through the same training pipeline, and the CCTs' washout rate is similar to that of the PJs. Combat controllers are there to control the airspace in combat operations, deconflict the airspace between aircraft, (that is, keep the aircraft safely apart), direct calls for fire on targets, and provide ground-to-air communications for command and control. They are the vital link between the ground and air assets to make sure things don't run into each other and to ensure that hot steel gets put on target.

Both PJs and combat controllers are capable of working unilaterally in small teams or can augment Army and Navy special operations forces. We determine job responsibilities according to mission requirements. We go to and from "work" via all the normal military infiltration and exfiltration methods: parachuting, diving, all types of surface vehicles, all-helicopter insertion techniques (alternate insertion/extraction or AIE), and of course, via the most basic of all, the MK-1 combat boot. Each method has its advantages and disadvantages. The method used for any given operation is situation-dependent. To us, it doesn't matter what method is used, although some are definitely more fun than others. However, they are all merely different ways to get to and from "work." For PJs and combat controllers the job really begins once you get to your workplace.

The "workplace" for PJs specifically means whatever environment the isolated individuals happen to have the misfortune of finding themselves in. We treat any medical conditions they may have—enough to stabilize them—and provide survival escort by whatever means are available and necessary to bring them back to friendly territory.

The combat search and rescue mission, like firefighting, is one of those missions that everyone hopes they never have to execute. The best day on the job I ever have is the day I don't have to do anything at all except be *ready* to do my job. That means everything has gone right that day for everyone else. Like a firefighter who gets the call in the middle of the night, you don't get to pick the time and place. You do not have the luxury of walking the ground ahead of time to rehearse for every potential twist in the event. You get what you get. The majority of the time you must assess the situation as it is happening, prioritize your response options, and then act. It is a very dynamic situation. CSAR is a time-critical event in which seconds and minutes mean lives lost or saved. As a professional who has trained throughout his career to do a specific job right, you want to test your mettle, test your skills, and contribute. You never wish any ill to fall on any of your teammates, but still, you *always* want to get in the mix. It is a constant state of conflict. The reality of doing business in combat, though, is that it is not a matter of *if* some catastrophic event is going to happen; it is a matter of *when*. And when it does happen, I don't know of any PJ who wouldn't want to be there, smack in the middle of it, to do what he has trained to do.

The aircrew and the team had done extensive rehearsals and we choreographed our procedures to rapidly fast-rope out of the helicopter. If there were no open areas in close proximity to a target big enough to land the helo, our only other infiltration option would be the fast rope. A fast rope is a coarse braided rope about four inches in diameter. They come in lengths ranging from 40 feet to 120 feet. Luckily, the buildings in Mogadishu weren't very tall, and we would only have to fast-rope perhaps sixty feet at most. We carried an eighty-footer with us, although I think that was just to ensure we would be able to fast-rope anywhere in the city.

The basic fast-rope procedure is pretty simple. There is a big loop at one end of the fast rope, and it is attached to a heavy-duty clevis pin on the fast-rope bar. The fast-rope bar is bolted to the roof of the helo, perpendicular to the cabin door. The remainder of the rope is positioned in a neat coil inside the cabin but close to the door. If the situation looks like it will require a fast-rope insertion, the fast-rope bar is extended out the side of the cabin door about four feet and locked into place. The coiled portion of the rope, still remaining inside the helo, is then slid to the edge of the cabin door. As the helo approaches the target the pilot begins to slow the helo from 110 knots to about 40 knots. At this point the helo is still moving along at a pretty good clip. As the helo gets into the terminal objective area the pilot conducts a maneuver called a flare. He pitches the nose of the aircraft up at about a thirty-degree angle, to bleed off more airspeed. Right at the end of the flare, as the nose of the helo starts to come back down to assume a hover position over the insertion point, the crew signals for the fast rope to be thrown out. The man designated to throw the rope kicks the coil out of the cabin door and ensures the end of the rope is on the ground. Then, one by one, out we go out as rapidly and as close together as possible.

Fast-roping is like sliding down a flexible fireman's pole. Doesn't sound hard, and it's not; however, keep in mind that with all your equipment you weigh about 260 pounds and you're holding on to the rope with just your gloved hands. The gloves are thick leather with heavy wool inserts to protect your hands from the intense heat that is produced by the friction of sliding down the rope as you pick up speed on the way down. The end result of all of that is a controlled fall from however high the hover was. But it is a relatively quick way to insert a team when you can't land the helo. We normally throw ropes out both sides of the helo to expedite the infil even more. The faster we get out of the helo the better. A helo is most vulnerable in a hover, and we owe it to the aircrew to exit with maximum speed.

Picture those same fifteen men in full combat kit packed into that seven-foot-square elevator trying to move the coiled fast rope into position, extend the fast-rope bar, and position themselves to quickly grab the fast rope and exit the helo, all while in flight, with the helicopter yanking and banking and maneuvering to get into the target area. It can be a very difficult process. In fact, it requires a specific sequence of actions from each team member to make it happen quickly and safely. The two men sitting on the fast ropes have to half stand up (the cabin ceiling is too low to stand fully upright) and move the fast rope from beneath them while the man next to them holds on to them to keep them from falling out of the aircraft. The people sitting on the floor of the cabin below the fast-rope bar have to extend the bar and lock it in place and move into a squatting position, then grab the rope to exit. Everyone who is sitting on the floor of the interior of the cabin has to reposition themselves into a squat so they can duck-walk to the cabin door they are going to exit out of and grab the rope. It was a good thing we practiced.

It was approximately 1600 hours, and the hit was going down according to plan. The two principal target detainees and some twenty others had been rapidly acquired, and the ground convoy had moved into position adjacent to the target building (across from the Olympic Hotel) to begin loading the detainees and the assaulters for exfiltration. The goal was to be off the target area in thirty to forty minutes if possible. The men on the ground were heavily engaged by small arms fire and rocket-propelled grenades. We had not merely stepped into the enemy's backyard to snatch him out; we had stepped into his living room. The target was in the heart of Mohammad Farrah Aidid's stronghold, the area adjacent to the Bakara Market, in what was known as the Black Sea district. Unlike the other UN and U.S. forces who were in Mogadishu, Task Force Ranger was not there to feed the starving and keep the peace. We were there to take down Aidid and his SNA command-and-control infrastructure. The UN had determined that Aidid and his forces were the primary roadblock to peace in Somalia. We were there to remove that roadblock.

From my limited view I could see RPGs streaking through the sky below, more RPGs than I had seen on any of the previous missions. Some exploded in midair, while others impacted buildings around the target. I knew the men on the ground were locked in mortal combat. Using surprise, speed, and violence of action, Task Force Ranger had capably handled all the previous missions, and I hoped this one would be no different. I said a silent prayer.

We droned through the air, engulfed in the deafening whine of our aircraft engine and rotor blade slap, boring what seemed to be endless holes in the sky. All that snapped into harsh focus when the team leader across from me blew his whistle and showed us a grease board with the message "Five-ton hit—ground evacuation of casualties." This was the first indication I'd received that the situation on the ground had begun to deteriorate.

The next call, however, which we got twenty minutes later, was the call every PJ lives for but hopes and prays will never come: "Super 61 down—four souls on board." That call meant that people we knew by face or by name were wounded, dead, or in grave danger.

Immediately everyone began to prepare for insertion into the crash site. A few minutes later another message was passed around the helicopter: four souls on board was changed to eight. After what seemed like an eternity, we received the call to go in. It would be a fast-rope insertion.

The CSAR team leader yelled out to everyone, "Six minutes!" then: "Fast rope! Fast rope! Fast rope!" The air was charged with excitement. Immediately everyone put on his thick, heavy leather fast-rope gloves. Super 68 began to weave and hook as we maneuvered into the area where Super 61 had crashed. Moving about in the helicopter became more difficult as we all strained against the Gs. And so began the chore-ographed dance to get everyone into position to fast-rope out of the air-craft. I would be the last man out, on the right-side rope. With the muzzle of my GAU-5 pointed at the floor of the helicopter, I reached down to the charging handle, pulled the bolt back, and released it, snapping a round into place in the chamber. Instinctively I checked the safety. I checked to make sure the sling was clipped into my LBE (load-bearing equipment). As I raised my head I locked eyes with Scotty, who was sitting across from me along the back wall of the cargo compart-ment. No words were said, but the message that passed between us was unmistakable. We knew the gravity of the situation, had our resolve, and would meet the challenge with confidence. We nodded to each other and looked over at Pat, and the three of us smiled at each other. *This is for all the marbles—this is what we have trained for. Let's go do it.*

The inbound run-in was north to south. Super 68 banked hard, and then the nose of the aircraft came up as the pilot started his flare. I was now on about a thirty-degree incline, still sitting facing the rear of the cabin. Dust was everywhere. The vast majority of the streets in Mo-gadishu are nothing more than hard-packed dirt topped with a layer of sand and fine dust. The downwash of the rotor blades created an instant dust storm, swallowing us whole. Brownout had engulfed the helo and obscured any view I had of the world outside the helo cabin. We roped into a north-south-running street called Marehan Road, approximately forty meters north of the crash site.

According to Ray Benjamin, a combat controller and fellow team-mate flying in the C2 bird, the CSAR/SST fast-roped in seven minutes and forty-eight seconds after the downed-helo call came in, but it seemed as if it took forever to get into the area. As we made our prepa-rations to fast-rope in, ground elements from the blocking positions around the target building—approximately five blocks away—were moving on foot to help secure the crash site.

What I was not aware of at the time were the valiant efforts of Star 41, a MH-6 Little Bird crew. They had landed in the street just a few meters south of the intersection of the alleyway that Super 61 lay in and Marehan Road. The MH-6 had set down in the street with minimal clearance between the rotor tips and the buildings on either side of the street. The pilot held the aircraft steady with one hand and provided cover fire up the street with his MP-5 while the copilot got out and helped pull two of 61's victims onto the external passenger seat. He then departed for the airfield. Words cannot adequately describe the enormous courage, professionalism, and tenacity on the part of that MH-6 crew.

I was the third-to-last man out of the helo, and the last man out on the right side. Scotty was the last man out on the left side. As I approached the rope I noticed that the medical bags—which were to have been thrown out when the ropes went out—were still in the aircraft. We had practiced and practiced the sequence of events needed to offload the helo, but in all the excitement, with rounds flying and all, the designated person had forgotten. I was able to throw the bags out as I moved toward the fast rope, but it cost us time, and time in a hover is precious to a helo in a combat zone. As I began sliding down the right rope, Super 68 took an RPG round in the main rotors just aft of the cargo area. Even though the natural tendency would have been to transition to forward flight in an attempt to save the aircraft and get it back to the safety of the airfield, the pilots, Chief Warrant Officer Dan Jollata and Major Rodriguez held their hover until the gunner crew chiefs, Kenny Hickman and Kenny Mikeman, confirmed that we were safely down and had cut the ropes.

They departed trailing smoke. The aircraft limped its way back to the airfield with no oil pressure remaining in the engines, and the pilots were forced to basically perform a controlled crash landing. The entire crew climbed out of that helo, moved over to the only spare Black Hawk we had left, and fired it up to rejoin the fight. I was on the rope when 68 was hit. I owe my life, at least in part, to those pilots for not slinging me down Marehan Road.

I have seen Dan on several occasions since that day. I always try to remember to thank him for holding that hover. In his typical good-natured style he smiles and gives me a wave that says, *Get outa here, you.* I thank the entire aircrew for their incredible bravery, coolheadedness, and airmanship they demonstrated that day. I would fly with them anyplace, anytime.

• • •

As soon as my feet hit the ground I quickly moved toward the wall on the west side and tried to orient myself as the dust settled. I couldn't see shit. The area was still blanketed under a thick cloud of dust. It just hung there, even though Super 68 had long since departed. It was hot. I was sweating, and the dust was sticking to me already. Despite the heavy leather fast-rope gloves, the forty-foot fast rope had left my hands smoking hot from the friction of sliding down the rope. I just wanted to get the damned gloves off.

Over the course of several years I have lost countless fast-rope gloves, sometimes the pair, but usually the glove from the right hand. My right hand is my shooting hand, so I almost always take my right glove off as soon as I hit the ground. I am constantly forgetting to clip the gloves into my LBE after taking them off, so I have a pile of left-hand fast-rope gloves in my gear bag. On October 3 I was determined to keep this pair intact. I made a conscious move to immediately clip them into the carabiner on the left shoulder strap of my LBE. I don't know why, but I did.

Even though I could not see well, I could hear the unmistakable cracking sound of rounds splitting the air as they went by my head. Gunfire this close sounds like someone is smacking two-by-fours together next to your ears. I was having a hard time determining where exactly the rounds were coming from. Hell, the more appropriate question was, where *weren't* they coming from?

I had no idea where Super 61 was located. I had not been able to see anything prior to going out the cabin door. Between the yanking and banking, doing the insertion, and the dust cloud that consumed us, it had been all I could do to get myself out from between the two gunners' seats and move to the rope without getting thrown out of the helo.

Visibility was still poor, but I saw a bunch of the team guys on the east side of the street come out of what appeared to be a courtyard gate. They moved south up the street to a corner about forty meters away, turned it, and were gone.

I decided to follow the team. I didn't want to get separated and cause a bigger problem. Besides, with the rounds snapping everywhere and the dirt getting kicked up around me, it was probably a good time to move. I picked up the medical equipment bags that were lying in the middle of the road and ran up the street and around the corner to join the rest of the team.

As I rounded the corner I was taken aback by what I saw. I am accustomed to seeing helos neatly parked on a ramp. A Black Hawk is a good-sized helicopter, but in the confines of the alleyway, Super 61 looked enormous, like a beached whale.

The helo was in an east-west-running alley with the nose to the east and the tail to the west. She was fairly intact. I was surprised. She was on her left side, and up against the ten-foot-high north wall of the alley. The main and tail rotors were both gone. The tail boom was cracked where it joined the main fuselage but was still attached. The tail section was angled down toward the ground at about a fifteen-degree angle, resting on the rear stabilator. There was approximately five feet of room to pass through between the belly of the aircraft and the south wall. The ten-foot wall on the south side was broken and crumpled where Super 61 had impacted before she rolled onto her side.

We have established standard operating procedures for executing this type of operation. The security element, the Ranger and Special Forces shooters, establish a perimeter around the incident site as best they can. Just before the security element disperses to establish a perimeter, a choke point is established by the team leader. All personnel on the team flow through the choke point. This establishes a point of reference for everyone on the team. Having such a choke point helps the command-and-control elements account for everyone.

As I arrived, I could see that the choke point had been established at the tail end of the helo. The casualty collection point (CCP) had also been established in this area. The choke point and the CCP lay between the aft portions of the cargo area and the end of the tail boom, about fifteen feet from the entrance of the alleyway off Marehan Road. I dropped off the equipment, then took off my medical rucksack. Bob Mabry, a Special Forces medic on the CSAR team, was at the choke point and cleared me into the site. It became obvious that there were more people around the crash site than had fast-roped in on our team. I was surprised to see the other Rangers. I really didn't know where they'd come from or how they'd gotten there; I assumed that they had moved in on foot from the target area at the crash site. I was happy we had more firepower. From the look of things, we were going to need every bit of it.

I pulled a couple of litters out of the equipment bags I had dragged across the road. I set them up so we could quickly load the wounded and move to the ground convoy when it arrived from the target area. I believed that the convoy would be there any minute. I proceeded around the south side of the aircraft between the belly of Super 61 and the wall. AK-47 rounds were snapping in the air. The volume of fire was heavy and loud. The alleyway we were confined in was unfortunately channeling these rounds into Super 61 and all of us who were around her.

At the belly of the aircraft cargo area I saw Scotty being shoulder-carried to the choke point by two of the Rangers from our CSAR team, Mike Collins and Ron Galliette. I thought we would have twenty to thirty minutes to get the wounded out and loaded before the locals would really be able to zero in an effective offense. I was wrong about how much time we had, as I was about everything else that day. We were decisively engaged right from the start. I did not realize it at the time, but Super 61 had crashed about five blocks away from where the initial hornet's nest had been stirred up. We would now have to stand and fight right in the living room of Aidid's forces.

One of Super 61's two crew chiefs, Charlie Warren, was walking and standing in the middle of all this, a dazed and disoriented look on his face. I asked Luke, a Special Forces explosives ordnance disposal guy assigned to the CSAR/SST team, to grab him and take him to the CCP at the choke point.

After working my way through the rubble in the alleyway between the crumpled courtyard wall and the belly of 61, I found one of the Special Forces snipers who had been in the helo when it crashed. He had several facial lacerations visible, but despite his own wounds he was trying to pull the copilot out of the top right side of the wreckage. He said the copilot, Chief Warrant Officer Donovan Briley, was dead. With the help of Sergeant John Belman, one of the Rangers on our CSAR team, we managed to get the copilot out, and I carried him to the choke point. When I returned to the nose of the aircraft, the Special Forces sniper was attempting to get to the pilot, Chief Warrant Officer Cliff

Wolcott, in the left seat. The pilot was pinned in his seat from the waist down by the control console and the collapsed roof of the wrecked aircraft. The left front side of the helo had taken the brunt of the impact when it rolled off the south alley wall.

I moved around the wreckage to the north side against the wall. Removing the sliding front engine cover, I tried to crawl under 61 as far as possible to try to get to the pilot. It was no use. I could only reach up to my elbow into the cockpit area. I could not feel the pilot, and fluid from the helo was running out of the area. I caught some of the fluid on my fingers and smelled it. It wasn't fuel, which made me very happy. I think it was hydraulic fluid. I crawled back out and around the nose of the aircraft again. The sniper said that he had checked on the pilot and determined that he was dead. I told him I wanted to check the pilot also. He said he was a Special Forces medic and knew what he was doing. I said okay and helped him out of the wreckage. Sergeant Belman helped the sniper back to the choke point.

Even though the pilot did not appear to be alive, I didn't have a good feel for the level of medical experience, to say nothing of the mental state, possessed by the Special Forces sniper, so I needed to verify the pilot's status myself. I slid headfirst down into the cockpit. It seemed like everything that had not been tied down had been thrown forward into the cockpit area on impact. Debris was piled on top of the pilot. Bracing myself on the left seat and hanging nearly upside down, I could just reach his face and neck with my right hand and fingers. I could feel no pulse at the carotid artery and no breath coming from the nose or mouth. It seemed deathly silent inside the cockpit, with the sunlight filtering through the dust and the fractured windscreen. I crawled back out to the top of the wreckage. I tried to stay low and not present too big a target as I crept over and looked into the cargo area.

It was then I saw a small piece of desert camo cloth under debris at the bottom of the cabin. It looked like someone might still be in the wreckage. It was difficult to make out, but it looked like the uniform was in the left side gunner's position at the bottom of the wreckage, and it looked like the crew chief/gunner was still strapped in his seat. As I maneuvered down into the cargo area, I called to him. I could see his hand move slightly. I worked my way down to him. As I talked to him, he moved his hand and tried to move his head. All kinds of debris from the wreckage and equipment from the right side of the helo were piled up on top of him.

I was right. The left side gunner/crew chief, Sergeant Ray Doughty, was still in his seat facing the ground. I pulled debris off of him and began cutting him free from his restraint straps. At this time I could hear Bob Mabry, a Special Forces medic on our CSAR team, outside the aircraft. I told him I had one more inside. Bob went around the nose of the wreckage to try to reach the cargo compartment from the underside. I could see his hand waving on the underside of the wreckage, but that was all he could get inside the fuselage. I continued to cut the crew chief out in order to free him. The crew chief was moving his hands and trying to help himself out. Unable to get into the cargo area any other way, Bob climbed into the cargo compartment over the top of the wreckage to assist me. I pushed and pried the crew chief's seat until I finally freed him. I had just handed the crew chief off to Mabry when the interior of the helo exploded in a flurry of rounds and shrapnel. (It looked like the inside of one of those little snow globes that you shake and watch the flakes swirl about.) I froze as the world around me erupted.

Flying shrapnel wounded all three of us. Bob suffered some nasty lacerations on his left hand. The crew chief lost the tips of two of his fingers. In his dazed state, he stood there staring at his hand. It was covered with the blood that was running out of his fingers. I quickly clamped my hand over his and said, "Hey there, partner, why don't we sit down here on the ground."

I received a small laceration on the left side of my chin and a small piece of shrapnel in the right forearm. The arm stung and smarted somewhat. My jaw felt like someone had slapped me good and hard. I wiped the blood away with the back of my hand and asked Bob if I had any other injuries that he could see. He said no, that I looked good to go, and we all decided to drop down to the ground in the event we took another large volley of fire. The whole time we had been working in and around the aircraft, there had been a steady string of *plat, ting,* and *ping* sounds as rounds impacted the helo. The last volley from the east side seemed to travel straight through the hulk. Bob suggested we put up a Kevlar floorboard in front of us. It was an outstanding idea.

The floor of the cabin/cargo compartment was blanketed with thin pieces of canvas-covered Kevlar, the same material our vests were made from. Depending on the thickness of the Kevlar, it could provide some protection against bullets. While the boards might not have been able to stop all the rounds, it was more protection than what we'd had before.

I ripped the boards off the floor and set some up in front of us. Several more rounds cut through the nose and cockpit area, knocking the floorboards over. We put them back up each time. The damned helo was a bullet magnet. Hell, if the Somalis couldn't pick out anything else to shoot at, they had no problem finding and shooting the helo.

Bob and I called for a litter team to take the crew chief to the choke point. Bob cleared a hole big enough to crawl through at the back of the cargo area next to the ground. We slid the crew chief out to the litter team. They took him to the CCP at the choke point. I crawled out next and went along to check on the injured.

At this point we were heavily engaged with Somali shooters. Rounds continued to snap. We'd been on the ground about forty-five minutes and we still thought that the ground convoy was going to get through to us soon. Because most of my dealings had been at the casualty collection area to the rear of the tail boom, I did not know how the men at the nose of the aircraft were doing.

At approximately 1710 I told the senior Special Forces sergeant major I was going back into the wreckage to get the Kevlar floorboards for cover at the choke point. When I arrived back at the hole we'd slid the crew chief out of, I found Bob still inside. He slid the floorboards out through the underside of the aircraft. Belman, Luke, and I took the boards back to the choke point at the tail of the aircraft and set them up to protect the wounded.

The sergeant major asked me if I was sure the pilot was dead and asked if there was any way to get him out of the wreckage. I told him I was sure he was dead but would check to see if we could get him out through the cargo compartment. I had to take off my LBE and body armor in order to crawl through the wreckage where the crew chief had been trapped to get to the pilot. I checked the pilot once again and tried to remove as much of the debris as possible to facilitate pulling him out. It was no use. He was pinned in hard. I crawled back out and put my gear back on. About that time a frag grenade or an RPG exploded outside the nose of the aircraft. Bob and I decided it was time to get the hell out of Dodge City. I reached into the radio console area and zeroed out the secure communications codes. We both grabbed as much gear, weapons, and small medical kits as we could carry, and returned to the choke point.

At the choke point Scotty was alongside me, laying down suppressive fire with his GAU-5. I remember Ron and John beside him firing off rounds. It is safe to say Scotty looked real pissed off about getting shot in the leg and having to stuff his calf muscle back into the hole. On top of all his other outstanding PJ skills, he is a deadly shot.

Pat Rogers, our combat controller on the team, continued to pass status reports to the Special Forces captain at the choke point and spotted targets for the AH-6 Little Birds to take out. All the Rangers at the tail of the helo were either suppressing fire from the west, north, and south, or helping get the wounded on the litters. We did another head count to make sure we had all the aircrew and passengers from Super 61. Once completed, I started to prep more IVs for the wounded at the CCP. Bob, Scott, and another Ranger medic who had moved into the area on foot from the original target area had been treating the wounded in the CCP, when they weren't suppressing enemy threats.

At one point while I was working on a guy I looked over at Scotty, who was closer to the entrance of the alleyway. He was so involved with putting rounds downrange that he hadn't noticed the Kevlar boards we had put up for cover and concealment. He ended up in *front* of the protective boards, intently picking off targets. I said, "Hey, Scott, you may want to get behind the floorboards."

He glanced back over his shoulder with a surprised look on his face and smiled. "Good idea," he yelled back.

I helped him slide back behind the boards. At that point, the board next to where Scotty was sitting fell over with a thump as a round impacted it. He stood it back up and we both laughed. The volume of fire would rise and fall somewhat, but there was always a steady bang and crack to remind you that this was a bad situation.

Shortly after we had set up the floorboards for cover at the choke point, a frag grenade came flying over the ten-foot wall next to us. My mind captured the view of the grenade in stop-frame photography mode. Frame by frame I watched as the grenade tumbled through the air, landing between the south wall and the rear belly of the helo. Then everything was a blur. Everyone dove for the ground. All of us who were working on the wounded draped ourselves over them. The grenade exploded with a bang that sucked the wind from my lungs, so extreme was the concussion. When I looked up, Scott; Bob, the Ranger medic; and I were all staring at each other, totally stunned. We snapped out of it and immediately began calling out to see if anyone had been wounded. Luckily, everyone had escaped injury. To this day I'm not sure if we helped the wounded when we threw ourselves over them or whether we simply squashed them, adding to their misery.

I tapped Scotty on the shoulder and smiled. "Hey, be careful what you wish for—it just may come true."

He laughed and said, "No shit!"

I was finishing an IV on one of the wounded when Scotty yelled over his shoulder, "Did you see that?"

"What?" I replied as I looked up.

"That," he said again as he laughed and pointed at another quarter-size hole that had just opened up in the sheet metal of the rear stabilator. Then another and another appeared. Holy shit, the rounds were coming through the metal just above our heads.

The mind is a funny thing. All I could think of at this point was the scene from *The Jerk* when Steve Martin's moronic character is getting shot at by the lunatic sniper on the hill. The sniper's rounds are hitting the cans of oil in the display rack next to Martin, and he utters the hilarious line "He hates the cans, he hates the cans! Stay away from the cans!" So I said it out loud. Scotty looked at me for a second, as if to say, *What in the hell are you talking about?* and then he burst into laughter with me. Like I said, the mind is a strange thing. Perhaps mine is a little stranger than most. I don't know.

In combat there is so much information coming at you all at once. You are bombarded by the deafening, violent noises surrounding you while having to carry out tasks that simultaneously require your attention. In order to survive and be productive you are required to maintain control, assess the situation, prioritize what needs to be done, and then act quickly and efficiently to complete the most pressing task. Maintaining situational awareness and constantly reevaluating priorities is critical. If you have ever been in combat or out on a firing range, you know that the sound of weapons firing in close proximity to your head can be deafening, and I was not wearing earplugs. But the mind has the ability to block things out. Even with all that noise, my mind filtered out what I didn't need to hear, allowing me to focus in to hear others. It seemed that I could talk with the others around me in what I remember as being only a slightly raised voice.

Because of bleed-over (interference from another radio source) of the emergency locator transmitter signal from the aircraft wreckage, Pat Rogers's ability to pass information to the C2 bird over his radio was limited. While he was standing next to the north corner of the intersection of the alleyway, looking north down Marehan Road, trying to spot where all the RPGs were coming from, the enemy fired one at him from farther west down the alleyway. The RPG slammed into the wall above and behind him with a tremendous bang and a blinding flash of orange and yellow-white light. Pat's back and right shoulder were peppered with shrapnel. The rest of us were showered with pieces of cinder block and mortar. Pat was dragged back to the CCP. He caught his breath, reoriented himself, and went right back out to try to call in the spot where the RPG had come from.

The RPGs seemed to come in waves. There would be a ton of them for a short while, then a lull, and then another large volley would come smashing into our area. We knew they had RPGs, but we'd had no idea that they had as many as they did. I believe their main warehouse was about ten minutes or so away from our location, since it was just about double that amount of time between the volleys of RPGs. During the lulls in the RPG activity, you just knew the bastards were running back to the warehouse to get more.

Thank God for poor quality control in Russian-built munitions. There were several frags that were thrown by the enemy over the wall into the crash site that did not explode, but there were plenty that did. I recall one instance where an RPG was fired at us and we experienced the excitement of watching it travel toward us, hit the ground about thirty meters away, slide through the dirt, and come to a halt just in front of our position at the tail of the helo. It did not explode. Everyone just looked at each other with big eyes.

At about 1730 hours there was another call for a medic. Scotty nudged me and said, "Hey, Wilky, they need a medic over there." I asked where, and the Special Forces captain told me it was across the intersection of Marehan Road to the south, approximately forty-five meters.

A group of about a dozen Special Forces assaulters and Rangers who had fought their way on foot from the target building to our location were now holed up in a small courtyard across and down the road. They had casualties and no medic to treat them. From the courtyard they saw me. I motioned to them that I was coming over. I grabbed my med ruck, moved to the corner of the intersection, looked back over my shoulder at my teammates, and delivered the classic stupid line. Yes, with my best serious face I said, "Cover me!" and ran across the road to the courtyard. Pat later told me that he and Scotty just looked at each other and laughed. Months later Scotty said, "How the hell were we supposed to cover you when we were taking fire from every direction?" Well, it seemed like the thing to say at the time. I mean, what the hell— that's what they say in the movies, isn't it?

As I made my break for the other side with my med ruck over my shoulder, I remember thinking: *Just put your head down and go—it's like stealing a base.* As I crossed the road, my boots felt like lead weights. It seemed like I was moving in slow motion. I could hear the familiar crack of rounds passing by, but I did not know how close they were coming. Luckily, I arrived at the courtyard across the street unscathed. There were three wounded. Some of the Special Forces assaulters were providing aid to two of the wounded Rangers. The third, Ben, a Special Forces assaulter, had a relatively minor wound to the arm. He was applying self-aid. The most critically wounded was Ranger Carlos Rodriguez. I immediately proceeded to work on him. He had received a gunshot wound to the hip and groin area. There was an entrance wound on the lower outside of his right butt cheek and an exit wound on the inside of this thigh that had left a gaping hole. He was writhing in pain and bleeding profusely.

I was concerned that the round had shattered his femur and taken out the femoral artery. If that was the case, he could bleed to death in a matter of minutes. I tried to calm him as I stuffed as much Curlex gauze as I could into the exit wound. Moving his leg as little as possible, I put another bandage over the Curlex already stuffed into his thigh and wrapped it as tightly as I could with an Ace wrap to try to make a tight pressure dressing. The entrance wound on his butt cheek was smaller and not bleeding as badly. More Curlex for it and another dressing applied on top. All I could do was plug the holes, try to stop the internal bleeding with pressure, and get some fluids into him. While I was packing the wounds, I asked one of the assaulters to start an IV on Carlos. I saw he was having trouble getting a good stick, so I took over the IV and asked him to get a baseline on Carlos's vitals. A quick blood pressure reading, pulse, and respiration count would give me a starting point to work from. As time went on I would be able to determine if Carlos was getting worse or holding his own. We got the IV in and pumped up the pressure infusion cuff that held the IV bag to force the fluid in faster.

Trauma medicine is what PJs are good at, and that means having your med equipment rigged for maximum efficiency. I had all my bags of fluid already set up with infusion cuffs. If I was going to have to use my med ruck, it meant that there was an emergency, and that almost always calls for massive amounts of fluids.

I moved over to check on the other wounded Ranger, Staff Sergeant Boorn. He had a gunshot wound to the lower left leg and ankle area. One of the assaulters had already applied a bandage and wrap. The bleeding was not too bad, and the wound looked like it would hold for the time being. Boorn was in obvious pain but would make it. I would come back to him in a minute.

I returned to Carlos and did another survey to make sure I had not missed any other life-threatening wounds. I found some minor facial lacerations, but that was it. I was very worried about the wound to his hip. Every time I put pressure on the area to try to determine whether he had broken bones, he screamed. There wasn't a whole lot more I could do out in the field. I started another IV and changed out the first IV with another bag. Ten minutes later, I put my last two bags of fluid in him. His vitals were holding. I decided to put some military anti-shock trousers on him as a splint for his uncertain pelvis and femur.

I went back to take another look at Boorn. I removed the dressing, cut off his boot, and assessed his wound. The bullet had ripped all the way through his lower leg and shattered the bones in the process. I packaged his leg and foot with some dressings and applied a splint to stabilize the ankle and leg.

I had no more IV fluids and had used over half of my bandages. I needed more medical gear. I called over to the CCP on the interteam radio and informed Bob and Scotty of the status of the wounded over on my side. I told them that I needed more fluids and asked if they had any they could spare. Bob said that they had a couple of extras. Initially, the Special Forces captain was going to try to throw them over to my side of the road. That sounded good to me until I looked back out of the courtyard gate down to the choke point. There was no way he was going to be able to heave one of those 1,000 cc IV bags all that way. If he threw them and they didn't get to my side, that would mean I would have to go out in the middle of the street, and the shooting, to pick them up. Hell, those IV bags would probably break open when they hit the ground anyway, and then they wouldn't do anyone any good. I yelled at him to hold up—I was coming across. I told the assaulters who were at the entrance to the courtyard to throw some rounds downrange to keep the bad guys' heads down. Then I put my own head down and ran back to the casualty collection point by the tail boom of 61.

The familiar sound of small-arms fire greeted me. I didn't know who was shooting, them or us, and I didn't have time to look. I just ran like hell. I was greeted by my teammates on the other side with the normal quota of sarcastic remarks about my lack of lightning speed. I talked with Scotty and Bob about the wounded I had on the other side. We tried to come up with a quick game plan for loading the wounded on both sides of the street into vehicles when the ground convoy arrived. I collected the three bags of fluids they could spare, threw a few battle dressing pads in the cargo pocket of my pants, and got ready to make another trip across the great divide.

I let Scotty, Bob, and the Special Forces captain know that I would probably have to stay with the wounded on the other side until we were all exfiltrated. As I moved up to the corner I remember thinking, *Here we go again.* I put on my best deadpan face, called for cover, and ran across the open road to the courtyard for the third time.

My teammates have come up with a couple of theories to explain my success in transiting the hostile no-man's-land between the two isolated groups of the task force. One theory suggests that while I was running across the road I was clumsily dropping pieces of my gear and had to stop to pick them up, thereby creating a stop-start, up-down target that the enemy couldn't get a good bead on. The other theory is that an exaggerated rate of arm swing combined with a pathetically slow rate of movement created the optical illusion of moving faster than I actually was, so the enemy was constantly leading me too much. I don't think either theory holds much merit. I think God just watches over fools.

Back in the courtyard I resumed monitoring Rodriguez, checking his vitals and the wounds that had been bandaged to see if the bleeding had stopped. I applied more bandages and an air splint to Sergeant Boorn. When it became apparent that the ground convoy was not going to get to us anytime soon we decided to move Carlos and Boorn inside the house the courtyard was attached to. We used the room closest to the courtyard as a CCP for our location. The room would provide a measure of protection for the wounded from small-arms fire as well as the traffic flow in the courtyard.

As it turned out, the collection of assaulters and Rangers I had joined contained the assault force element commander and one of my CCT teammates, Jeff Bray. He had come in with the assaulters on the original target takedown. He was working the communications for the assault head and coordinating the calls for fire. I could hear him talking with the AH-6 Little Birds, which were constantly making gun runs on targets around the area of the Super 61 crash site.

The assault force element commander, a Special Forces captain, asked what the status of the wounded was. I told him I had one immediate, Rodriguez, who needed to be evacuated as soon as possible; one delayed, Boorn; and one minimal, Ben, the Special Forces assaulter. I told him I didn't know how long Carlos would hold. I asked if we couldn't get anyone out, could we at least get some more medical supplies dumped off to us somehow? With the exception of the few bandages remaining in my med ruck and what I had been able to carry over from the CCP on the other side of the road, I was out of medical gear. The night was still young, but already we were down to counting magazines of ammo, and we were out of water and medical supplies.

The Rangers and assaulters continued to engage the enemy and defend our position despite a heavy concentration of small-arms fire and RPGs from the Somalis. At one point, an RPG set the house on fire. It was going to be an interesting night.

It was about 1910 hours and darkness was beginning to blanket the area as Super 66 came into the area to dump a resupply of ammo, water, and medical equipment. We could hear the helo making its approach. Unfortunately, that also meant the Somalis were aware of her and had prepared a reception. The volume of fire picked up rapidly as the helo approached, and it reached a crescendo as Super 66 flared and hovered above the middle of the street to deliver the much-needed supplies. Floating there motionless, she took a heavy beating from the Somalis but managed to make it back to the airfield.

I needed to start a new IV on Carlos and give him some morphine. As much as I appreciated the medical supplies, they included no IV administration sets or needles. I had discontinued the first IVs on Carlos earlier that day when I ran out of fluids the first time. Now I had to use an old IV administration set off an empty bag, and I had one IV catheter left to start an IV again on Rodriguez. I slowly administered some morphine to help ease his pain. He was drifting in and out of sleep.

Out in the courtyard I could hear Jeff Bray calling in the Little Birds on gun runs. He came in several times to check on me and the wounded.

Not long after dark, the front of the building took an RPG round that left several more wounded. We dragged two more Rangers and one Special Forces assaulter into the back room where the other two wounded were located. I checked everyone out. One of the Rangers, Sergeant Stebbins, had shrapnel wounds from the top of his left foot up his entire left side, including the back of his left arm. He looked like a cartoon character that had just survived an exploding cigar. The left side of his uniform was all shredded and charred, and his face was covered with black residue from the explosion. Despite his appearance, however, he was remarkably okay. His leg was bleeding pretty badly, and he had a good chunk of shrapnel sticking out of his foot. He also had a laceration under his left eye. The other Ranger, Private Heard, could not hear and had a minor shrapnel wound on the left forearm. The Special Forces assaulter, after removing his armor and equipment, looked to be okay. He was stunned and disoriented by the RPG blast, but I could not see anything that looked life-threatening. I returned to work on Stebbins to stop the major bleeders. When I turned back around to check the assaulter out again, I found he had already put his kit back on and returned to the outer room, where the RPG had hit, to continue the fight.

I bandaged and splinted Ranger Stebbins's shrapnel wounds. At around this time, another RPG had started a fire in one of the adjacent rooms, and smoke filled the entire house. One of the assaulters managed to put out the fire, open some shutters, and clear the smoke.

I now had four wounded. Carlos was on a good dose of painkiller, but I could not get Boorn or Stebbins to take anything. I wanted to give them each a small dose of Percocet, just a little something to take the edge off the pain. I told them it would not knock them out like Carlos. No one wanted any. I asked them about every fifteen or twenty minutes. Every time one would say no, the other would follow suit. Finally, after about an hour and a half of this tough-guy stuff, I talked one of them into taking some Percocet. Almost immediately the other one said, "Okay, I'll have some too."

Our position continued to take fire. By coordinating with the spotters at the strong point positions, Jeff was able to talk the Little Birds onto the targets. Several danger-close missions were called in and executed. We had hot brass raining down on our heads several times. Some targets were less than fifty meters away. The Little Birds' guns and rockets were on time and on target. The AH-6 Little Birds, guided by Sergeant Bray, and our soldiers sparkling (designating with infrared pointers) targets from the strong points, kept the enemy at bay throughout the night.

• • •

By 2230 hours things had quieted down a good bit; the volume of enemy fire seemed to be lighter and more sporadic. The calm was shattered by a flash of orange and white light and a deafening bang that reverberated throughout the small cinder-block structure when a grenade exploded against the outside wall of our CCP. There was a small centered window, about two feet by two feet, about three-quarters of the way up the wall. I thought the Somalis had been trying to throw the grenade in the window but hadn't quite made it. I had my 9 mm Beretta pistol out covering the window. Everything was silent for a minute or so after the explosion. In a whisper Stebbins asked me for my M-16 to cover the window in case anyone tried something again. I handed him the weapon after checking to see it was loaded, charged, and on safe. "As your health care provider, I need to advise you that narcotic pharmaceuticals and automatic weapons are not a sound combination." I played it perfectly straight.

He looked at me for a few seconds with a puzzled look. Then he smiled. "Roger that, Sergeant! Hoo-ah." I think even Boorn smiled.

To pass the time and keep their minds off their wounds and the pain, we had whispered debates about what the per diem rate was for downtown Mog this time of year. We all agreed we were entitled to file for missed meals.

Three and a half hours later, early morning October 4, word came that the ground reaction force (GRF) was moving to our position, so I prepared the wounded for movement. We had one poleless litter and had improvised another litter with a tablecloth. When the GRF arrived, Sergeant Glen Ivory linked up with me. He had a couple more splints and bandages, which we applied to Sergeant Boorn and Sergeant Stebbins. Finally a Malaysian BTR (a Russian-designed armored personnel carrier) pulled up. We moved ourselves and the wounded into the vehicle. The BTR moved a ways up the street and stopped. It was still dark. A medic from the GRF motioned the BTR to stop and said he had an immediate litter patient who needed to be taken out. The litter patient was the crew chief on 61, Sergeant Warren, who had initially been loaded into a Humvee for exfiltration but then offloaded and deposited on the side of the road with the medic to watch over him. I didn't know why they had done that, but there he was. The BTR was already packed with the wounded from my CCP, but we moved some litters around and were able to just slide him in. The wounded who were already in the BTR were caused considerable more pain in having to move but all who could helped to get the litter in and hold it in place.

The BTR remained at that location for about an hour and a half. The sun came up before we started to move again. As the day broke, the RPGs increased in volume. The BTR rocked back and forth as it took hits. We were stuck in there, counting on the gunner on top to provide security. Because we had no windows, we had no way of knowing how bad the situation really was, but the concussion of the RPGs impacting the walls around us was enough to give us a hint. Finally we made it out to the Pakistani stadium.

As I climbed out of the BTR at about 0800 hours, I was surprised to see how many of us were gathered there. Those who were uninjured moved up into the bleachers so that the commanders could get a good head count. The medical augmentation unit attached to Task Force Ranger had been flown into the Pakistani stadium to set up a casualty collection point to stabilize the wounded so they could be flown to the UN compound, where further medical care was waiting. Doctors, physician's assistants, and medics were moving quickly among the wounded lying on the soccer field.

I immediately began to move my patients out from the BTR to the casualty collection and triage area. There were wounded everywhere. I coordinated with Dr. Marsh, the doctor in charge, so that he understood the condition and priority of each of my wounded.

From that point on I stayed with my patients and monitored their status. I pitched in to help others start more IVs on other wounded personnel in the triage area. I looked for teammates and familiar faces. I found Dan (Dano) Schilling there. He was helping to move litters. I had not seen him since the day before, when we'd wished each other luck before we launched on the hit. God, it was good to see him! We talked for about a minute, each of us hoping to get an update on our fellow teammates.

Scotty was among the wounded, lying on a stretcher next to the soccer field. He looked drained. In accordance with proper PJ bedside manner, I told him he looked like shit. He smiled and gave me the finger. He was still in his combat gear. I began the standard procedure of removing his gear so we could get a good assessment of his leg and have him flown to the UN compound hospital as soon as his time came. As I began to cut the boot off of the foot on his injured leg, he began to object violently. "Don't cut my desert boot! This is the only pair I have." I smiled as I sliced through the boot material next to his leg. "You know the deal. If I can't get the laces undone, I cut the boot! Besides, a prudent operator would have another pair stashed somewhere already." I laughed, and he cussed at me some more. Dan and a couple of other guys came over as I was cutting the remainder of his gear off, and they razzed him about his predicament. I got an IV in him, and we wrapped him up to keep him warm.

After all the wounded were loaded into helicopters and departed the stadium, I found myself sitting in the back of a Humvee with Dan Schilling. He had persuaded me to ride with him on the ground back to the airfield—I must have been dehydrated or something and so not fully able to see what a dumb move that was. We had no sooner taken the left-hand turn out of the Pakistani stadium when we heard that familiar snap and crack of rounds passing over our heads. All I could think was, *Holy shit, here we go again!* Fortunately, though, that was the last of the rounds shot at us. We were able to move around the outskirts of the city back to the airfield without further contact.

When we arrived back at our base hangar on the airfield at about 1230 hours I was shocked by what I saw. There is an old saying that you only know what you know. In the battle I had just experienced, I'd had a very limited view of the world. My piece of the battle was but a small sliver. I did not have a good grasp of what had happened to other parts of Task Force Ranger. The Humvees now parked in the courtyard in front of the hangar were bullet-riddled and bloodstained. There were piles of weapons, our weapons, on the floor of the hangar. The place was a beehive of activity, with everyone moving purposefully around the hangar. My first job at hand would be to rearm myself and repack my medical ruck. We all knew we still had teammates missing out there in the city. First and foremost, I needed to be ready to go again should we receive information on their whereabouts. After finding and cleaning my GAU-5, I loaded thirteen magazines with 5.56 ammo and repacked all my medical gear. With all my equipment staged and ready to go, I then took stock of my own person. God, did I stink. I was caked with dirt, and my uniform and boots were stained with blood. My jaw and arm were a little sore from the shrapnel wounds I had received while in the downed helo. As the afternoon wore on, I began to realize just how tired I was. After letting my boss know I was ready to go again, I returned to my cot at the back of the hangar and lay down to try and get a little rest.

When I awoke at about 1800 hours, it was dark out and several hours had passed. As I attempted to get out of my bunk, I became painfully aware of what seemed to be every muscle in my body. Adrenaline is a wonderful thing—up until this point I had felt very little pain or strain. Now, however, I had muscles screaming at me that I didn't even know existed. As I got up to walk out of the hangar to go to the bathroom, I surveyed the hangar floor. It was then that I became aware of just what a huge impact this battle had had on Task Force Ranger. There were so many empty cots, so many men in the hospital, or worse. I sat back down and put my head in my hands. As I would come to find out later, we had lost eighteen men that day, and seventy to eighty of us had been wounded in varying degrees of incapacitation. It was a sobering view.

I could see small pods of men gathering and talking—everyone trying to piece together the big picture, trying to find out what had happened to others who hadn't been with them during the battle. It was through these discussions and the after-action briefings that I truly began to understand the complexity of all that had happened—all the dynamics of the battle. We learned that Task Force Ranger had become task-saturated, which the text books define as a unit having to deal with several catastrophic situations simultaneously. It had been immensely complicated.

As I look back on the events of those fateful days some ten years later, I am filled with a sense of pride, softened with sadness. I think often of the teammates I served with, of the men we lost and their families. I remember them in my prayers. I pray that God will hold them and their families close to His heart.

All of the illusions of combat and any notion of glory have been dispelled. The reality of war and combat is that it is pure violence and graphic brutality. It is ugly and painful. These days I have a much greater appreciation for the sacrifices of those who have gone before me. We had a bad day or two, but think of those who went through World War II and moved from theater to theater. They were fighting for the duration. Their experience was so much harder than ours was. And yet I still can't express how it felt to hear taps played in the days after our battle.

Over the course of time I have been given many accolades. People have been wonderfully kind to me, and I appreciate that kindness. But I was only holding up my end of the deal, just like everyone else. I did what my fellow teammates expected me to do. I did what the American people pay me to do. It was merely my turn at bat. I would like to think that I did my job well. But it was my job nonetheless.

The heroes in my book are the aviators and crews that kept the bad guys off our backs all night. The heroes were those men who, after surviving the melee of the initial ground convoy and making it back alive, turned around and went back out to get our sorry butts. It is said that you can easily get a man to go into combat willingly the first time, but it takes courage, dedication, and tenacity to voluntarily go back and risk death once again.

In the weeks that would follow we would continue to fly signature flights over Mogadishu and train and integrate the reinforcements that arrived on October 5. The world looked different, though. When I watched the sunrise or looked up at the stars at night I understood how precious each day was. We all looked at the world through a different lens. I remember how alive I felt sitting on the sandbags outside the hangar, looking at the ocean and smoking a cigar with Dano.

ON FRIENDSHIP AND FIREFIGHTS

Dan Schilling

My promise of undying faithfulness to you and yours to me,
though made with all solemnity, is unlikely to survive the tricks
that fate has in store—all the hidden landmines that beset
human life. What we can rely on are the comeliness and iron
virtue of the short-lived hero: his loyalty to cause and comrades,
his bravery in the face of overwhelming odds, the gargantuan
generosity with which he scatters his possessions and his person
and with which he spills his blood.

—**Thomas Cahill**

*Dan Schilling was a thirty-year-old U.S. Air Force staff sergeant at the time
of the Battle of Mogadishu. As one of four combat controllers from Air Force
Special Operations Command involved in combat operations, one of his
responsibilities in Task Force Ranger was to provide close air support in the
form of AH-6 Little Birds and MH-60 Black Hawks. His other responsibilities were to facilitate communications between ground and air forces, control
air traffic on the battlefield, and survey sites for aircraft use. Dan was
assigned to the Ranger battalion commander and served in the rescue vehicle convoy.*

Combat controllers or CCTs, as we're collectively known, employ air-
land-sea tactics to infiltrate and operate in forward, nonpermissive en-
vironments to establish and operate assault zones. CCTs provide
ground-based, time-critical fire control for AC-130 and helicopter gunships and fighter-bombers. In addition, CCTs provide vital command
and control radio capabilities in the forward area, perform surveys of
austere landing/assault/drop zones, and are qualified in demolitions to
clear obstructions and hazards.

Combat controllers are all scuba- and airborne-qualified to include HALO (high altitude, low opening). Our initial training is more challenging than most special ops organizations. It's a thinking man's game. You work with the finest warriors in the world, including SEALs, Green Berets, and Rangers. But that's only the beginning. You have to make quick decisions while integrating fighter jets moving at 530 knots, coordinating suppressive ground fire, and relay all of this to the Army or Navy commander you're working with—all accomplished while you're suffering the same sleep deprivation and fatigue as the other guys. Oh yeah, and all the white keeping your nine different frequencies, secure communication codes, and twenty-two call signs straight. Combat controllers can do anything, anytime, anywhere, with anybody, and often do.

Ask a returning combat veteran of the Afghan or Iraqi campaign who is a Green Beret, Ranger, or SEAL and they'll all know a combat controller. They may forget the name but not the man. A CCT is the most fully integrated, modernized fighter on the battlefield. Controllers have conducted more parachute operations behind enemy lines than any other force. There are many great tales of combat controller bravery and operational feats of daring from Afghanistan and Iraq. In Afghanistan, for example, per man, combat controllers have inflicted more damage and casualties on the Taliban than any other force. And we lost guys in each of those campaigns.

Our mission in Somalia also had deadly consequences . . . if not deadly intentions. We knew we'd be killing someone in Mogadishu; it only remained to see whom. At the time it was just another deployment. Yet, like so many things, something much grander—U.S. foreign policy—became eclipsed by something smaller, in this case the Battle of Mogadishu. In the ten years following the operation in Somalia, U.S. foreign policy has been almost completely driven by that single event.

The afternoon before our deployment all the Air Force guys stationed at Fort Bragg stopped to have a beer at a place we called the shootout. We called it the shootout because a few years earlier, when it was a Dairy Queen, some locals had robbed the joint and shot some patrons, then duked it out with the authorities. Now it was an Italian joint. Lieutenant

Colonel Oeser, our commander, informed us prior to leaving the compound that when we reported for duty in the morning all of us would have Ranger haircuts, as our deployment cover would be that of a Ranger battalion going to Somalia to assist with the trouble there. Having a cover story lowered the profile of other units involved in joint operations.

These were men, mind you, who were used to flouting conventional military regulations and grooming standards. Tim Wilkinson and I in particular took great pleasure in sporting Fu Manchu mustaches. The time had finally come, and we were going to war. Not war like the first Gulf War, but a no-shit chance to hunt other men down and pit ourselves and our training against the other guy. Rusty Tanner, Scotty Fales, John McGarry, Pat Rogers, Tim, and I had a couple beers and steeled ourselves for the impending trauma: not combat, but haircuts. Fort Bragg, North Carolina, is home to over eighteen thousand soldiers and countless places to get an Army buzz: high and tight. Well, we all strode into the Drop Zone on Yadkin Road, an Army standard for military haircuts. I believe it was John who went first. He stepped right up to the barber there and said, "Give me your best high and tight."

By the time all of us walked out we looked like abominations of military standards. True, we had regulation hair, but most still sported highly irregular mustaches. When Pat and Tim dropped me off at the house and I rang the bell, my wife screamed when she answered the door. She didn't recognize me. Tim, Pat, and I laughed hysterically. Then they both left me there alone with a highly distressed woman.

It was then that my wife realized something big was really happening. Like most wives, she knew it was always a possibility. I wouldn't tell her where I was going; indeed, I'd never told her where all the late nights and early mornings of the past few months were heading. But she was a savvy woman and had narrowed it down to Bosnia or Somalia. I wouldn't budge. I knew the unit would call her and reveal all that was necessary in time, probably a few weeks after we deployed.

In the morning when it was time to go, I bade my wife a loving farewell and promised to be careful. But I still hadn't shaved my mustache. I'd been on enough goat ropes to know that we weren't on our way until the plane was actually wheels up, and even then it wasn't a sure thing. So I arrived at the compound only to find that Tim hadn't shaved his either. When the time came to depart the compound for the aircraft, the jig was up. Just before we walked out the door, Tim and I stepped into the bathroom in the team room and shaved. Then it was off to Green Ramp at Pope Air Force Base to meet the plane.

The Rangers were there, looking comfortable with their high-and-tight haircuts. Interspersed among them were the Army Special Forces operators, looking quite obvious with their newly shaved heads shining in the sun. It would be obvious to anyone with even a modicum of intelligence that the rest of us were anything *but* Rangers. No matter—it would work for CNN. They never knew as much about us as they thought they did.

Our flight was uneventful. We stopped in Germany for an evening meal at Ramstein Air Force Base feeling tired and a bit bored. We'd all been through this drill before. We arrived at the Mogadishu airport on the afternoon of August 26, a bright day with a breeze off the Indian Ocean. I remember walking off the front of our C-5 and surveying the surroundings. We moved into a hangar at the airport, the only hangar. The advance party had to remove a DC-3 from our new home by ripping off the wings and carting it to places unknown. It was your standard hangar, constructed of corrugated tin over a bare steel frame with a shape like a Quonset hut. In the rear was a once mobile maintenance scaffold for use on airplanes; it refused to budge, and so it was left there for us to live around.

The Air Force guys, being the fewest in number old hands at this and more adept at garnering the best living quarters, immediately staked out a place in the rear under the scaffolding, as it would provide a bit of seclusion from the other 350 guys living inside. We even managed to construct a small prep/storage/cooking area from nesting crates (small steel boxes used by units to transport equipment and supplies). One of the first things we realized about the austerity of our surroundings was that there were no shower facilities. For that matter, there was no *anything*. No chow hall, no real shitters, no laundry, nothing. In fact, the next evening, in order to take a shower, I snuck into the adjoining shed area, inhabited by some Russian helicopter pilots, and stood next to a tin building under the runoff from a rare rainstorm to bathe. A bit cold, but it beat two days of grunge.

On the twenty-eighth, around noon, I made my first foray out into the city with a Ranger vehicle convoy to the UN compound situated on the site of the old Somali University. I'd been in third-world countries before, but this place lent a whole new meaning to the term. There were the usual potholes, houses in various stages of deterioration, and aimless people. But Mogadishu had a smell about it that was unbelievable, which contained within it a palpable desperation. You could feel it on your hands and face. We drove along the edge of the city to circumvent the problem areas, and the locals mostly ignored us. They were too caught up in living or perhaps surviving to give much notice to another military vehicle convoy. We linked up at the university compound with some other local forces for purely administrative purposes and to get a feel for the AO (area of operations) and give the drivers and convoy members a chance to settle in. The architecture gave me the sensation I was in the Italian countryside. There was a Mediterranean feel about the place—low-slung shrubbery and grass, whitewashed walls.

Later in the day Mike Pringle, the Ranger who operated the .50 cal on my Humvee, retrieved me from my bunk at the behest of Lieutenant Colonel McKnight. When I reported to the Joint Operations Center (JOC), McKnight informed me that Captain Steele was taking the Second Ranger Platoon on a foot patrol out into the neighborhood above the airport to search for LP/OP's and mortar tubes. He explained that they would be out for several hours and thought it best to send me along in the event of trouble.

I reported to Steele, who greeted me in his usual gruff manner. I did some last-minute coordination with the commo guys trying to unfuck the confusion surrounding communication. Things were still in a state of flux, so it wasn't clear whether in the event of trouble I would be talking on some nets in the clear or using cipher text. As I was already carrying two radio systems, the thought of carting a KY-57 secure voice device wasn't appealing. My rucksack weighed well over 75 pounds with spare batteries, NVGs, and ammo—so anything I could jettison would be welcome.

The Rangers lined up for precombat inspection, and I fell in with them. Steele came out, said a few words, and asked if there were questions. As an operator with access to the JOC, I knew more than most. I still wasn't sure on a few details but figured it would all fall into place, for me at least. I knew my job. I turned to the Ranger next to me, a kid no more than nineteen, and asked him if he knew the mission. He didn't. I turned to the kid on the other side and asked the same question. Same response. What was apparent was Steele's anxiousness to get outside the wire and start the mission, as he had some artificial timeline to meet.

We walked out of the Task Force Ranger compound and made for the airport gate. As we cleared the sentries everyone locked and loaded their weapons. I carried my CAR-15 (a type of telescoping M-16, a bit primitive by today's M-4 standards, but at the time a well-respected weapon) and a .45 caliber Springfield pistol. We entered the city and moved a couple streets away from the gate, then made a left turn into an alleyway. Once we were out of sight of the airport we stopped, sat down, and talked the mission over. I couldn't believe it. We had waited until we were in bad-guy territory to conduct a question-and-answer session. I remember Steele having an animated argument with his senior medic—an ex-Delta guy and Vietnam vet, I think. Regardless, this guy knew his shit and was visibly agitated by the situation, as was I.

Eventually we moved out, heading uphill into a residential area overlooking the airport. We stopped once or twice so I could survey some emergency helicopter landing zones (HLZs) in the event a contingency required a helo exfil. It was now dusk. We passed through a few shantytowns. The dwellings there weren't houses in any traditional sense of the word, just tarps stretched over thorn bushes with an entrance low to the ground on one side. I remember walking among them thinking, *Shit, what a way to live,* and then realizing shitting was something these people did in and around their dwellings. You couldn't blame them, but we were getting it on our boots.

We arrived on the ridgeline, where the houses stretched downhill to the north away from the airport. We searched a few dwellings, but many of the Rangers were inexperienced in room clearing, and I decided to stay outside while they conducted their searches. For me it was safer that way, and besides, most of the houses were unoccupied anyway. It was just after one of these searches that we heard a firefight start up away to the east, down in one of the neighboring districts. We stood on top of the high ground looking down the road at the battle taking place ten or twelve blocks away. At one point a vehicle passed through the fight from the far side toward our position. When it arrived, the Rangers stopped the car—an old Datsun or perhaps Toyota—to question the occupants. The car was shot up and one of the passengers was wounded. The Rangers let them go, and Steele asked me to call in a helo to investigate.

After requesting an MH-60 from the JOC, I gave the aircraft that showed up a brief description of the situation down the road and asked him to do a flyby. He made a pass from our location over the Somalis and so was flying away from us. We were looking down the road at the gunfire being exchanged between the locals and then watched in amazement as both sides stopped shooting at each other and began engaging the helicopter. The pilot reported he was taking fire and was exiting the vicinity. The 60 returned to base and left us to our own devices. It was my first experience with a culture that placed less weight on their internal conflicts than their resentment toward Americans. I mean, really, why would you stop shooting someone who was trying to kill you just to fire some ineffective rounds at a passing helicopter? Inexplicable.

We spent another four or so hours patrolling the hills above the airport. In truth, we found nothing worth engaging—much to the disappointment of the Rangers, I'm sure. By the time we passed the sentries on our perimeter I was exhausted. The Rangers were carrying only their combat gear, no rucksacks, and I'd been carting my full ruck. Every time we stopped to rest or consider our next move I'd take a knee or lean up against a wall. In the dark I didn't realize it, but I was squatting in shit. Mogadishu was a city, but a city without electricity, running water, or sanitation services. So people dumped their garbage and defecated in the alleys where we were walking. When I got back to the hangar in the early hours of August 29 it became obvious to me that I wouldn't be able to use that uniform until we had some laundry service. I placed it in a bag and stored it way in the back of my gear. Several of my teammates commented on my smell. Still no showers either. I washed off with some bottles of water. Then I went to sleep.

The next day I learned that Steele had fired his medic; the guy went home on the next supply plane, never to be seen again. This was a shame, as he was one of those men you want around in the event of the shit really hitting the fan, as it did six weeks later.

I slept in a little that morning, but generally that was difficult to do— when you're living with 350 people who each have approximately three by eight feet of personal space, whoever gets up earliest sets the day rolling. After inspecting my boots in the daylight I was even less inclined to use them again, since it was nearly impossible to distinguish the shit from the dirt and mud on them. Several guys made comments about them too, but there wasn't much to do about it. I had only two pairs and needed both. I didn't dare take my pants out of the plastic bag for a look-over.

That afternoon we took our first shot at implementing our rules of engagement. We were authorized to engage any crew-served weapons (weapons requiring more than one man) and any technicals. Technicals are vehicles, usually dilapidated trucks, with some type of heavy weapon mounted in the rear. And it was for technicals that we went hunting. We went back up into the neighborhoods above the airport with several Humvees and a couple dozen Rangers, all with itchy trigger fingers. The mission was a bust, though, but not for a lack of trying. We didn't find anything as we tore ass around the city at high speed. We arrived back at base in the late afternoon. The Rangers started to post-op the vehicles, and I returned to the hooch and reported my impressions to Pat Rogers and Tim Wilkinson.

At 1930 hours that same evening we received our first mortaring by the Somalis. Those guys were poor mortar men, but two rounds landed on the tarmac, a hundred meters from the hangar, and the incoming rounds sent people scrambling for cover. Steele took most of the Rangers from the hangar to an area above our compound that we had turned into a chow hall and which had cinder-block walls. I went to the front of the hangar to have a look. Tim, Scotty, and the other medics, never missing an opportunity to cut people open, all went in search of casualties. I saw Colonel McKnight come out of the JOC and walk out toward the aircraft ramp where all the helicopters were parked. Running over to him, I asked where he was going.

"General Garrison wants to know what type of rounds they are, so I'm going to look for one."

"Wait a minute," I said, "don't go by yourself. I'll go get my Kevlar and weapon and be right back."

I'd been assigned to McKnight since before we left Fort Bragg and considered him to be my personal charge when it came to operations. By that I don't mean I felt personally responsible for his safety, but when we were on missions I was his link up the food chain and was his go-between for anything that might require close air support. It wasn't a good idea for him to go running around by himself. If he got hit by shrapnel out there on the tarmac, no one would see him or know where he was. On the other hand, the thought of going out there and running around with incoming mortar rounds just to look for a tail fin sounded like a bad idea. But what could you do?

First we ran across the street to where the Air Force had a medical station called a MASF (a sort of MASH, if you will) and checked on several Air Force people taking cover behind pallets in front of their station. These people were scared shitless, but I think McKnight's presence as one of the Rangers, and his inquiry as to their status, really boosted their spirits. I just stood around, waiting for a mortar to come and take us out.

We left the medical folks and ran out among the MH-60s. And there in the middle of the ramp, in the dark, lying between two helicopters, was the tail fin of a mortar round. I couldn't believe it. McKnight scooped it up, inspected it briefly, and then we trotted back to the JOC to show our prize to Garrison. The General knew what kind of mortar round it was as soon as he looked at it, which impressed me. This wasn't a complete round, mind you; it was the destroyed tail of an already detonated Soviet munition. But Garrison was an old hand at this, so nothing he did ever really surprised me.

I should pause here a moment to say a few words about General Garrison. Many know his record and command history. I'm not the person to expound on his exploits; in fact, I don't know the man well. But I will say he is the finest general officer I ever worked for or probably ever will. He understood his men and how we thought, what we wanted and needed, and he understood the situation. And it wasn't just Mogadishu. That man could understand the situation anywhere he was, immediately and completely. He is the finest leader an operator could ask for. It wasn't just a shame that his career was derailed after our deployment; it was a criminal act committed by political cowards.

After another hour passed it seemed apparent the attack was over. But Garrison was pissed off about the whole thing. I remember the staff talking about it and Garrison making the decision to launch on the best intel we had on any available targets.

This was what I had been waiting for. Time to kick some ass, and we'd only been in country for seventy-two hours! This would be different from the missions I'd been conducting. The intel guys picked out the most reasonable target for us to address. The Special Forces assaulters were planning the attack on the building, and the Rangers were working out the final details on cordoning off the target perimeter. The vehicle convoy (to which I was assigned) was to drive to a point just short of the objective and stand by for contingencies.

Our lager point turned out to be K4 Circle, a major landmark in the city and only about a mile up the road from the airport. We arrived there close to 0200 hours and watched the helos swoop in and drop off the assaulters in the distance. It was a quiet, dark night with a clear sky and little breeze. The evening was cool. All the homes around us were dark and there was no movement. Night is the preferred operating time, as our night vision capability allows us to enjoy an unfair advantage, as it should be. Even our .50 cal guns had active laser aiming systems. This allowed the gunner to point his weapon in any direction, and wherever the red dot landed, there you go.

The Humvees dispersed around the intersection and our vehicle, as the command and control element, sat in the middle. And we sat. It occurred to me that our vehicle was sitting smack in the middle, and any sniper worth his salt could correctly identify our crew as a worthwhile target. I was getting frustrated with McKnight, who had a tendency to stop in the open as he moved from position to position checking his men. Whenever he'd do this, I'd guide him subtly to the nearest vehicle, usually ours, for cover. Bear in mind, I was tied to him at the hip and didn't want anyone confusing this NCO with a lieutenant colonel and putting a round through my head by mistake. When you consider the income disparity, it just wouldn't be fair.

We were standing near our vehicle, and Mike Pringle was on our .50 cal up in the turret when he called to McKnight and said he had movement on the rooftop to our west. We all looked at the couple of bodies moving back and forth along the edge of the building—definitely a bad sign. Pringle wasn't happy about it, and even the naked eye could pick out the fact that these people were carting handheld equipment on their shoulders—one with a red light. The discomfort was understandable. McKnight kept everyone in check by reminding all that there was no preemptive firing. The movement went on for fifteen or twenty minutes. We could all see our laser sight dots clearly on the guys up there. The guys on the roof were the only ones who didn't know they were under threat.

Around this time some of the Rangers had managed to capture a Somali who was in the wrong place at the wrong time. They brought him over. We had an interpreter who rode in the back of our vehicle under the shell. After a couple brief exchanges McKnight demanded to know what building that was with the movement on top. The Somali explained that the building all our crew-served weapons were trained on was the only hotel still working in town. The guys on the roof were a television news crew capturing us on video.

Eventually the assaulters finished their mission and picked up nine Somalis from the target building. Our first raid and it didn't require a single round. The next day we saw ourselves on the television that the task force kept in the back of the hangar. Fucking CNN.

Most days in Somalia were uneventful, full of false starts, poor intel (or none at all), and very little to do. Much emphasis was placed on mail and the receipt thereof. For some reason the Rangers, assaulters, and helicopter crews all got regular mail, and their parent units were not even in the same state. Back home, our unit was just down the road from the assaulters' and yet we couldn't get *any* decent mail service. To fully appreciate the grave nature of this exclusion, one must have served in the military and relied on it for all communication with loved ones at home. It defied logic. Our unit insisted on dealing with our mail separately even though we begged them to lump our correspondence in with the assaulters'. The great irony was that everyone in the Task Force, if not the entire special operations community, believed that the Air Force guys always got the best of everything. Our reputation was at stake!

During deployments, time not spent in preparation for or in engagement on a mission inevitably leads to a constant search for humor, especially when you're dealing with predominantly type A personalities. This can result in extensive planning and bizarre twists, but the necessity to avoid boredom is the mother of invention. One such occasion was the impending birthday of Pat Rogers. Of the six Air Force operators (Tim Wilkinson, Scotty Fales, John McGarry, Jeff Bray, Pat Rogers, and me) engaged in actual combat missions, only Pat didn't have a woman at home. He got mail from his parents and care packages addressed to "the single guys" from other supporters of the unit, but nothing romantic. One such constant flow of packages came from the widow of one of our former teammates, Mark "Scrogg" Scholl, who'd been killed on a training mission nine months earlier. Regardless, Pat complained incessantly: no woman and no good mail. So my wife and Bray's girlfriend stopped in at a sex shop back in Fayetteville, North Carolina, and purchased Pat a girlfriend in the form of a blow-up doll, along with other goodies.

When we finally did get mail in September, Pat came over to my bunk to gloat over the fact that my wife had sent him a package and was obviously interested in a romantic liaison. Before you draw the wrong conclusion about this apparent affront, you have to understand the tight nature of our team. Pat spent Christmas with my family and was like an uncle to my son. My wife and Pat were close friends. It was just good-natured ribbing from one guy to another—until he opened the package and found Gina, the Love Goddess inside. I'd tipped off Scotty and Tim as to the contents and we were all present for the revelation.

Pat hung a sign around Gina's neck advertising prices for various types of services and placed her on a chair near the Air Force planning table in the middle of the hangar. I don't believe she was ever deflowered, but one never knows in a hangar of 350 men. She *was* quite lovely. She stayed up for several weeks until we had a congressional visit and we were instructed to remove Gina from the chair before the dignitary's arrival. Unfortunately, we had a call for a mission and kitted up and left before Gina could be hidden. When we got back (another dry run) our distinguished visitor had already come and gone, and Gina was probably the only person to greet him in that part of the hangar. Colonel Oeser, our commander, read us the riot act when we got back, so down she came.

We went out on another night mission on September 6, which is worth noting for several reasons. It was the first firefight between Task Force Ranger and the Somalis. It was also the first time I ever experienced friendly fire. The assaulters were again taking down a building north of K4 Circle. Ranger security had cordoned off a four-block area, and our convoy was parked adjacent to a place called the reviewing stand, where Aidid used to make speeches before we began hunting him. My C2 Humvee was in the middle of the convoy of vehicles, which were all in a line pointed north in case we were needed. McKnight, as was his habit, got out of his vehicle, and I went with him. There was a major road leading off to the east called National Street (which we would visit again on October 3), and the Somalis were lighting tire fires about four blocks down, as was their custom. McKnight, his convoy NCOIC, and I were watching this through our NVGs, but the Somalis didn't seem to be a direct threat to us. While we were standing there I looked to the north and could see some Somalis running down the backside to the reviewing stand parallel to our vehicles. The reviewing stand was made of cinder blocks and concrete, none of it quality work.

The Somalis, who were probably no more than a hundred or so yards away from us, crouched down near the base of the backside of the stands, and all of a sudden opened fire on the convoy. Nothing much, just a couple quick bursts from their AK-47s. The response was immediate and overwhelming. The entire convoy opened up on them with .50 cals, MK-19 40 mm grenade launchers, and small arms. The Somalis fired back, but it was mostly a one-sided affair. The amazing part for me was that I was positioned so that I could see both sides of the fight simultaneously. Tracers always appear to move in slow motion, and it was mesmerizing to watch the exchange. I realized the Somalis who fired on the Rangers were unconcerned with collateral damage, because directly behind them was another one of those thorn-bush-hut villages, and it received the brunt of the Ranger fire. I have no idea how many casualties this caused, but almost certainly people were hit.

We had moved back to the vehicles when out of the blue we could all clearly see .50 cal tracer arcs coming from the American base a mile or so away. Some stupid son of a bitch over there could hear the firefight and I guess figured it was a Somali-versus-Somali affair and so was lobbing rounds in our direction. I couldn't believe it. How dumb could you be? This went on for a few minutes while we were getting ready to load up and depart. The assaulters were finishing up and extracting via helicopter, so we were no longer needed.

As I got into my Humvee and we drove off, Mike Pringle, still on our .50, called down to me. "Dano, I think I got shot in the head." I didn't know what to say. I thought for a moment. "Do you want me to look at it?" I said this as we trundled down the road toward K4 and home. As the only guy on board with even cursory medical training, I had designated myself vehicle medic.

"No, I think I'll be all right till we get back."

When we got to the compound I looked at his head. The round had come straight at his face and hit the edge of his helmet where the Kevlar dropped down level with his eye on the left side. The round had splintered, and part of it had ricocheted off into space. The other piece had gone down the side of his head and left a crease, which was bleeding. He was fine, but if it had been a fraction of an inch to the right, it would have gone in through his eye socket and killed him.

I started calling him "One Inch" after that. He and another guy who received a superficial wound to the leg were our first casualties.

At approximately 1430 hours on October 3 we received intel that two targets from our primary hit list were meeting near the Olympic Hotel in the Black Sea district. The Black Sea was adjacent to the Bakara Market, one of the largest arms markets in East Africa, and was saturated with Somali National Alliance (SNA) regulars and sympathizers. The plan was the typical template used on our other raids: helos with Ranger blocking forces and assaulters departed separately for the target, followed by our ground reaction force (GRF) convoy as an exfil platform for the "precious cargo" (PC) and all task force personnel. Aside from the challenging target location, right in the middle of town, this raid was mostly indistinguishable from the previous raids we'd conducted.

The GRF on this day was comprised of seven Kevlar Humvees, two cargo (unarmored) Humvees, and three five-ton trucks. The convoy was manned by Rangers, assaulters, SEALs, and me as the combat controller. I was located in my usual spot, the C2 vehicle, third in the order of march. My job, as usual, was to provide mobile command, control, and communications in addition to fire support direction for the convoy or other forces as needed.

The personnel assigned to my vehicle were Lieutenant Colonel McKnight (ground reaction force commander), Staff Sergeant Bill Powell (forward observer), Sergeant Pringle (.50 cal gunner, vehicle radio operator, and all-around deadeye shot); Specialist Joe Harosky (driver), and one interpreter. I occupied the right rear seat in the vehicle and was armed with my modified CAR-15 and .45 cal pistol as a secondary. I wore a large ALICE ruck containing my two radios, COMSEC, NVGs in a padded case, spare batteries, and a small med kit. Around my neck I carried a COMSEC fill device with various codes and an execution checklist. The rest of my gear was carried on my first-line belt: two spare 5.56 mm magazines (all tracer for marking targets when calling fire missions), flare gun with green and red flares, four spare .45 cal magazines, and survival radio with spare battery. I finished out with my body armor, which contained a front plate only. I reasoned that I would always be wearing my ruck and therefore could dispense with a rear plate, which was uncomfortable to wear under the ruck. And besides, I didn't have a rear plate. The only other equipment I had in the vehicle was a medical kit that I had put together in an MRE case. Everyone in my vehicle knew I was the designated medic. I was no PJ, but I was the best we had.

When we came out of the JOC I discovered that the armored doors we had been repeatedly requesting for the rear seats in the Humvees since our arrival in Somalia had come in on the morning resupply plane and were now in place, thanks to Pringle. Through some Army glitch the Humvees had all come originally with front doors rated for 7.62 mm rounds but no back doors at all. On every previous raid and all my other trips around the city I had traveled without the protection of an armored door but had become accustomed to the freedom and ease of movement that went with the exposure.

I'd taken to sitting in my seat sideways, facing out. In this manner I could wear my ruck all the time and use it as a backrest by resting it on the center console between the rear seats. It was quite comfortable. I'd prop my feet on the doorsill and rest my weapon on my knees while driving. For getting in and out I merely needed to lean forward and, likely as not, the momentum of my ruck would carry me out of the vehicle. For getting in I could plop down while still on the move and be ready to return fire. A door would only complicate this process, and I viewed it as an undesirable trade-off of mobility for perceived protection.

Still, I was happy to see they cared enough to send doors for us lowly backseaters, until I discovered that my window was jammed in the up position and I couldn't lower it. The other Humvees were beginning to reposition near the gate of the Ranger compound as I started removing the door. It was a heavy goddamn thing, but easily separated from the vehicle by lifting it straight up off the hinges.

"Hey," Pringle yelled at me. "I just got those doors and put them on this afternoon." He'd even had Harosky paint the new door to match the Humvee's camouflage scheme. "Why are you taking it off?"

"The window's stuck. I can't get it down."

"Wait a minute." Mike disappeared into the back of our Humvee, rummaging around among the flotsam of the vehicle: cans of .50 cal ammo, cases of water and MREs, my medical box, and assorted other miscellany. He emerged with a hammer and held it aloft, rather like a symbol of victory, jumped down, opened my door, and began banging on the window and latch with the hammer until the window dropped into place with a solid thunk. Satisfied with himself, he hopped back up into the turret, tossing the hammer into the back, nearly hitting our interpreter.

We left the compound simultaneously with the helos. It was always a comfort to see the helos lifting off. They projected a sense of power and awe that was impossible for the vehicles rolling through the city streets to match. A large formation of helicopters lifting off at once resonates for a half mile around. You can feel them. And for me it was a comfortable feeling.

As was normal practice, I locked and loaded both my CAR-15 and .45 cal as we passed the front gate of the airport. Passing through the gate, we began to pick up speed, and I got that pregame excitement you feel when you're doing something for real. We moved through K4 Circle without incident, went up Via Lenin, and were passing the reviewing stands (where we'd had our first firefight weeks before) when the first two vehicles made a right turn onto another street, but not the one McKnight had intended. McKnight's pilot vehicle, commanded by Ranger Jeff Struecker, had made the turn prematurely, and it put him on the wrong side street. McKnight quickly gave Harosky instructions to continue driving straight. This put us in the lead, and Harosky put us on the north-south road that led to the target building and the Olympic Hotel. We stopped short of the target, and most of the troops dismounted. The volume of fire was light. You could see the target buildings where the helicopters were just departing. Dust was everywhere, and the movement on the street was mostly Ranger blocking forces getting into position.

I found myself next to one of the SEALs, Homer Nearpass. He was standing at the entrance to a side street, and when I caught his eye we both grinned at each other. I liked Homer; he was a good shit, for a non–Air Force guy. Homer had already racked up a couple kills with his partner on this deployment and embodied all that people assumed to be true about SEALs. It seemed to me he didn't really give a shit about the people here or the Army's running of the show. I thought he was clearly just interested in getting confirmed kills and having a good time. I don't know why we grinned at each other. It was almost as if to say, *What the hell.* We didn't say anything, but the sensation was already different than on any other mission I'd been on. You could feel it but not define it. I couldn't help myself. I hadn't even fired any rounds yet. In fact, I'd never fired a round in anger, ever. I could have, but it was never a necessity. Now, mostly I was monitoring the different nets and occasionally relaying pertinent calls to McKnight.

I relayed the next checklist call to McKnight, and he made the decision to move the vehicles up to the objective. We remounted the vehicles, and the convoy rolled up to the target with us in the lead. The helo force had already established orbits over the objective. You could see them running their patterns at varying altitudes and sweeping the city blocks around our force. If the exchanged gunfire didn't advertise our location to everyone in the city, the aircraft patterns certainly would. Not that I cared. Having the helos overhead provided the in-control feeling that always worked as a sort of security blanket.

The vehicles were now spaced out on the target road and pointed north. Our vehicle was still in the front of the convoy, and that placed us at an intersection slightly past the objective building, which was on the right/east side of the vehicles. And while Matt Eversmann's Ranger chalk was near our position, it still wasn't a good place to park.

From our vantage point, parked in the middle of a four-way intersection, you could readily observe to the front, left, and right. Off to the left I could see an olive tree in the intersection one block down. It was a light-green-and-gray-barked affair. It looked almost biblical, like one of those drawings you see in an illustrated children's Bible. Tied to it, looking just as biblical, was a donkey. His muzzle was facing the tree, and I had a perfect profile view of him. Behind him, of course, were many Somalis, moving and shooting at us intermittently. He was stock-still, almost as if he were drawn there, with his ears pulled straight back and his tail hanging straight down. *You're fucked, donkey,* I said to myself.

The Somalis could fire at our vehicle from three directions, and that put Pringle with the .50 in an undesirable position. Harosky, as the driver, was even worse off, as he couldn't do anything but point his weapon out the driver's window and wait for targets to come into view. It must have been miserable, trapped there like a rat in a cage waiting for an RPG to come from behind a building or some direction he couldn't see.

I got out of the vehicle. I didn't want to be part of the grand target, and I could do my job just as well from any location as long as I stayed within talking distance of McKnight. Usually I felt more secure being near the vehicles and their heavier weapons, but not today. A parked vehicle is an RPG magnet and an easy target for even the most inaccurate of small-arms fire. Even poor shots had a better chance of hitting a vehicle than a single soldier, so you just knew that every Somali in the neighborhood was aiming at our Humvees.

I assumed that the assaulters were still clearing the objective since none of them were outside the building. When they did come out they were going to have to move the precious cargo down the line a hundred yards or so to get them to the five-ton trucks for exfil. The line of vehicles spread out along the road several blocks, and somewhere down that line one of our five-tons had already been disabled by an RPG. You could see it smoking. The volume of incoming fire was now higher than I had ever seen before; however, in relation to what we would experience later, it can only be described as moderate. Bullets were impacting buildings and vehicles from every angle. You wondered how so many bullets could miss so many people so many times.

I was moving around near our vehicle watching for bad guys to shoot when I caught Homer Nearpass's eye again and we both grinned, the same stupid shit-eating grin as before. All I could think to say was, "This is fucked up."

"Yeah," he replied, and we both shook our heads.

After twenty minutes on the objective we had three casualties that needed evacuation. One of them, Blackburn, was a Ranger who had fallen out of his helicopter as it hovered over the insertion point. Bart Bullock, one of the assaulters' medics, ran up to McKnight and me as we stood by the wall of the building next to the target. He said something along the lines of "I've got a guy that needs to come out and unless the mission's over now, we need him evacuated." I got all the pertinent data from him and relayed it through the C2 net to Lieutenant Colonel Harrell, the assault force commander, and his crew in the C2 helo so they could pass the information along to Doc Marsh, the assaulter flight surgeon, and the medical folks back at the hangar. By this time there were two other small-arms casualties, and McKnight decided to send a three-vehicle convoy back with the wounded.

When the three Humvees left, I found myself getting anxious about our time on target. What the hell was taking so long? Anything over thirty minutes was asking for trouble. Looking around, I could see my donkey was still standing there. *One lucky motherfucker.* I also could see the assaulters inside the target building doorway, which was just behind my vehicle, but they weren't moving. I ran down to the nearest assaulter, who turned out to be the sergeant major, a silver-haired guy whose name I couldn't recall.

"What are you waiting for?"

"Waiting on the Rangers," he said from inside the doorway. I could see all the Somalis they'd captured, flex-cuffed and lined up along the wall inside the building's foyer. Several assaulters were in there with them, the rest probably maintaining security elsewhere.

"Well, the vehicles are all here, what's left of them"—we were down by four when you combined the medevac convoy departure with the destroyed five-ton—"but I'll go ask McKnight what the holdup is."

I dashed the 150 feet or so back to McKnight, who was standing by our vehicle. "The assaulters are ready; they're waiting for a signal from us."

"We're waiting for them."

Fuck. I can't believe it, I thought. *Typical Army shit, each group waiting for the other.* Army communication was always so much more cumbersome than it needed to be.

Dashing back once again to the sergeant major, and a bit out of breath, I told him, "Go ahead and load the PC, we're waiting on you and ready to go as soon as you are." I don't remember what he said, if anything. I just turned around and started back for my vehicle as they began filing the precious cargo out of the target. We'd now been on the target for thirty-seven minutes.

As I ran back to my vehicle again I noticed Howie Wasdin, one of the SEALs, lying in the road partway down an alleyway on the other side of the street from me. He was on the ground, grimacing and holding his leg. Apparently he'd moved down the alley to engage people, I supposed, and had been shot. Now he was lying there in the open and, it looked like to me, waiting to get shot again. One of the assaulter medics, got there when I did. Homer showed up from somewhere behind me with his CAR-15 and immediately began putting down Somalis on the road leading away from us. The medic was prepping Howie's leg and setting up to work on him. It was not the place to treat casualties. It felt like sitting in a carnival shooting gallery halfway between the shooter and the targets.

"*Fuck* that. Drag him around the corner," I said. With my weapon slung over my shoulder and a grip on both sides of his running gear, I dragged him back down the alley and around the corner to the main street and the relative safety of the vehicle convoy. Homer was calm as always, and I could see him getting off good shots, not just slinging lead downrange. It was tasks like this that made wearing a large ruck full of radios undesirable. Typical downside to being a combat controller. When you really needed to move, that commo gear got in the way. No one else—except for medics with their med kits, which didn't weigh nearly as much—had to run around with so much shit on their backs.

I left Howie with Homer and the medic, and as I turned to run back to my vehicle and McKnight, I caught Homer's eye again. We didn't smile, just shook our heads again. When I got there I was greeted by another casualty. Bill Powell, our other Ranger, had done the same thing as Howie, with similar results. "You stupid fucks," I mumbled. "Why would you move *down* the alley toward people?" He'd managed to make it back to the vehicle under his own steam and was sitting in the left rear seat, his normal position, looking quiet and rather pale.

"Sit back and I'll check you out." I didn't like the idea of turning my back to all the hostile fire, but Harosky was still sitting in the driver's seat and seemed to have my six. They must have been indirect strikes (ricochets) because the damage to Powell's legs was not severe. But you never know about these things—small holes can kill a man—so I was preparing to cut his pants open and do a better search when McKnight called for me.

I decided Powell would be all right in the truck, so I told him to stay put and went to McKnight's side. "One of our helos is down," he said.

"Which one? What's the plan?"

"We're going to load up and drive over to pick them up."

I'd missed the entire thing while I'd been assisting with Howie. When not listening or making calls, I kept my handsets hooked on the shoulder straps of my rucksack, where they'd be within easy reach. I didn't use high-speed earpieces or throat mikes—too complex and prone to trouble. Handsets were easily replaced in the event your comms stopped working and could be handed across to someone else or made for expeditious transfer to another individual if I was incapacitated.

I hadn't seen the helicopter and didn't know where the crash was. I asked, but all I got was a general wave of the hand by McKnight, indicating somewhere east of us. "Fine," I said. *Let's go get those guys and get the hell out of here.*

The word from on high to move took a couple minutes, but the C2 helo requested we proceed to the crash site and extract the personnel there. It took another *ten minutes* to get the convoy ready for movement.

During this time Matt Eversmann and the remaining four Rangers of his chalk were pinned down north of our vehicle on the next east-west-running alley. I left McKnight again and went to cover their movement back to the convoy. The Rangers had Blackburn's gear with them and were trying to decide how to get it across the street without getting shot. From my side of the alley (south) I told Matt—who was clearly in charge of the Rangers there, even though he wasn't the ranking man—that I would provide cover fire for them so they could get across without having to fire their weapons. Pringle was in the turret having difficulty covering three directions.

"Pringle, why don't you cover the front and left side of the vehicle and I'll take the right?"

From that point on I covered the right side of the vehicle and Pringle would cover the left and front since he had the heavy weapon. It sounded reasonable to both of us at the time. Days later, when we had the chance to look our vehicle over, we discovered that my side of the vehicle had received twice as many rounds as the other. Still, all four Rangers had been able to cross without further incident and move down the convoy.

By this time the volume of fire had dramatically increased. I had already seen numerous RPGs pass our position up and down the alleys, mostly from the right and left. While waiting for the precious cargo to be loaded, I noticed two of our fast ropes lying in the street near our vehicle. We had always recovered them on the previous raids, and command guidance had made it a point to retrieve them since we were running short. I started to pick up one of the fast ropes to load it on the Humvee because I knew we were leaving soon. A ninety-foot fast rope has the diameter of a fire hose, weighs about seventy-five pounds, and is bulky to move when not coiled properly. The closest was in the middle of the road, where it had lain since Chalk Four's infil. I retrieved it and dragged it back to my Humvee, where I was busy stuffing it in the back under the shell with our interpreter (a man who was as animated as a chunk of wood). I was already sweating and dusty and saw SEAL John Gay behind cover, shooting at some Somalis nearby. I asked John to give me a hand with the fast ropes. He stopped shooting, looked right at me, and shouted, "Forget about the fucking ropes."

His comments put things in a different light. It's like when you're about to fall in love with a girl at a bar after one too many, or perhaps about to put money down on a ring for a woman you have no business marrying, and one of your friends steps in and saves your ass by shutting you down. Instantly, you look at things through a different lens. It suddenly seemed silly to be out there in the middle of the road with all those AM General bullet magnets, risking your life for a piece of green braided nylon. Combat lesson number one: never risk your life for an inanimate object.

When I finally got in the Humvee to depart, Bill Powell was in his seat across from me and in a state of shock. Our interpreter was still in the back under the Kevlar shell, doing his best to disappear back there. He never left the truck the whole time we were on the objective. Pringle was doing fine, but it was Harosky that I felt bad for. It was Ranger policy, I believe, for the driver to remain behind the wheel of the vehicle at all times. That poor guy had to sit in the front seat of the lead vehicle, exposed to everything from three directions, and all he could do was point his M-16 out the driver's window.

As we passed out of the east-west intersection where we were parked,

I saw the donkey for the last time. He was in the exact same position as when we arrived, and in spite of the volume of incoming and outgoing fire that had passed over, under, and around him for forty-five minutes, he was still standing there—not so much as a scratch on him.

We departed en masse with our vehicle in the lead and McKnight giving directions relayed from the C2 helo on his radio net. One thing was certain, though: whoever was at the crash was going to need all the fire support they could get—which left me with little to do on the ride. I figured the convoy, with its stock of heavy weapons and now seventy men strong, was more than capable of taking care of itself. So I decided I wouldn't be calling in any fire while on the road. I directed my attention out the window at the passing streets and openings, looking for targets.

The convoy went east first, and then we turned south on a paved road. Here we made our first stop, with the convoy pointed south, while McKnight got further directions. The convoy then suddenly came under exceptionally heavy small-arms and RPG fire. Some of the vehicles closer to the center of the convoy were really taking a beating. Sitting in one of the Humvees, Sergeant First Class Grizz Martin was hit by an RPG and was mortally wounded. I heard and felt the impact of that second direct hit we received in this operation (the first being on the five-ton nearer the objective). It came from the side of the street opposite from where I sat.

Howie Wasdin was in the front seat of a Humvee, which I called the SEAL Humvee, and which had no armor or even windshield; it was a completely open vehicle. Poor SEALs always got the crappiest missions and equipment from the Army. Theirs was the only Humvee like it, but they hadn't minded before this mission. It gave them complete control of a vehicle and there were four of them, so it worked out well enough. A couple of assaulters without a position on the assault helos joined up with them.

Howie's leg was propped up on the hood. He'd been shot in the same leg a second time. No surprise. It was just lying out on top like some sort of hood ornament. Prior to that he'd been doing pretty well, but after the second impact, he started to deteriorate. He was obviously in great pain and started to slip into shock. He kept talking to Homer and saying, "Get me out of here!" I remember Homer was very reassuring and promised Howie that he'd get him home. As things started to get worse, one of the assaulters began giving orders to vehicles, trying to reposition them out of the deadly cross fire in the intersections. Several others were severely or mortally wounded at this stop. Howie would eventually get shot a third time in the same leg.

We stayed at this stop for what seemed like an eternity; it was one of those occasions when time slipped into slow motion. The vehicles were all taking rounds, and we were sending out a volume of suppressive fire like I had never witnessed before. I remember the .50 caliber—normally loud enough to make it uncomfortable to your ears—sounded muffled. Here I was standing outside my door watching down the street and to my right and Pringle was sending rounds down the street whenever someone would show their face or cross in front of us, yet Mike and I were exchanging words in a normal tone of voice, as if there weren't two hundred weapons and dozens of RPGs going off around us. It was surreal. To this day I can't explain it.

I was trying to conserve ammo. As a combat controller, whose job was to perform communications functions, whether it be air support, information relay, or integration of ground and air forces, I carried only three magazines for my CAR-15. And two of those were made up of 100 percent tracer, meant for distinguishing my rounds from everyone else's in the event I needed to mark targets for the Little Birds. I always figured that as long as I had enough ammo to defend myself up close, I'd be too busy directing fire when the shit hit the fan to be firing much at anyone. Wrong again. No matter how much your equipment weighs, pack extra ammo. My second combat lesson came the hard way—the manner in which I learn all my most valuable lessons. Since I had used all my ammo, I was now working my way through Powell's. He wasn't shooting, so when I needed a new magazine he would just give me one.

In front of us, people would come out of alleys farther to our south and try to cross the street. I have no idea why it was so important for them to cross. I thought the Somalis were all crazy even to be on the streets. *If I had a family or was in town as a civilian, I'd be staying put,* I thought.

I also discovered at this stop that if I rolled a fragmentation grenade down the side street, it would keep people from sticking their heads out from their hiding spots. I wasn't worried about the shrapnel. Out here I didn't think I would have much trouble with shrapnel from my own grenades, in spite of the hard surface, if I rolled them far enough down the street. We only had a few in the vehicle, so I used them sparingly.

A few weeks before, I had seen some Rangers at the training range get hurt by shrapnel when they were throwing grenades downrange without any protection, and some of them had gotten little bits of shrapnel blown back. At the time, I had walked off to where I was in defilade, away from the situation, and shaking my head the whole way. Rangers. You gotta love 'em, but they're still Army.

I also learned that the people farther away from our location seemed to be more interested in running across the street, while those closer to us (under two hundred meters) were more interested in shooting at us. It became a rule of thumb for me to not waste ammo on people farther away. But everybody in Mogadishu seemed to have a weapon, and I was not going to take chances with anyone who paused out in the open; these people did not seem to believe in taking a real bead with their weapons, only in squeezing a few shots off in our direction.

Someone stuck a weapon out from around a corner somewhere in front of us and sprayed our windshield with a burst. I didn't even get a chance to fire a round. One of the bullets penetrated the windshield, and another was stopped by the glass. So much for our 7.62-mm-rated, government-guaranteed, lowest-bidder-awarded bulletproof windows. McKnight must have had his hand already up, for the round grazed his arm and exited through my window past my head. McKnight and I were both cut by flying glass. I took over the comms for the colonel while he collected himself and allowed me to bandage his arm with Curlex and a cravat from my med kit. He had no broken bones from the round, and his wound was not debilitating.

"Good to go, Colonel," I told him, and he took comms back from me. Shortly thereafter another wild burst from around a corner managed to hit our interpreter, who—taking no chances—had maintained his fetal position in the back of the Humvee. He never uttered a sound when he got shot or at any time during our drive through the streets, so I never knew he needed treatment. It wasn't until we got back to base and he offloaded that I realized he had been shot. He went to get treated, and I never saw him again. The funny thing was, he was from southern California too, or at least that's where he lived, and was going to UCLA for graduate school. He was a native Somali and had only come back to work as an interpreter and make a little money. As I saw it, the joke was on him.

When McKnight got new tentative directions to the crash, he had Harosky move out. I assumed the word went down the line along all the vehicles. Unfortunately, internal comms within the convoy were breaking down. The internal Ranger communications net was one of the few I wasn't on.

The direction from the C2 helo was sketchy at best. I remember McKnight saying only that it was farther to the east and north. That was not very precise, but once we started moving I felt better. Anything was better than stopping. Every time we stopped, the increase in the volume of fire was just incredible. There were sometimes so many rounds passing by our vehicles that the walls looked like they were being sandblasted.

We turned and drove east, but only a couple blocks. As we made a left turn (north) I saw a group of about six or eight Somali men with weapons—mostly AK-47s—on the same street we were turning onto. When we rounded the corner and came fully into their field of view I could see the startled look on their faces. Pringle opened up on the group, and I remember watching one of them, a tall skinny guy, maybe in his twenties, wearing a bright yellow shirt, holding an AK-47 in one hand, come apart. His chest and head just seemed to explode. The holes in his shirt looked like dark red flowers in contrast to its bright yellow color.

The rest scattered, most of them stumbling into the alley on our right as we came onto the street. I knew they were going to be there, waiting to fire on us from the next intersection farther down the alley. Harosky accelerated rapidly, and as we came abreast of the alley I saw four of them still in the open, short of the safety of the next intersection. They were maybe ten meters from our vehicle. They all turned to fire; one of them was half crouching, lying on the street. Whether he had been hit by Pringle or not, I don't know. It looked like he was hurt; he had a grimace on his face.

I shot him first, two rounds in the chest. I drew a bead on the guy next to him and shot him in the chest with two more rounds in rapid succession. They were such big targets I couldn't miss. I didn't even use my sights. I wasn't fast enough to shoot all of them, as we passed the alley too quickly.

As I was shooting, at least one of the Somalis loosed a couple shots at me. My government-guaranteed 7.62-mm-rated door took two rounds. The first round hit my door right at chest level and didn't strike me only because the window was down and the combination of the door and window stopped the bullet. The second one, which came through while I was shooting the second guy, hit me in the foot, slamming it back against the transmission cover from where I had it wedged against the door. It hurt in a dull way. I reached down and felt my boot, then looked at it and realized the door had just enough armor to absorb the energy of the round while still allowing it to pass all the way through. As for my foot, it didn't get a scratch. After the mission was over, when I finally had the opportunity to inspect it I found the only indication I'd been shot was a dark purple bruise.

I hoped like hell the vehicle behind mine would completely waste those guys. I was starting to get angry and frustrated. I wasn't required to make any calls on the radio during the time since we had left the objective, and the lack of anything to occupy my attention was having an adverse effect on my morale. As it was, all I had to do was look for people who were shooting at us and shoot them first. I was mindful that I was dipping into Powell's ammunition while trying to conserve my own supply, but at the same time I wanted to send out as much fire as I could. It was a difficult balance.

When we arrived at Armed Forces Street the situation deteriorated further. McKnight asked for a smoke grenade to mark our position. Someone popped a purple smoke and threw it out onto the street in front of us. Behind us, the convoy was taking a beating. From our position, in the lead, we were relatively protected at this intersection. But Harosky wasn't taking any chances and stopped short of the road. Matt

Rierson, an assaulter in the convoy, ran up to the side of McKnight's window yelling about us stopping. He wanted to know what was going on. He and McKnight had a quick conversation, and McKnight explained that he was trying to get clarification from above on directions for the convoy, but that from up in the helo they weren't sure where we were, as somebody else had also popped smoke. Rierson ran back in the direction he'd come from, disappearing into the mass of confusion that was now the convoy.

I think the confusion was far greater than anyone realized. On top of that, the leader of this gaggle, McKnight, still seemed dazed and was slow to respond to issues. I think also that the situation was overwhelming to him, as it put him a bit out of his element. Ranger commanders aren't used to working vehicle convoys, or so I've been told. By now the second helo had already gone down. Adding to it all, the CSAR helo had also been forced back to base by an RPG hit on its tail.

Because of this, communications were getting congested. Combat lesson number three: in a dynamic combat situation, when communication is the most important, it's going to be the most difficult. I was attempting to stay emotionally cool, but it was getting harder as the situation continued to deteriorate. I found Rierson's visit agitating. Why didn't the leaders have a better handle on it? McKnight wasn't nearly as assertive as I'd known him to be at other times under duress. Of course, I'd never seen anything like this, so he'd probably never seen it either. I dialed into the command net, and nobody had a definitive plan to implement. In my normal capacity I would have been on the radio calling fire missions or getting vectors from the aircraft in the area. I thought, *If it's this bad here, it must be hell at the crash sites.* I had no idea we were taking the majority of the casualties right here in the convoy. I remember looking out of the vehicle, waiting for the convoy to roll, thinking: *We're going to keep driving around until we're all fucking dead.*

I decided that the information we were getting from within the chain of command was not working, and took matters into my own hands. I switched to helo common, a frequency utilized by the helos to talk amongst themselves.

"This is Uniform six four Charlie on helo common. I'm in the lead Humvee in the convoy and I need vectors to the crash site. Request assistance." U64C was my call sign; it designated me as a combat controller attached to the ground forces commander, McKnight. Immediately one of the reconnaissance helicopters came up. He had our position and was anxious to help. Those were his buddies in the crashed helicopters. "Colonel McKnight, I've got a recce helo who's going to give me vectors to the crash."

"Go ahead, Dan," said McKnight.

"Six four Charlie, turn left on Armed Forces Street and proceed west," said the helo. That would put us on a street at least wider than the roads we'd been on. I felt better already.

I assumed McKnight would disseminate the information to his Rangers in the convoy. When we had traveled a few blocks, the helo gave me another left turn to the south. Shortly after we turned south, I realized that we were back on the target building street. I could see the abandoned five-ton truck coming up, close to the Olympic Hotel. As soon as I saw the smoking five-ton, I realized the helo was taking us to the second crash site. I couldn't blame the pilot; he knew no one was on the second crash to provide security and had taken it upon himself to send us there.

I wasn't sure if we should now proceed on to the second crash— since I didn't think there were any friendly forces there with the downed crew—or redivert back to the first.

"Colonel, we're going to the wrong crash site. We're headed to the second crash. Do you want to go there, or do you still want to go to the first helicopter?"

"We need to go to the first helicopter."

"Negative on the second crash. I need vectors to crash site one," I said to the helo.

It was my fault. I'd not specified which crash site we wanted to go to upon initial contact. I assumed that the helo was aware of our intentions since we had been trying to get to crash site one for at least the past twenty minutes. My lack of clarity with the helo forced us to make this pass by the objective. I'd made my first real mistake. A stupid and, I suppose, easy one, but it was still my fault. The problem was compounded by the fact that I hadn't seen the first helicopter crash and so didn't have any idea where the hell it was. I only knew it was "over that way," a vague reference to the area east of us.

On my command, the whole convoy made a U-turn and proceeded back up the target street until the helo gave me a right turn to the east. None of this can be placed on the shoulders of McKnight. He gave me control of the convoy and I took it. It was my responsibility to get the convoy to the crash. After only a couple blocks, the helo gave me another left turn to the north. All this time nobody in my vehicle was saying anything, not McKnight, Powell, Harosky, or Pringle. Harosky would just listen to my directions, and Pringle was busy shooting Somalis with the .50. Everybody else was just quiet.

In retrospect, I wish I'd kept going to the second crash. We might have gotten there in time and picked them all up while they were still alive and before the resistance stiffened. Certainly we would have arrived long before any convoy leaving from the airport. The problem with hindsight, though, is that it allows you to perceive how things might have worked out, which of course is always perfectly. In truth, we might all have been killed attempting to get through the shantytown surrounding crash site two.

When we made this last turn to the north, I knew we would be passing with the crash on our right. On at least three occasions the helo attempted to give me a right turn toward the crash, and each time I told him we couldn't accept the turn because the alley wasn't big enough.

Our exchanges went something like this: "Six four Charlie, take your next right."

"Negative on the right turn. I need a bigger street."

"Six four Charlie, turn right at the next alley."

"Negative, not big enough. Give me another one. Or different directions."

Every alley he gave me as an option was too small to support the five-ton trucks. I was afraid if we lost another vehicle it would become a giant steel plug, effectively cutting our force in two. If the convoy got divided into two sections, we'd be through. There just wasn't enough room for a vehicle to get around another if one of them became disabled. After multiple attempts on our part to turn right, the helo sug-

gested we try our approach from the north. I gave Harosky the instructions, and we accelerated until we approached Armed Forces Street. By
this time our vehicle was already pretty beat up. For some reason the
right side of the vehicle was taking the brunt of the rounds. Whether
this was due to the fact that I was supposed to be providing security for
the right while Pringle covered the front and left with the .50 or
whether it was due to most of the resistance being to the east of us, I'm
not sure. In any event, both tires on the right side were already flat and
the Humvee just sort of bumped along the road. You could hear the
tires; they sounded like rubber belts being slapped against a wall.

We arrived back at Armed Forces Street again. When we got there it
looked as if we had driven into a ghost town. The street, unlike the
small side roads we'd been driving on, was completely deserted. We
slowed as we approached the street. It was a large four-lane affair with
concrete dividers but not a soul on it.

"Turn right onto the main drag here, Joe," I said to Harosky. "We're
going to go east a few blocks and then turn right again." I assumed that
we had the rest of the convoy behind us, but communications had completely broken down within the convoy. We turned right and were
limping along at about twenty miles per hour waiting for the helo to
give us a right turn. We only went a few blocks, maybe three or four,
when the helo told me to take the next right coming up.

"Right turn, Joe."

We slowed to take the corner, and as we rounded it a Somali about
thirty or forty meters down the alley with an RPG stepped out from behind a building on our right side. He had it aimed straight at us. I
started yelling, "RPG, RPG, RPG!" Silence from the .50. Why wasn't
Pringle shredding this guy? I was struggling to get a bead on him with
my CAR-15 out the window, but I had only one hand on it since I was
using my left hand to talk into the handset with the helo.

I dropped my handset and was frantically attempting to get my front
sight on the guy, wondering why Mike still wasn't shredding him and
yelling at Harosky, "Go! Go! Go!" all at the same time, when I noticed
that Pringle had run out of ammo and was down inside the vehicle with
us, getting a new can for the .50. He just sort of hunched down with his
hands up by his head when I started screaming, "RPG!"

To make matters worse, if that were possible, Harosky started driving down the alley right at the guy with the RPG! Where I meant for him to "GO" was *past* the entrance to the alley so we'd be out of this guy's line of fire. I'd thought this was obvious. Again, poor communication on my part, I suppose. But before anything else could be done, the guy fired his RPG. When it leapt out of his launcher it left a little puff of smoke, but the round itself looked huge. We were on a collision course with that grenade. Because the Somali was directly in front of us I could see the round traveling all the way to our vehicle. When it launched I even stopped trying to get my weapon out the window. I was frozen by the sight of that round coming right at us. In what seemed to be an eternity the round came straight at me, and then went just wide of our vehicle at windshield level past the right side of the Humvee. I saw and then felt it as it went past. It couldn't have missed my head by more than two feet.

Right as the RPG went past the window I started screaming at Harosky, "Back up! Back up! Back up!" and got my weapon out the window to get off a few rounds at the RPG gunner. Pringle recovered quickly and was putting a new can on his .50 even as we started backing up. He was incredibly cool despite being the only guy in our vehicle who was completely exposed for the entire mission. When we started backing out of the alley's entrance, I looked back out the right side of the vehicle to make sure we wouldn't hit the Humvee behind us. But there was nobody there! I was dumbfounded for an instant. How could we possibly be alone? But there we were, just our Humvee, the guy with the RPG, and an empty street. Not another vehicle in sight. I had no idea where everybody else was. Why weren't they behind us? All I could think was, *We're going to get hit by an RPG any second and we're all going to die right here.*

"Spin around, Joe, head back the way we came, and let's see if we can't find everybody else."

I wasn't even talking to the helo now. My first priority was to get back with the other vehicles and then we could try to get to the crash after that. As we passed the intersection we had come out of onto Armed Forces Street I saw the other vehicles still lined up facing north toward the street. They had stopped short of the street and had stayed there the whole time we'd been gone, maybe five minutes. I'm not sure, but I think the vehicle behind ours had been disabled by an RPG or small-arms fire and so, as a result, the convoy hadn't moved. McKnight had not said a word since I'd asked him if he still wanted to go to crash site one. But as we pulled up to the rest of the convoy he snapped out of his stupor. Maybe it was all the excitement from the RPG near miss. It certainly worked for me. I was now hyperalert in a way I hadn't been before. I felt like I could see through buildings and around corners.

Sergeant First Class Gallagher, the convoy NCOIC, came over to our vehicle as we rolled to a stop. Our vehicle was now facing the opposite direction to the rest of the convoy. Gallagher was agitated because Mc-Knight had not been telling him what was going on over the convoy radio net, and that forced him to leave his vehicle at the trail end and actually run over and speak to him face-to-face. McKnight got out of the vehicle and the two started discussing options over the hood of our Humvee, a bit heatedly. I got out and was standing near the right front tire listening to them.

Gallagher was standing in front of our Humvee leaning on the hood facing me and McKnight when he got shot. It knocked him over, and he was lying on the ground near the right side of our Humvee at my feet. I half dragged, half helped him to my door, where I got in and started rummaging through my dwindling medical supplies. His right arm was pumping bright red blood out of the wound in distinct spurts. It was so bright red, it looked fake. I had never seen blood that color before, but I knew that it was arterial and that if we didn't stop it he would bleed to death before we ever got back to base, whenever that might be—if ever. Again I had the distinct feeling that we were going to drive around in circles until we were all dead.

I patched his arm as best I could by stuffing it with Curlex and then placing a cravat over it and tied it as tight as I dared. His arm didn't appear to be broken, but I was afraid to tie it so tight because if it was broken, tying it might cause more damage. While I was fixing Gallagher up, I caught part of McKnight's call to Higher Command that we were packing it in: "This is Uniform six four. I have numerous casualties, vehicles that are halfway running. Gotta get these casualties out of here. . . ."

So we were finally heading for the hangar, if we could make it. The convoy had more wounded and dead than able-bodied, and we were, all of us, running very low on ammo. I finished working on Gallagher and sent him back to his vehicle under his own steam, but kept his weapon. I needed the rounds. I had gone through everybody else's ammo in my vehicle except Harosky's.

The rest of the convoy passed us and turned left onto Armed Forces Street for the drive home. We turned around to bring up the rear of the convoy as the last vehicle. I didn't bother calling the recce bird back to tell him we were going home. It didn't seem important anymore. I'm sure he knew.

What I couldn't believe was that we were going back without all of our people. Still, starting back to the hangar now made me feel like we might actually make it out alive. As we pulled onto Armed Forces Street for the third time, the only magazine I had left was the one I had gotten out of Gallagher's M-16, but we were on our way back and, as the last vehicle in the convoy, I suddenly felt very vulnerable. If we became disabled, I had no doubt that there wouldn't be anyone coming back to get us since, obviously, no one on the convoy was talking over the radio anymore, at least not to each other. Each alley we drove by, I would send one round down in the hopes that it would keep whoever was down there hidden until we could get past. It seemed to make perfect sense at the time.

After we passed the reviewing stands, the preferred Aidid propaganda platform, just north of K4 Circle, I saw Humvees coming our way from the airport. "Who the hell could that be?" I said to no one in particular. It was the rescue convoy. The vehicles in the front of our convoy had stopped and appeared to be talking to the rescue convoy. Homer, the other SEALs, and guys on their Humvee had to abandon their vehicle there. It looked like hell, and I think one of the rims was on fire. Ours wasn't doing well either—by this time all four tires had been shot out and we had numerous bullet holes, but compared to theirs, our ride was clean, one owner.

"You need to keep moving," McKnight yelled at the other vehicles as we came alongside. He told Harosky to drive up to the head of the convoy and take the lead. All the time McKnight was telling Harosky that it was going to be all right and to just keep going, we'd get to the hangar okay. I think he said this as much to boost his own spirits as for Joe's benefit. I knew that if we could get through K4 then we'd make it back to the airport alive. Sure enough, as we got closer to the airport the volume of fire dropped off to almost nothing.

We rolled, or maybe lurched, to a stop between the Task Force Ranger hangar and the Air Force MASF, where McKnight and I had searched for casualties on our sojourn to find a mortar round. It was 1810; we had been gone maybe three hours. All the other vehicles pulled up behind and around ours, and guys started to pile off. Our vehicles were blocking the road used by all the other UN coalition members inside the airport perimeter, but we didn't care. There were dead guys and wounded everywhere. I couldn't believe that we took that many casualties on the convoy. We were simply not prepared to deal with an entire city of a million people, on their own streets, bent on our destruction. As I got out of our Humvee I congratulated Harosky and Pringle on getting us back alive. McKnight left the vehicle immediately, went to supervise the unloading of his Rangers, and then departed for the JOC. I went over to help carry the wounded into the triage area that the Air Force had prepared; those people knew we were coming in with a lot of wounded and were ready for us. I helped Homer carry Howie and assisted a few others. I refused to help unload the Somali prisoners off the five-ton. I could see that one of them was definitely dead, but I didn't give a damn. I left the Somalis to the assaulters; they were the professional snatchers, let them take care of the PC.

The first place I went from the MASF was the JOC. As I passed, Pringle and Harosky were standing next to the Humvee; our interpreter had left to get treated, under his own power, I imagine. I sure didn't help him. I never saw Pringle and Harosky again either.

In the JOC the situation seemed to be mass confusion. I think General Garrison and his people were already on top of their next move, but I sure couldn't tell. I found my commanding officer, Lieutenant Colonel Oeser.

"O.R., what's the status of W.K., P.R., and F.A. [Tim, Pat, and Scott, respectively]? Have you heard anything?" All the Air Force guys used operating initials as identifiers, which made for a more efficient system than the Army's. These were our guys on the CSAR helo, and so they would be in the middle of whatever was going on out there at the first crash. Tim and Pat were the best friends I had.

"Sorry, Dano, no word. Don't know the status of any of our guys except you." As the lone Air Force guy on the convoy, I was the only one to have made it back in.

I had heard Pat on the radio earlier, so I figured he was still okay. I had also heard Jeff Bray on the radio calling fire missions, but that had been a while ago. Where were they now? One thing was sure—they had not all been overrun, as I had feared, because we were planning a rescue mission. I knew I was going to go back out. I wanted to get to my friends. I was also scared. I had made it back to the hangar alive once and was aware that if I went back out, then I was really pushing my luck. The difference between life and death could be measured in nanoseconds out on the streets. But the way I saw it, it wasn't really my choice. They were out there. We had to go bring them back.

I found McKnight. "What's the plan, Colonel?" He explained that he wasn't going back out, but that Major Nixon, his second in command, would lead the Ranger contingent on the rescue. Lieutenant Colonel Harrell would lead the overall rescue and command the assaulter contingent. This meant he was in charge overall. Sounded like the typical Ranger/assaulter problem to me. Fuck it. I'd go with whomever they'd assign me to.

I left McKnight for the last time and went in search of Nixon. I'd worked with him in the past and liked him. He was an affable, down-to-earth guy from Texas. Probably meant that Garrison liked him (Garrison was from Texas). My original vehicle was ruined; in fact, many of the vehicles were in no condition to go back out. I remember the mechanics had one of the Humvees with a shot-up fuel tank in front of the hangar leaking diesel all over the place. They were trying to contain the flow with sandbags. I suggested they move it away from the hangar, as it smelled up the entire front of the building. I found Nixon outside the hangar.

I said to him, "McKnight's not going back out. So I'm your man for comms and air if you need me." He said that his vehicle was already full but that he would throw somebody off to make room for me. He seemed happy to have me along. Knowledge is power, and our guys tend to carry most of the plans with them in their heads since we have to be familiar with the entire flow—all frequencies and call signs, air routes, ground routes, and fire support issues. Our guys also tend to be older than most of the Rangers. Nixon told me to load up and get some water because it would be some time before we pulled out.

This time I remembered one of my tough lessons learned earlier in the day. No matter what your primary job is, you can't carry too much ammunition. I went into the hangar, back to my rack, and dug out every magazine I could find. I also got all the magazines that I had dropped on the floor of my shot-up Humvee. I now had twelve mags in all, only some of which had started out as mine. I went to the folding table in the middle of the hangar that doubled as our planning and card playing area and found Homer there, loading magazines.

The hangar was mostly empty. With all the dead and wounded that were being evacuated and many of the rest of the guys pre-staged on their vehicles ready to go out on the rescue, there was no one left. I sat down on the opposite side of the table from Homer, where we'd played some wicked games of spades and hearts, and started loading magazines. He had a couple cans of ammo, which came in bandoliers, and was sitting quietly by himself.

I sat down without saying anything at first. Finally I looked up at him and said, "Man, I don't want to go back out there."

"I know," he said. "This is fucked up." Then he grinned. I grinned back. We just kept loading ammo. This went on for about twenty minutes.

After I had loaded all my magazines, I grabbed a couple bandoliers and stuffed them in my ruck, then went out to my new vehicle to check it out. Unlike my first vehicle, I wasn't afforded a seat and so had to sit in the back, where the Rangers had removed the rear Kevlar hatch. I climbed in, took off my ruck, and sat down facing out the rear on the right side next to the Ranger already sitting there. After I'd situated myself, I asked the kid next to me his name, and in true Ranger fashion he replied with his rank (private) and last name. I said, "My name's Dano, and if we were going to have to work together I'd like to know yours, because we're definitely going out." He told me his name, which I've since forgotten.

"You watch out the left rear side and I'll watch out the right rear side. That way we can cover each other's six. Sound all right to you? Were you on any of the convoys earlier today?"

"No." He looked about nineteen.

There really wasn't anything I could add to that, so I said nothing. We just sat in the back of our Humvee, waiting to go.

We knew that going out the front gate of the airport was a mistake and also that command had requested armor support from the Malaysians and Pakistanis. There were five-ton trucks and Humvees all over the place outside the Task Force Ranger compound, all loaded with Rangers, assaulters, and regular infantry or personnel from God knows where. They certainly weren't part of our task force—that was obvious. We spent a long time lining up in some semblance of order and finally departed around 1930 hours. The plan called for us to move to the new port facility past the east end of the airport. This was where the armor was and we could get to it without having to expose ourselves to enemy fire by staying inside the friendly perimeter.

We arrived over at the new port facility without incident, and most everybody offloaded their vehicles and stood around. There was some talk, but mostly guys just stood around in small groups. We waited here for over three hours while our leadership worked out the details with the Pakistanis and Malaysians. As I understood it, the language barrier was proving difficult to overcome. After about an hour of standing around, I got so cold I started to shiver, which struck me as odd since I had never been cold here at night before. I spent more time looking over my position and thinking about what I was going to do when we got back out there. I had seen the damage caused by getting hit and started to get nervous about my exposure in the back of the Humvee.

It wasn't my head and torso that I was worried about, it was my groin. The way I was situated, with my back toward the front of the vehicle and my crotch facing the tailgate, I was scared to death that I would get shot there. At least sitting in a seat afforded the illusion of protection. But in the back, man, there was nothing between your future family and high-velocity rounds but a tin tailgate. I took off my ruck and dragged it up between my legs and rested it there. Two radio systems designed to be exposed to small arms and inclement weather and drop-tested from twelve feet should absorb a direct hit by an AK-47, I reasoned blindly. Didn't matter; it was the only plan I could see.

Many troops volunteered to go into the city with us, and loaded onto the vehicles only to be told later that they wouldn't be coming along. I appreciated their willingness to go downtown. That willingness is truly the American soldier's legacy. Others loaded onto the Malaysian APCs for the ride into the target areas. From the Pakistanis and Malaysians we got two very ancient M-48 tanks and a number of armored personnel carriers, called BTRs.

I remember briefly thinking it would be better to be closed inside one of those APCs, where the bullets couldn't reach you. But it was just a fleeting thought. Combat lesson number four: Never get into anything that was manufactured and has moving, mechanical parts if you know you're going into a gunfight. That goes for anything with wheels or wings: tanks, planes, APCs, Humvees, you name it. You're better off on your feet.

We launched somewhere between 2300 and 2330 hours—almost midnight—heading straight north from the new port, which was situated east of the target area. The tanks went first, followed by the APCs, with the rear brought up by seven Task Force Ranger Humvees. No five-ton trucks went out on this mission. By this time I was resigned to always going last.

When we arrived at National Street, the whole convoy turned left toward the two targets: to the second crash site, in the unlikely event that anyone was still alive there, and to the first crash site, where things were very much still happening. As we started down National, the volume of fire we were receiving really started to increase. We responded with as high a volume of fire as could be sustained, with the Malaysians really sending out the rounds. This time we weren't taking any chances with fire suppression. By the time the Humvees passed the same streets there wasn't any resistance. The progress was slow but steady. We kept stopping as the armor in front of us cleared everything out of the way.

When we reached the intersection of National and the north-south-running street one block east of the Olympic Hotel, we stopped. Here the force separated; some of the APCs went north to crash site one, while some others went south to check out crash site two. We occupied the intersection with both Pakistani tanks and a number of APCs to serve as a central choke point for the other rescue troops to pass through on exfil. At our location we received only light fire through the night. Occasionally one of the Pakistani tanks would let loose a round, and it was deafening. Also the Malaysians at our location launched flares over the target area to the north, which really upset our guys there since any illumination worked to the Somalis' advantage. We all used NVGs and they didn't; any light only helped illuminate our people. It took a while for the word to get passed to the Malaysians that we wanted them to stop firing flares.

We waited all night for the troops to consolidate at the first crash site and for the removal of Cliff Wolcott's body from the helicopter at crash site one. Cliff had been the pilot of the first helicopter to crash, and that was the reason we were waiting all night. The troops at crash site one couldn't get his body out from under the helo. No one was about to leave without him.

As it started to get light the Pakistani tanks started up their engines. I thought they must know something we didn't, as we were waiting on word of the extraction of Cliff's body from the first crash. But the tanks both turned around and drove off to the east without us. Their departure could not have been more poorly timed, because as the sun came up the volume of incoming fire increased. In spite of the fact that the fire we'd been receiving during the night was light by comparison with what we'd sustained during the initial assault, we still lost one of our Humvees at the intersection to small-arms fire. It turned out to be the one Homer was riding in; poor bastard had lost another vehicle.

We were sitting all alone without any support, feeling naked, when a pair of Cobra gunships flew overhead. The Little Bird gunships were tied up at the first crash site, where they had been making gun runs since the previous afternoon. Where the Cobras came from or were assigned to, we didn't know. The Cobras made several gun runs over our

position at targets we couldn't see; I didn't know who might be controlling them from the ground, and no one was talking to them on the fire
net. I never did find out what they were shooting at. On one run, one of
the Cobras rolled out on a straight line right at us, shooting at the building just short of our position to the south. I just about crawled under
the pavement. I could see the rounds from his cannon walking toward
us—I couldn't believe this guy was making a run at a friendly position.
He must have been a hell of a shot because the rounds stopped right before they would have slammed into our vehicle. Whether it was just a
mistake or he had indeed eliminated the threat, I don't know, but that
was the only run he made at our location. Thank God for that.

It was shortly after this episode, around 0630 hours or so, that I witnessed one of the strangest things to take place throughout the entire
mission. From out of the alley to our south an old man came walking
up the street cradling a little girl who couldn't have been more than four
or five years old. She appeared dead. She was limp in his arms, with her
head flopping back and one arm hanging down below his waist in front
of him. He walked right up to the intersection with all our vehicles and
men there and then turned left and proceeded west down the street
away from us. He never so much as looked in our direction; he didn't
flinch when weapons were fired, and incoming rounds didn't bother
him in the least. Although rounds were impacting in his general vicinity, he didn't pay any heed to them, and he never got a scratch. The last
I saw of him he was walking out of sight to the west, straight down the
road headed God knows where. Poor man—I somehow knew that she
was his grandchild. It was one of those situations where you intuitively
know something. I couldn't really feel his loss, though; I was too tired
and worn too thin.

Finally, around 0700 hours, the first of the APCs from the crash site
started to pass through our position. They came in a straight line and
were really moving fast from west to east en route to the Pakistani stadium, a safe location not so far or as difficult to get to as the airport. The
stadium was an abandoned Olympic-style sports arena with high walls
that made it safe from everything but mortars. Behind the APCs I could
see some of the rescue force running down the street toward us. There
wasn't enough room on the APCs for all of them. Some of the poor bas-

tards were running down the street trying to keep up with the last APC but were failing to maintain the pace. The APCs weren't going slow enough for anyone to keep up anyway. They zoomed right past us on their way to safety.

On top of one of the BTRs, I saw a Task Force Ranger trooper lying dead with his arm hanging off the top of the vehicle. He had to be one of ours because he had aircrew cammies on. Blood had run all the way down the side of the vehicle from where they had thrown his body, and it reminded me of the little girl in the old man's arms. What a waste.

When they finally arrived at our location the last of the task force troops were scrambling on top and into the back of the vehicles waiting at the intersection. There were now only a few Humvees left and no APCs, and the volume of fire was increasing in direct proportion to the rising of the sun. We were now the last vehicle in the convoy, and I hollered at Nixon's driver to back up so we could get some of these guys. They were obviously exhausted, and we didn't want to be the only vehicle left out on the street.

All the other vehicles had passed us, and ours was starting to draw more fire. The last couple of troops on the street were climbing onto our Humvee when I saw Bob Rankin—another combat controller who wasn't on the initial assault but who'd volunteered to come out on the rescue—looking for a place to climb on. He was standing at the back of our tailgate facing us. There was absolutely no place left for him, so I and a Ranger who had climbed up partially onto my lap reached over, grabbed him by the shoulder straps, and pulled him halfway onto the rear of the vehicle. Hands came from all over to help hold him in place. All Bob said was, "Don't let me go."

I answered him: "We've got you, Bob."

He was wedged facedown among all the guys in the back and he couldn't see anything, but he obviously recognized my voice. "Dano, is that you?"

"It's me, Bob."

"Just don't let me go!"

He rode like that all the way to the Pakistani stadium, with his ass and legs hanging out of the back. I'm sure it was quite a sight to behold for all the Somalis near the stadium, of which there was no shortage. We were coming off the mission from hell and these people were walking around the streets as if nothing unusual were going on.

We arrived at the Pakistani stadium at approximately 0800 hours. There was already a triage set up, and the Pakistanis were knocking themselves out trying to help us. When I arrived there were already American helos on the ground and the exfil of our people was in progress, some to the hospital and the rest back to the airport. I found Tim Wilkinson and Jack McMullen (another controller who'd come out on the rescue mission) and talked with them for a little while. The Pakistanis were passing around a rice dish with either lamb or beef in it. I hadn't eaten since breakfast two days earlier, so I ate some.

I sat down for a bit in the stadium stands and looked upon the scene. The Pakistanis had mortar tube positions dug into the former soccer field. Our vehicles were parked haphazardly along the side nearest me. Men were milling about. A couple Pakistanis in white uniforms were distributing tea. I could see several groups of task force guys clustered around each other. I sat for a while just looking, not thinking much.

There were three or four American bodies lying on the ground under ponchos waiting to be loaded. When it was time I went over and helped carry them to a waiting helicopter. It seemed like the least I could do for them, and I didn't want them to be carried by non-Americans. These men had lost everything, and it didn't seem right for them to be loaded for their last trip home by anyone other than those they'd been out with when they died.

I found Tim again a bit later. I was surprised to see him, and we exchanged some news. He told me all our guys had made it through. Scotty had been shot. Pat got some shrapnel, as did Tim himself, but otherwise all our guys were safe and everyone was going to pull through.

Finally, by 1100 hours, all the personnel going out by helo were loaded, and there was nothing left but our Humvees. Before the last helo had lifted, I'd asked Tim if he wanted to ride back with me to the airport in my vehicle instead of flying back. To my surprise, he said yes. Prior to this raid, Tim had been complaining to me about how all he ever got to see was the city from the CSAR helo and how I got to go all over the city and see it up close. Our vehicle was to bring up the rear, as usual, and as we clambered onto the Humvee I noticed Tim didn't have his CAR-15.

"Where's your gun?" He sheepishly replied that he hoped Scott Fales had it but that he wasn't really sure since he hadn't seen it all night, because he was completely occupied with treating wounded. And now Scotty had been evacuated with the rest of the casualties. I couldn't believe he was going back out into the city without a long gun of some kind.

Our vehicles lined up within the safety of the stadium in preparation for departure. Tim was now seated where my new Ranger buddy had so recently sat. I didn't know where that Ranger was now and didn't care, nor did I care about the others. Hopefully they were smart enough to catch rides on a helo. Fuck having to drive back through hell. Still, it was great to be with an Air Force teammate. It was the first time I'd been with any of my own guys during the entire mission. Combat lesson five: One of the problems with combat control is that you invariably end up working with people you know only a little about or sometimes not at all. As tired as I was, it was the best I'd felt in hours. At the moment I didn't care what was coming next.

As the first of our vehicles pulled out of the stadium, sure enough, we could hear the volume of fire start up again. Something was coming for us. Tim looked at me, pulled out his M-9 pistol, shrugged, and said, "I can't believe you talked me into this."

But we weren't spoiling for a fight. Not anymore. We'd accomplished our mission, picked up all the bad guys we'd set out to, and then come back out to get the rest of our people, dead or alive. And now it was time to go back to the hangar. *You can keep your shitty little city, fight among yourselves, and starve each other, for all I care,* I thought. No matter how bloodied we were, we knew we were still militarily far superior to anyone there and had dished out more than we took against people who liked to dish it out.

The convoy route we used to get home took us around the city to the north, west, and then south, along an established resupply route the Americans utilized to get between the several compounds we occupied throughout Mogadishu. At one point along the drive, around the north end of the city, a child of maybe five or six who was standing on the side of the road made a face and pointed a finger at us. Tim held up his pistol and made a motion with his head as if to say, *Uh-uh*. As he receded we could see the kid just standing there, smiling.

We arrived back at the hangar at 1230 hours on October 4. Tim and I were the last two men at the very end of the long line of warriors who'd gone out and come back.

I don't remember much about October 4 after we got back. I know I reconfigured, loaded ammo, replaced batteries, etc. We waited for a bit to see if we were going back out again. We were definitely missing people, and it was only a question of when and where we would go to get them back. Eventually the word came to stand down. I went to sleep on my cot but don't remember what time or for how long I slept.

On the fifth I remember being up early in the morning, rechecking my gear, and talking with a couple others, mostly Tim and Pat. The rest of the day is a blur, indistinguishable.

On the morning of the sixth, while I was standing at the rear of the hangar, a mortar round, a single round, exploded on the concrete just outside the hangar entrance. It really jerked the hangar to life, with people running everywhere, grabbing their gear, unsure what to do. Most were still unsettled from the mission. I ran to the front of the hangar and saw a couple PJs and some medics working on Doc Marsh, the assaulter flight surgeon, and Matt Rierson. I went back to my bunk to grab something when I heard Staff Sergeant Struecker urgently calling my name from a few rows away near the center of the Rangers' cot area. He had a guy with shrapnel wounds and there weren't any medics available—would I come and look at his guy?

I got my newly refurbished med kit from my cot and ran over to where a knot of Rangers were standing around a guy on the floor. I knelt down and started to check him over. He had entrance wounds in the neck but no exit wounds and didn't seem to have any other problems. *Potentially serious,* I was thinking, but I didn't want to alarm the guy, so I started talking to him while I checked him over. He needed a thorough check before we could move him to the MASF.

"What's your name?" I asked.

"Specialist Moynihan."

Good, I thought, *he's cognizant and calm.* I asked Struecker to move his buddies back and everyone stepped back sharply. With Rangers there's never a hesitation. You gotta love 'em.

"Where you from, Moynihan?" This drew a blank. I started to think perhaps he wasn't fully aware when he blurted out, "Uh, I'm from all over."

"Well, Moynihan from all over, you're going to be just fine. You've got some shrapnel in your neck, but nowhere else, and it isn't serious. We're going to take you over to the Air Force folks and they'll fix you right up."

I stepped aside with Struecker and told him the shrapnel didn't seem to have severed anything serious, but that since it'd gone in the side of his neck it could be resting close to something potentially more dangerous. "You need to keep his neck as immobile as possible and get him over to the MASF." He thanked me and then got his guys to take Moynihan away.

Now in full medical mode, I went to the front of the hangar, where Rusty Tanner (another PJ and our quasi–first sergeant) and another medic were working on Matt Rierson. He had a big hole in his back where a golf-ball-size chunk of shrapnel had ripped through his body. They were talking to him and working feverishly to plug the hole and stabilize him for movement. Someone brought up a litter and I helped them get him onto it. He was trying to talk and I could see him fighting to stay aware. His determination was more than inspiring, it was astounding.

Four of us lifted him and carried him to a medevac helicopter that arrived for the short flight to the hospital on the other side of the city. We were moving him to the helo as quickly and smoothly as possible. A couple guys were talking to him and telling him to hang in there. I could see him struggling to stay with us, but then his eyes started to change. They took on that dull, opaque appearance you see in a dead deer or elk. They turned just as we put him on the helicopter. Later I heard that he died on the way to the hospital or shortly after arrival. I didn't believe it, though. I know what I saw. He died as we loaded him, with his friends still telling him to hang on.

I didn't really know Matt, other than who he was, what position he filled, and from the numerous times I'd seen him during our nightmare drive through the city. But his death really affected me. That's not to diminish the memory of the other fine soldiers we lost during the battle. I saw some of them die as well. But Matt's the only person I've ever watched die, so close I could touch his face. And he was trying so hard to stay. I could see it in him, but I could see death coming for him as well.

I used to think about him and his family regularly the first few years after the battle. In fact, for a long time I thought about the battle every day. Not so much anymore; too much time has passed. As for Matt, well, wherever his family may be now, they should know that I admired that man as a stalwart operator and valiant human being. But then, they already know that better than I.

After that and the two separate memorial services we held for our dead, we learned that the political winds were shifting. No more missions, it was rumored. Sure, we were configured for fighting, and we still had to get Mike Durant back—our pilot who'd been taken alive by the Somalis. But once we retrieved him that would probably be it. And it was. What bullshit. Only politicians would let you fight to the death and *then* decide the price was too high.

As the days passed, Tim and I returned to our favorite pastime, a type of self-therapy: smoking cigars on the sandbags and sipping a little gin. Yes, alcohol. My wife, Liz, had smuggled me some Tanqueray disguised as a water bottle weeks before. I've always been a gin drinker, and my favorite is a glass on the rocks with a couple olives. When a package arrived from my wife with a jar of olives and two water bottles, I knew what she'd done. I carefully unscrewed one and took a sip: water. I couldn't believe it. How could she send me olives and two bottles of water? It didn't matter, I rationalized; they were still from home and I could munch on the olives from time to time. I drank that first bottle slowly over a few days. Then, after one of our raids I came back to my bunk looking for something to drink (all we had in Somalia was bottled water) and there wasn't any around my cot. I reached into my care package, pulled out the second bottle of water, took a huge chug, and nearly choked on a mouthful of gin! Bless her heart!

In the evenings I would covertly mix myself a canteen cup of Tanqueray with a little olive juice and a couple olives. Ice was out of the question, as it probably didn't exist anywhere in the country. Then Tim and I would hurry from our cots at the rear of the hangar and as nonchalantly as possible saunter through its length, me with my hand over my canteen cup so that no one might catch the scent of gin. Alcohol-deprived men have an acute sense of smell.

Safely through the gauntlet, we'd settle on a short sandbag wall on the perimeter of the task force compound to have a smoke. Tim would clip them for us. My usual smoke was a Royal Jamaica Churchill Maduro and Tim typically had an H. Upmann or Punch. Tim was the man with all the cigars, but it never bothered me to mooch off him. Hell, it's his fault I even smoked good cigars. What it did was help to create an atmosphere where we could talk things through. I believe that sitting on those sandbags and talking, over the next few weeks while we waited to go home, was beneficial. It gave us a chance to relax in a manner that would otherwise not have been possible. With an offshore breeze and a good smoke, it was even pleasant.

After Durant's release we were going home. We lost eighteen guys on Somali soil, killed hundreds of Somalis, and took down half of Aidid's leadership, and we were calling it quits. The sad thing is, we had the Somalis on the ropes psychologically. The advantage was all ours. The Somalis were scared to death we would come back out. I firmly believe that if we had pressed our advantage home over the next few weeks, Aidid would have been in our hands. In war you never voluntarily give up the advantage. Ever. We broke one of the cardinal rules. Clausewitz was rolling over in his grave.

For the task force it was even worse; it was personal. We were made to stop short of our objective.

We headed home from Somalia on October 21. Our return mirrored in many ways the whole operation. For the Air Force guys it was another exercise in neglect. Tim, Pat Rogers, John McGarry, Tom "Turtle" Terlikowski (a PJ who came over with the relief forces after the battle), and I got on a C-5 with the remaining Rangers, who were going all the way to Georgia. The plane entered the States at Seymour Johnson Air Force Base in North Carolina. The plan from there was for someone representing the assaulters to meet us, who would then ferry us back to our compound at Pope AFB, a two-hour drive.

No one was there. It was six o'clock in the morning, we were back after the mission from hell, and we were left hanging. Pat called the squadron; nobody there either. He woke up one of the ops guys, Matt Donnelly, who was incredibly apologetic but had nothing for us, at least nothing that would resolve the situation to our satisfaction. The Army, in a show of all its bureaucratic glory, informed our unit they would take care of getting us back. Ah, the big A, as we called it, always coming through for us.

However, we weren't the only Department of Defense assets offloading in North Carolina. The assaulters had vehicles on the plane as well, and their unit sent over some guys in a van to drive the vehicles back. We commandeered the driver of the now empty Ford Econoline and piled in. At the first convenience store we saw I had the driver pull in so we could get a twelve-pack of Miller Lite and some Genuine Draft. Our first beer in many months, and it tasted great.

Almost home, but our driver had another plan. He insisted we go to the assaulters' compound first because those were his instructions. Finally we got him to run us up the road to our place and drop us off in front of our main building. It was now about nine in the morning. And there in front of the building was about a dozen and a half folks from the unit waiting for us. The Army had called over to say we were on our way.

The biggest surprise was Scotty Fales. He'd been shot during the battle and shipped back to the States two days later through Germany. He was with the others, moving around in his hyperactive fashion and doing well on crutches. I wasn't in the mood to stand around and bullshit with everyone, so I went to my locker and changed into the Levi's and T-shirt I'd arrived in on the day we deployed. I didn't even take anything else with me. I called my wife to tell her I was back and to come get me and walked down the hill toward the compound gate. As I was approaching the security building I noticed one of the maintenance workers putting up a banner across the road with something written on it facing the front gate. As I walked underneath I turned around to see what was written. It said: "Welcome Home." One more day late and another dollar short. I laughed out loud and walked out the front gate.

APPENDIX

SPECIAL OPERATIONS WARRIOR FOUNDATION

The Special Operations Warrior Foundation (SOWF) was founded in 1980 as the Colonel Arthur D. "Bull" Simons Scholarship Fund to provide college educations for the seventeen children surviving the nine men killed or incapacitated at Desert One, the Iranian hostage rescue attempt. It was named in honor of the legendary Army Green Beret, Bull Simons, who repeatedly risked his life on rescue missions.

Since that tragic day in the desert of Iran, the special operations community has lost more than four hundred special operations personnel. Special Operations Forces include, but are not limited to, Army Rangers, Special Forces, Navy SEALs, and Air Force special operations personnel.

The Special Operations Warrior Foundation believes that no child should be left behind if their parent is killed in a mission or training accident. The foundation provides college scholarship grants, *not loans,* as well as family and financial counseling to the children surviving special operations personnel killed in an operational mission or training accident. The scholarships cover tuition, books, fees, room and board. At the beginning of 2004, the Warrior Foundation had five hundred children of fallen special operations personnel in the program, including sixty-six enrolled in colleges across the country.

The Warrior Foundation is a 501(c)(3) tax-exempt nonprofit organization that provides college funding for surviving children of special operations service members killed in the line of duty.

Contact information:
Special Operations Warrior Foundation
P.O. Box 14385
Tampa, FL 33690
www.specialops.org
e-mail: warrior@specialops.org
telephone: 1-866-600-SOWF

GLOSSARY

Aerial medevac The action of evacuating the wounded by helicopter.

Aid-and-litter team A small number of troops designated to carry wounded from a battle.

Aimpoint sight A battery-operated sighting device mounted on small-arms weapons.

Air controller A person or sometimes aircraft designated for controlling close air support (*see* CAS).

AK-47 A 7.62 mm small-arms weapon used by Somalis, usually manufactured in Russia or China.

AO (area of operations) The geographic location where operations are taking place.

APC (armored personnel carrier) A lightly armored vehicle, either tracked or wheeled, used to carry troops and provide protection from small-arms fire.

Bakara Market One of the largest arms markets in East Africa, located in Mogadishu.

Battle of the Black Sea Military historical term used to describe the Battle of Mogadishu.

BDU (battle dress uniform) Uniform used by U.S. troops in combat which can be either desert or green camouflage.

Black Sea district The area adjacent to Bakara Market, an Aidid stronghold, and the area where the Battle of Mogadishu took place.

Blocking position A designated point on the ground where troops establish dominance and can prevent enemy forces from entering or leaving an area.

Body armor A piece of equipment, usually a vest, that can be worn by the individual soldier to provide ballistic protection from small-arms fire.

BP *See* Blocking position.

Bravo Company B Company, Third Battalion, 75th Ranger Regiment.

Brownout The dust storm effect created by rotating helicopter blades.

BTR Russian-designed armored personnel carrier.

C-5 Galaxy A U.S. Air Force military transport plane used to carry heavy equipment and troops.

CAR-15 A 5.56 mm weapon carried by Task Force Ranger troops.

CAS (close air support) The act of providing fire support to troops on the ground from any aircraft.

CCP (casualty collection point) An area designated for the treatment and evacuation coordination of casualties on a battlefield.

CCT *See* Combat controller.

Chalk The term identifying the troops to be carried in an individual helicopter.

Chem-lites Fluid-filled plastic light sources that emit light when bent for a number of hours. Can be overt or infrared.

Choke point Term used to identify a CCP or other area controlled by friendly forces, which personnel or vehicles must pass through in order to verify identity and body count.

Clevis pin A four-inch pin that holds a fast rope in place when attached to a helicopter.

CO Commanding officer.

Cobra A helicopter gunship used by conventional Army or Marine forces. No Cobras were attached to Task Force Ranger.

Combat controller An Air Force operator who coordinates communications for air support and information relay between ground and air forces.

Command and control The process of providing direction to forces from military leaders on the battlefield.

Command net A communications frequency designated for use by commanders on a battlefield.

Command post The area designated for decision making and planning.

Commo Communications.

COMSEC fill device A device used to load a secure code into a piece of communications equipment.

Cravat A band of cloth or sling used for treating the wounded.

CSAR (combat search and rescue) The crew or aircraft designated to recover or assist with search and rescue on the battlefield.

C2 *See* Command and control.

Delta Force An Army Special Forces unit used for classified or sensitive operations.

Drop zone Any area designated for parachutes or parachutists to land.

ELT (emergency locater transmitter) A device used to identify the location of an aircraft or pilot in an emergency.

EOD (explosives ordnance disposal) The personnel or procedures used to remove or destroy explosives.

Evac The act of evacuating wounded personnel from a battlefield.

Exfil (exfiltration) The act of extracting forces from a battle or area.

Fast rope A coarse braided rope approximately four inches in diameter used to insert personnel into areas from a helicopter.

Fire net A communications frequency designated for use by combat controllers or forward observers to direct close air support assets.

Fire support Providing additional or heavy weapons support to troops on the battlefield via aircraft or indirect weapons such as mortars or artillery.

Flash-bangs A grenade used to temporarily disorient enemy forces but not inflict injury.

Flex-cuffing Binding or trussing personnel in order to immobilize them.

FO (forward observer)/FSO (fire support officer) Army personnel designated to provide close air support coordination.

Front sight post The front sight on any weapon directly aimed at a target.

GAU-5 Air Force designation of a CAR-15, a 5.56 mm weapon.

GRF (ground reaction force) A precoordinated and staged force used to provide blocking position, heavy weapons support, and extraction of Task Force Ranger forces.

HALO (high altitude low opening) High-altitude parachute operations designed to introduce small numbers of special operations forces clandestinely into an area.

Helo common radio channel A communications frequency designated for use among helicopters to coordinate air movement.

Higher Command Reference to higher authority within a military force.

Howitzer A piece of military artillery.

Humvee A four-wheeled vehicle used by U.S. military for transporting small numbers of troops and which can carry crew-served weapons.

Infil (infiltration) The act of inserting forces into a battle or area.

Insertion point The geographic point at which troops are introduced onto the battlefield.

JOC (joint operations center) The area designated for coordination, command, and control of units not normally assigned to each other.

Kevlar Material found in equipment worn or used for ballistic protection.

Khat An organic amphetamine chewed to induce a high, often resulting in aggressive behavior.

KIA Killed in action.

Kill zone An area on the battlefield where firepower can be brought to bear, inflicting heavy casualties on an enemy force.

KPOT Kevlar helmet worn by U.S. forces for ballistic protection.

Lager point A designated geographic location on the battlefield used for troops on standby.

LAW (light antitank weapon) A handheld small rocket firing a projectile capable of disabling lightly armored vehicles.

LBE (load-bearing equipment) The vest worn by soldiers carrying their ammunition, water, and first aid and communications equipment.

LCE (load-carrying equipment) Another designation for load-bearing equipment (*see* LBE).

Live fire A mock mission utilizing live ammunition rounds.

LP/OP Listening post/observation post.

M-60 machine gun A crew-served weapon firing 7.62 mm ammunition and used for suppressing enemy fire.

M-203 grenade launcher A 40 mm grenade fired from under a CAR-15-203 or GAU-5.

M-249 SAW A crew-served weapon firing 5.56 mm ammunition and used for suppressing enemy fire.

MASF (mobile aeromedical staging facility) A staging area for treating and evacuating wounded troops.

MAST (military antishock trousers) A pressure system placed on wounded individuals used to treat shock.

MH-6 Little Birds Small helicopters operated by the 160th SOAR used for ferrying up to four troops.

MH-60 Black Hawk helicopters Cargo helicopters used for ferrying up to fifteen troops and providing fire support.

MILES (military integrated laser engagement system) Training devices attached to weapons and soldiers in simulated firefights, to indicate when an individual is wounded or shot.

MK-19 40 mm grenade launcher A 40 mm grenade fired from a vehicle-mounted weapon. Similar to an M-203.

NCO (noncommissioned officer) Any enlisted military member who has reached a position of authority through promotion.

Night Stalkers Informal name for 160 Special Operations Aviation Regiment (SOAR), which provided all helicopter support to Task Force Ranger.

NOD (night optical device) *See* NVG.

NVG (night vision goggles) Handheld or helmet-mounted optical equipment allowing the individual to see in the dark.

OOM (order of movement) The sequence or order by which troops conduct movement.

Operations center *See* JOC.

Operation Gothic Serpent Official name for the deployment of Task Force

Ranger in support of United Nations Operations in Somalia (UNOSOM) II in pursuit of Mohammad Farrah Aidid.

Operation Just Cause The U.S. invasion of Panama in December 1989.

OPFOR (opposing force) Designated enemy forces in mock battle situations.

PC (precious cargo) Term used to describe a person or thing to be obtained by Special Operations forces, often the objective of a mission.

PJ (pararescuemen) Rescue specialists from Air Force Special Operations Command.

QRF (quick reaction force) A prestaged and coordinated contingency force used to supplement the main forces in a military operation.

Recce helo A helicopter used for reconnaissance and observation or direction.

Resupply The process of equipping or replacing depleted supplies.

Rio Hato An airfield seized by U.S. Special Operations forces during the U.S. invasion of Panama.

RIP (Ranger Indoctrination Program) The initial training program completed by potential Rangers after basic training but prior to assignment to a Ranger battalion.

RPG (rocket-propelled grenade) A Russian-manufactured grenade launcher firing a projectile, capable of disabling a vehicle or downing a helicopter.

RTO (radio telephone operator) A soldier whose primary responsibility is to provide communication support.

Rules of engagement The rules by which U.S. forces are authorized or constrained in engaging enemy forces.

SAM (surface-to-air missile) Any missile fired from the ground to disable or destroy aircraft.

SAW (squad automatic weapon) *See* M-249.

SEAL A Navy commando.

SERE (survival, evasion, resistance, and escape) Term used to describe the process by which U.S. military forces avoid capture and conduct themselves as prisoners of war. Also the training process by which U.S. military personnel are prepared for these possibilities.

SINCGARS An Army radio system used to communicate between ground troops and aircraft.

Small-arms fire Any weapons or rounds fired from handheld systems.

SNA (Somali National Alliance) The name by which the quasi-professional military forces of Mohammad Aidid were known.

SOP (standard operating procedure) Any standardized method of conducting operations, usually formalized in writing or a manual.

Spectre gunship A C-130 cargo plane converted into a close air support platform and flown by the U.S. Air Force Special Operations Command. Also known as an AC-130.

SST SAR (search and rescue) security team A specialized team usually made up of combat controllers, pararescuemen, and Rangers used to rescue downed special operations aircrews and passengers.

TacLight High-intensity flashlight mounted on a weapon; often infrared.

10th Mountain Division An Army infantry division headquartered in Fort Drum, New York.

TFR (Task Force Ranger) The aggregate name for the joint forces deployed in support of Operation Gothic Serpent.

TOC (tactical operations center) *See* JOC.

Tracer A round fired from a gun leaving a light trail and serving as a reference for the point of impact.

Triage The process of prioritizing sick or injured people for treatment according to the seriousness of the condition or injury.

Turret gunner An individual manning a weapon system, usually vehicle-mounted, in which the weapon is moved or aimed by means of a turret.

Web gear *See* LBE *or* LCE.

WIA Wounded in action.

INDEX

DAN SCHILLING's military career spans eighteen years in Special Operations. He is the co-founder and chief executive of Kokopelli Western LLC., a successful consulting and development firm specializing in post-secondary institutions. He lives with his wife, Liz, in Springville, Utah, where he thoroughly enjoys the desert and the 500-foot cliff in his backyard.

MATT EVERSMANN currently lives in Baltimore, Maryland, with his wife and daughter. In August 2000, Matt was awarded an honorary bachelor's degree from Hampden-Sydney College in Hampden-Sydney, Virginia. Matt served with the Ranger Regiment from 1992 to 2000.

ABOUT THE TYPE

The text of this book was set in Berkeley, a variation of the University of California Old Style, which was created by Frederick Goudy. While capturing the feel and traits of its predecessor, Berkeley shows influences from Kennerly, Goudy Old Style, Deepdene, and Booklet Oldstyle, all of which were also designed by Goudy. It is characterized by its calligraphic weight stress, and its generous ascenders and descenders provide variation in text color and easy legibility.